WORK IN AMERICA

The MIT Press   Cambridge, Massachusetts, and London, England

WORK IN AMERICA

Report of a Special Task Force to the
Secretary of Health, Education, and Welfare

Prepared under the Auspices of the
W. E. Upjohn Institute for Employment Research

First MIT Press printing, January 1973
Second printing, November 1973
Third printing, March 1974

This book was set in Linotype Baskerville
printed on Nashoba cream white antique
and bound in natural finish #443
by The Colonial Press Inc.
in the United States of America.

Library of Congress catalog card number: 73–278
ISBN 0–262–08063–X (hardcover)
ISBN 0–262–58023–3 (paperback)

CONTENTS

FOREWORD

Most of the people in the United States will work, or have worked, forty or more years. To be concerned about the worker is to be concerned about the aged who, through their labors, brought this Nation to its present level of affluence and well-being; about the youth who have yet to choose from among a thousand occupations; about the disabled and others who are unable to participate in the economic, social, and psychological rewards of work; about the new role of women in our society; and about the rest of us who depart from our homes and return and who seek to fill the time in between with meaningful and well-recompensed activities.

While negotiations over wages and fringe benefits seem to have received the lion's share of attention in the past few decades, considerable interest has been displayed over the past year in our magazines, newspapers, and other media in the *quality* of working life. This is not, of course, an entirely new issue. One need only recall the novels of Dickens and the horrible lot he portrayed of children at work, Steinbeck's migrants and Caldwell's farmers, the sweatshops in our industrial cities, and more recently the efforts to improve the working conditions of coal miners—to realize how profoundly and broadly people care about the quality of work.

Yet, after following the searching exposition of this report, one cannot help but feel that however deeply we have cared in the past, we never really understood the importance, the meaning, and the reach of work.

When I asked last December for this report to be prepared, two things motivated me. The first was a general and enduring sense that the subject was vitally important to much of what HEW does. The second, and more immediate, was a statement President Nixon made on September 6, 1971, in his Labor Day Address:

In our quest for a better environment, we must always remember that the most important part of the quality of life is the quality of work, and the new need for job satisfaction is the key to the quality of work.

This report, I believe, confirms both the President's and my observations.

It is an unusual report; indeed, its only counterpart to my knowledge is the Newman Report on Higher Education, which I released last March. In the breadth of its perspective and its freshness of outlook, this report literally takes on everyone, not excluding some of the thinkers in the present Administration. Manpower policies, medical care strategies, educational and welfare concepts, and more, are intelligently scrutinized by the writers. I cannot recall any other governmental report which is more doughty, controversial, and yet responsible than this one.

Perhaps that is good enough reason to release it, for an open government such as ours can only be the better for a fresh breath of inquiry. Certainly, reasonable men may reasonably disagree with some of the particulars of this study (I do myself). One could wish that the data on which some of its conclusions are based were more adequate. Some of its suggestions, moreover, cannot, by their nature and extent, be lightly accepted. Nonetheless, the ideas are provocative and deserve a large platform for debate and discussion.

I also find much in this report that bears on other policy issues on the national agenda. Its attack on the categorization and fragmentation of manpower training and educational programs points up a problem that has long preoccupied my attention, particularly at HEW. I am more fully convinced than ever before that the only sensible thing to do is that which the President has proposed in his Special Revenue Sharing and Allied Services bills: to consolidate funding, increase the flexibility in the authority of State and local governments, and pull together programs to serve *whole* people and *whole* families.

Moreover, the interrelationships among health, education,

manpower, and welfare in relation to work, as shown in this report, provide additional evidence in support of the President's proposal to create a Department of Human Resources. The present organization of the Executive Branch constrains vision and thinking and acting; these constraints must be removed.

Finally, this report warns us of the great disservice done to the American people when we ignore the enormous contributions of work to health and education and concentrate instead on medical care and schooling. I would add this: We shall make very large mistakes if we fail to pay continuing and close heed to our basic institutions—work, family, and community. This report is a beginning, not a conclusion: it draws our attention back to matters from which we have been perilously estranged, and with which we must again feel familiar and comfortable.

Elliot L. Richardson

LETTER OF TRANSMITTAL

Honorable Elliot L. Richardson
Secretary of Health, Education, and Welfare
Washington, D.C. 20201

Dear Mr. Secretary:

On December 29, 1971, you charged us with the task of examining health, education, and welfare problems from the perspective of one of our fundamental social institutions—work.

At issue were three abiding and deepening concerns. First, the problems with which HEW contends have been fragmented into more than 300 separate categorical programs, with the consequent fragmentation of the services rendered by these programs, and the loss of a sense of wholeness and purpose of national social welfare policy. Second, the narrow categorical interests tend to give rise to equally narrow analyses, which then fail to identify those social and institutional interrelationships the understanding of which is vital to effective policy making. And third, our knowledge of what in fact constitutes or contributes to health, education, and welfare has become severely constricted, so that, for example, "health" much too quickly, and dangerously, is thought of as "medical care." As we hope this report demonstrates, work provides a broadening, enlightening, and useful perspective on many of the problems addressed by HEW.

In form and function, our task force was modeled on the Newman Task Force on Higher Education, which reported to you last year. As in that effort, members of our group were chosen for their ability to grasp quickly the significance of unfamiliar data and for their facility in understanding the policy implications of research. Members of the group worked part-time or in their free time on the project. All of them held other, full-time jobs. To insure the independence and autonomy of

the task force, it was agreed in advance that the report would reflect our own conclusions, and not the policies of any governmental agency or any institution for which the members
worked. To help facilitate this independence, the project was
administered under a contract with the non-profit W. E. Upjohn
Institute for Employment Research. Recognizing that it would
be impossible for the group to achieve consensus on a topic as
broad as the institution of work, we agreed in advance that we
need not be in total accord concerning every issue in the report.
In the end, however, we were pleased to find a high degree of
consensus among our group on the major issues.

Procedurally, the task force reviewed much of the literature
on the subject of work, and, for the variety of issues that were
then identified as requiring expert, practical, or differing opin-
ions, special papers were commissioned through the Upjohn
Institute. Some fifty papers were prepared by individuals in
business schools and other university departments, labor unions,
business, and government. These papers, which present much
of the documentary evidence on which our report is based, will
be published at a later date. Finally, we also interviewed a large
number of blue-collar and white-collar workers in order to
ground our effort in the workers' views of their problems.

We wish to acknowledge the invaluable cooperation of the
staff of the Upjohn Institute in the preparation of our report,
particularly the administrative assistance of Iona Meredith
Striner. We would like to thank Jonathan Moore, Counselor to
the Department of Health, Education, and Welfare; Laurence
E. Lynn, Jr., Assistant Secretary for Planning and Evaluation;
and Charles M. Cooke, Jr., Director of the Office of Special Concerns, for their support and encouragement for our study. We
are also grateful to Rita Dolan and the secretarial staff of the
Office of the Asssistant Secretary for Planning and Evaluation
for their help in preparing the report.

We are especially grateful for the opportunity you have given
us to introduce some new perspectives on work into the national

dialogue. A copy of our report is attached for your consideration.

James O'Toole, Chairman
Elisabeth Hansot
William Herman
Neal Herrick
Elliot Liebow
Bruce Lusignan
Harold Richman
Harold Sheppard
Ben Stephansky
James Wright

Attachment

SUMMARY

Our Nation is being challenged by a set of new issues having to do, in one way or another, with the quality of life. This theme emerges from the alienation and disenchantment of blue-collar workers, from the demands of minorities for equitable participation in "the system," from the search by women for a new identity and by the quest of the aged for a respected and useful social role, from the youth who seek a voice in their society, and from almost everyone who suffers from the frustrations of life in a mass society. Rhetorical, ideological, and partisan responses to these issues abound. But truly effective responses are far more likely to be made if the obscure and complex sources of discontent are sorted out, and the lever of public policy is appropriately placed.

This report examines the uses of one institutional fulcrum to move aside the expressed dissatisfactions of many Americans. We offer neither panacea nor simple solutions to the many social problems discussed in this report, but in locating our analysis in the institution of work, we believe we have found a point where considerable leverage could be exerted to improve the quality of life.

The first chapter of the report discusses the functions of work: its centrality in the lives of most adults, its contribution to identify and self-esteem, and its utility in bringing order and meaning to life. Work offers economic self-sufficiency, status, family stability, and an opportunity to interact with others in one of the most basic activities of society. Consequently, if the opportunity to work is absent or if the nature of work is dissatisfying (or worse), severe repercussions are likely to be experienced in other parts of the social system.

And significant numbers of American workers are dissatisfied with the quality of their working lives. Dull, repetitive, seemingly meaningless tasks, offering little challenge or autonomy, are causing discontent among workers at all occupational levels. This is not so much because work itself has greatly changed; indeed, one of the main problems is that work has not changed fast enough to keep up with the rapid and widescale changes in worker attitudes, aspirations, and values. A general increase in their educational and economic status has placed many American workers in a position where having an interesting job is now as important as having a job that pays well. Pay is still important: it must support an "adequate" standard of living and be perceived as equitable—but high pay alone will not lead to job (or life) satisfaction.

There have been some responses to the changes in the workforce, but they have been small and slow. As a result, the productivity of the worker is low—as measured by absenteeism, turnover rates, wildcat strikes, sabotage, poor-quality products, and a reluctance by workers to commit themselves to their work tasks. Moreover, a growing body of research indicates that, as work problems increase, there may be a consequent decline in physical and mental health, family stability, community participation and cohesiveness, and "balanced" sociopolitical attitudes, while there is an increase in drug and alcohol addiction, aggression, and delinquency.

The second chapter takes up the effects of work problems on various segments of our society. Here we find the "blues" of blue-collar workers linked to their job dissatisfactions, as is the disgruntlement of white-collar workers and the growing discontent among managers. Many workers at all occupational levels feel locked-in, their mobility blocked, the opportunity to grow lacking in their jobs, challenge missing from their tasks. Young workers appear to be as committed to the institution of work as their elders have been, but many are rebelling against the anachronistic authoritarianism of the workplace. Minority workers similarly see authoritarian worksettings as evidence that society is falling short of its democratic ideals. Women, who are looking to work as an additional source of identity, are being frustrated by an opportunity structure that confines them to jobs damaging to their self-esteem. Older Americans suffer the ultimate in job dissatisfaction: they are denied meaningful jobs even when they have demonstrable skills and are physically capable of being productive.

In the third chapter, we review the physical and mental health costs of jobs as they are now designed. Satisfaction with work appears to be the best predictor of longevity—better than known medical or genetic factors—and various aspects of work account for much, if not most, of the factors associated with heart disease. Dull and demeaning work, work over which the worker has little or no control, as well as other poor features of work also contribute to an assortment of mental health problems. But we find that work can be transformed into a singularly powerful source of psychological and physical rewards, so that work can be used to alleviate the problems it presently causes or correlates with highly. From the point of view of public policy, workers and society are bearing medical costs that have their genesis in the workplace, and which could be avoided through preventive measures.

The fourth chapter takes up the redesign of work. Several dozen well-documented experiments show that productivity increases and social problems decrease when workers participate in the work decisions affecting their lives, and when their responsibility for their work is buttressed by participation in profits. The redesign of jobs to permit participation must go well beyond what has been called "job enrichment" or "job enlargement," and there are specifiable roles for management, trade unions, and government in the redesign of work. For all, and particularly for government, it is necessary to recognize that if workers were responsible for their work decisions, each workplace would be an "experiment in redesign." And through experimentation of this type in a fundamental institution, we might gain the enthusiasm of living in an experimenting society.

The redesign of jobs is the keystone of this report. Not only does it hold out some promise to decrease mental and physical health costs, increase productivity, and improve the quality of life for millions of Americans at all occupational levels, it would give, for the first time, a voice to many workers in an important decision-making process. Citizen participation in the arena where the individual's voice directly affects his immediate environment may do much to reduce political alienation in America.

However, work redesign is not the only or a sufficient response to the problems we enumerate. For some workers, their jobs can never be made satisfying, but only bearable at best. Other workers may be in relatively satisfying jobs, but after many years on the same job, they may wish to change their careers. Still others, ill-prepared by their education, may want to enlarge their choices through additional education and training. The fifth chapter takes up these matters. Several worker self-renewal programs are suggested, along with training possibilities, and the concepts of vocational and career education are reviewed. With respect to the last, we note that high school vocational education has been unsatisfactory in this country, and that for the concept of career education to advance, it might be worthwhile to view schools as a workplace, as much in need of job redesign as other workplaces, and to understand that the proper precursor to satisfying work is a satisfying education.

In the sixth chapter, we examine Federal policy in relation to the creation of jobs, manpower, and welfare. Clearly, the first and most important element in job satisfaction is to have a job. The quality of work cannot be dealt with adequately until there is a sufficient quantity of work. Recognizing that a strategy calling for the creation of jobs runs headlong into the classic "trade-off" problem between inflation and unemployment, we point out that the productivity gains from the redesign of jobs and the dampening effects on inflation caused by a worker self-renewal program would probably keep inflation at reasonable levels and permit the Nation to adopt a vigorous job creation policy. Job creation itself is related to the many things that patently need doing in our society, but are not being done, and to the differential impact of governmental policies on the quantity and quality of both private and public jobs.

The manpower section points up the major deficiencies in current policy—the fragmentation of programs, their unfortunate amalgamation with welfare programs, and their failure to relate realistically to the demand for workers—and alternatives to these policies are suggested.

In the discussion of welfare, our analysis indicates that our welfare problems are predominantly definitional and familial; in the latter, work can play an ameliorative role. Providing decent work opportunities for lower-class men would contribute to family stability by enabling women to anticipate marriage to a steadily employed and self-respecting man. We conclude that the key to reducing familial dependency on the government lies in the opportunity for the central provider to work full time at a living wage. With regard to the definitional problem, it is time to give full recognition to the fact that keeping house and raising children is work, and it is as difficult to do well (and is as useful to the larger society) as paid jobs producing goods and services. Counting housewives in the labor force would be a useful step in redefining a portion of our welfare problem and constructing judicious alternatives.

This report does not contain a summary list of recommendations. There are, to be sure, implied recommendations throughout the report, but we have felt it would be best at this time to draw attention to some of the policy implications of the issues of work and its dissatisfactions, to provide a framework for viewing the interrelationships between work and other basic institutions, and to lay the groundwork for changes in policy, both private and public.

Without work all life goes rotten. But when work is soulless, life stifles and dies.

—Albert Camus

WORK IN AMERICA

1
INTRODUCTION

Homo Faber

It is both humbling and true that scientists are unable, in the final analysis, to distinguish all the characteristics of humans from those of other animals. But many social scientists will agree that among those activities most peculiar to humans, work probably defines man with the greatest certainty. To the archaeologist digging under the equatorial sun for remains of the earliest man, the nearby presence of primitive tools is his surest sign that the skull fragment he finds is that of a human ancestor, and not that of an ape.

Why is man a worker? First of all, of course, man works to sustain physical life—to provide food, clothing, and shelter. But clearly work is central to our lives for other reasons as well. According to Freud, work provides us with a sense of reality; to Elton Mayo, work is a bind to community; to Marx, its function is primarily economic. Theologians are interested in work's moral dimensions; sociologists see it as a determinant of status, and some contemporary critics say that it is simply the best way of filling up a lot of time. To the ancient Greeks, who had slaves to do it, work was a curse. The Hebrews saw work as punishment. The early Christians found work for profit offensive, but by the time of St. Thomas Aquinas, work was being praised as a natural right and a duty—a source of grace along with learning and contemplation. During the Reformation, work became the only way of serving God. Luther pronounced that conscientious performance of one's labor was man's highest duty. Later interpretations of Calvinistic doctrine gave religious sanction to worldly wealth and achievement. This belief, when wedded to Social Darwinism and laissez-faire liberalism, became the foundation for what we call the Protestant ethic. Marx, however, took the concept of work and put it in an even more central position in life: freed from capitalist exploitation, work would become a joy as workers improved the material environment around them.[1]

Clearly, work responds to something profound and basic in human nature. Therefore, much depends on how we define work, what we conceive work to be, what we want work to be, and whether we successfully uncover its meaning and purpose. Our conceptions (and misconceptions) of ourselves, the wisdom with which public policy is formulated on a range of issues, and the rationality with which private and public resources are allocated are influenced greatly by the degree to which we penetrate the complex nature of work.

Because work, as this report illustrates, plays a pervasive and powerful role in the psychological, social, and economic aspects of our lives, it has been called a basic or central institution. As such, it influences, and is influenced by, other basic institutions —family, community (particularly as a political entity), and schools—as well as peripheral institutions. Work, then, provides one institutional perspective—but a broad one—from which to view these interrelationships that affect ourselves and our society.

Toward a Definition of Work

We measure that which we can measure, and this often means that a rich and complex phenomenon is reduced to one dimension, which then becomes prominent and eclipses the other dimensions. This is particularly true of "work," which is often defined as "paid employment." The definition conforms with one readily measurable aspect of work but utterly ignores its profound personal and social aspects and often leads to a distorted view of society.

Using housework as an example, we can see the absurdity of defining work as "paid employment." A housewife, according to this definition, does not work. But if a husband must replace her services—with a housekeeper, cook, baby sitter—these replacements become workers, and the husband has added to the

Gross National Product the many thousands of dollars the replacements are paid. It is, therefore, an inconsistency of our definition of work that leads us to say that a woman who cares for her own children is not working, but if she takes a job looking after the children of others, she is working.

Viewing work in terms of pay alone has also produced a synonymity of "pay" and "worth," so that higher-paid individuals are thought by many to have greater personal worth than those receiving less pay. At the bottom of this scale, a person without pay becomes "worthless." The confusion of pay with worth is a result of historical events and traditions apparently rooted in the distinction between "noble" and "ignoble" tasks.[2] History might have been otherwise and garbage men, for example, in recognition of their contribution to health, might have been accorded monetary rewards similar to those received by physicians. Certainly, it takes little reflection to conclude that, except in crude economic terms, no one is worth nothing, nor is anyone worth a hundred times more than another merely because he is paid a hundred times as much.

We can come closer to a multi-dimensional definition of work if we define it as "an activity that produces something of value for other people." This definition broadens the scope of what we call work and places it within a social context. It also implies that there is a purpose to work. We know that the housewife is *really* working, whether she is paid or not; she is being productive for other people. Substituting the children a woman cares for does not change the nature of her work, only the "others" for whom she is productive. And voluntary tasks are certainly work, although they are not remunerated. Some people at various stages of their lives may be productive only for themselves, a possible definition of leisure.

The Functions of Work
The economic purposes of work are obvious and require little comment. Work is the means by which we provide the goods and

services needed and desired by ourselves and our society. Through the economic rewards of work, we obtain immediate gratification of transient wants, physical assets for enduring satisfactions, and liquid assets for deferrable gratifications. For most of the history of mankind, and for a large part of humanity today, the economic meaning of work is paramount.

Work also serves a number of other social purposes. The workplace has always been a place to meet people, converse, and form friendships. In traditional societies, where children are wont to follow in their parents' footsteps, the assumption of responsibility by the children for one task and then another prepares them for their economic and social roles as adults. Finally, the type of work performed has always conferred a social status on the worker and the worker's family. In industrial America, the father's occupation has been the major determinant of status, which in turn has determined the family's class standing, where they lived, where the children went to school, and with whom the family associated—in short, the life style and life chances of all the family members. (The emerging new role of women in our society may cause class standing to be co-determined by the husband's *and* wife's occupations.)

The economic and societal importance of work has dominated thought about its meaning, and justifiably so: a function of work for any *society* is to produce and distribute goods and services, to transform "raw nature" into that which serves our needs and desires. Far less attention has been paid to the *personal* meaning of work, yet it is clear from recent research that work plays a crucial and perhaps unparalleled psychological role in the formation of self-esteem, identity, and a sense of order.

Work contributes to self-esteem in two ways. The first is that, through the inescapable awareness of one's efficacy and competence in dealing with the objects of work, a person acquires a sense of mastery over both himself and his environment.[3] The second derives from the view, stated earlier, that an individual is working when he is engaging in activities that produce something valued by other people. That is, the job tells the worker day in and day out that he has something to offer. Not to have a job is not to have something that is valued by one's fellow human beings. Alternatively, to be working is to have evidence that one is needed by others. One of these components of self-esteem (mastery) is, therefore, internally derived through the presence or absence of challenge in work. The other component (how others value one's contributions) is externally derived. The person with high self-esteem may be defined as one who has a high estimate of his value and finds that the social estimate agrees.

The workplace generally, then, is one of the major foci of personal evaluation. It is where one finds out whether he is "making the grade"; it is where one's esteem is constantly on the line, and where every effort will be made to avoid reduction in self-evaluation and its attending sense of failure.[4] If an individual cannot live up to the expectations he has of himself, and if his personal goals are not reasonably obtainable, then his self-esteem, and with it his relations with others, are likely to be impaired.

Doing well or poorly, being a success or failure at work, is all too easily transformed into a measure of being a valuable or worthless human being, as Erich Fromm writes:

Since modern man experiences himself both as the seller and as the commodity to be sold on the market, his self-esteem depends on conditions beyond his control. If he is successful, he is valuable; if he is not, he is worthless.[5]

When it is said that work should be "meaningful," what is meant is that it should contribute to self-esteem, to the sense of fulfillment through the mastering of one's self and one's environment, and to the sense that one is valued by society. The fundamental question the individual worker asks is "What am I doing that *really* matters?" [6]

When work becomes merely automatic behavior, instead of being *homo faber,* the worker is *animal laborens.* Among workers who describe themselves as "just laborers," self-esteem is so deflated that the distinction between the human as worker and animal as laborer is blurred.[7] The relationship between work and self-esteem is well summarized by Elliot Jacques:

. . . working for a living is one of the basic activities in a man's life. By forcing him to come to grips with his environment, with his livelihood at stake, it confronts him with the actuality of his personal capacity—to exercise judgment, to achieve concrete and specific results. It gives him a continuous account of his correspondence between outside reality and the inner perception of that reality, as well as an account of the accuracy of his appraisal of himself. . . . In short, a man's work does not satisfy his material needs alone. In a very deep sense, it gives him a measure of his sanity.[8]

Work is a powerful force in shaping a person's sense of identity. We find that most, if not all, working people tend to describe themselves in terms of the work groups or organizations to which they belong.[9] The question, "Who are you?" often solicits an organizationally related response, such as "I work for IBM," or "I'm a Stanford professor." Occupational role is usually a part of this response for all classes: "I'm a steelworker," or "I'm a lawyer." In short: "People tend to 'become what they do.'"[10]

Several highly significant effects result from work-related identification: welfare recipients become "nobodies"; the retired suffer a crucial loss of identity; and people in low-status jobs either cannot find anything in their work from which to derive an identity or they reject the identity forced on them.[11] Even those who voluntarily leave an organization for self-employment experience difficulties with identity—compounded by the confusion of others—as the following quote from an article entitled "Striking Out on Your Own," illustrates:

No less dramatic . . . are those questions of identity which present themselves to the self-employed. These identity crises and situations usually come packaged in little episodes which occur when others find that they have encountered a bona fide weirdo without a boss. . . . You are stopped by a traffic policeman to be given a ticket and he asks the name of your employer and you say that you work for yourself. Next he asks, "Come on, where do you work? Are you employed or not?" You say, "Self-employed." . . . He, among others you meet, knows that self-employment is a tired euphemism for being out of work. . . . You become extremely nervous about meeting new people because of the ever-present question, "Who are you with?" When your answer fails to attach you to a recognized organization . . . both parties to the conversation often become embarrassed by your obscurity.[12]

Basic to all work appears to be the human desire to impose order, or structure, on the world. The opposite of work is not leisure or free time; it is being victimized by some kind of disorder which, at its extreme, is chaos. It means being unable to plan or to predict. And it is precisely in the relation between the desire for order and its achievement that work provides the sense of mastery so important to self-esteem. The closer one's piece of the world conforms with one's structural plans, the greater the satisfaction of work. And it follows that one of the greatest sources of dissatisfaction in work results from the inability to make one's own sense of order prevail—the assembly-line is the best (or worst) example of an imposed, and, for most workers, unacceptable structure.

These observations have been verified a number of times in investigations of mass and protracted unemployment. Loss of work during the Depression was found to produce chronic disorganization in the lives of parents and children, as documented in several studies of the 1930's.[13] Cynicism, loss of self-confidence, resentment, and hostility toward the Federal Government, helplessness, and isolation are all experienced during such difficult periods.[14] According to Charles Winick,

Inasmuch as work has such a profound role in establishing a person's life space, emotional tone, family situation, object relations, and where and how he will live, either the absence of work or participation in marginal work often makes it likely that he will develop a pervasive *atonie*.[15]

Atonie is a condition of deracination—a feeling of rootlessness, lifelessness, and dissociation—a word which in the original

Greek meant a string that does not vibrate, that has lost its vitality.

Besides lending vitality to existence, work helps establish the regularity of life, its basic rhythms and cyclical patterns of day, week, month, and year.[16] Without work, time patterns become confused. One recalls the drifting in T. S. Eliot's "The Wasteland":

What shall I do. . . . What shall we do tomorrow?
What shall we ever do?

When duration of unemployment has been prolonged, unemployed workers progress from optimism through pessimism to fatalism. Attitudes toward the future and toward the community and home deteriorate.[17] Children of long-term unemployed and marginally employed workers uniformly show poorer school grades.[18] And, despite the popular notion that unemployed people fill their "free" time with intensified sexual activities, the fact is that undermined egos of former breadwinners lead to diminished libidos.[19] "There are so many unconscious and group needs that work meets," Winick writes, "that unemployment may lead not only to generalized anxiety, but to free-floating hostility, somatic symptoms and the unconscious selection of some serious illnesses."[20]

Many of the studies revealing the disorganizing effects of unemployment during the Depression have found echoes in recent "ghetto ethnographies." Such studies as Liebow's *Tally's Corner* show these effects to be as much a function of unemployment and marginal employment *per se* as of economic catastrophe. This is so because to be denied work is to be denied far more than the things that paid work buys; it is to be denied the ability to define and respect one's self.

It is illusory to believe that if people were given sufficient funds most of them would stop working and become useless idlers. A recent economic analysis shows that as people increase their earnings and acquire wealth they do not tend to decrease the time and energy that they invest in work.[21] In another study, when a cross section of Americans were asked if they would continue working even if they inherited enough to live comfortably without working, 80% said they would keep on working (even though only 9% said they would do so because they enjoyed the work they were doing).[22] Some people may not want to take specific jobs—primarily because of the effects on their self-esteem —but working, "engaging in activities that produce things valued by other people," is a necessity of life for most people.

Some of the most compelling evidence about the centrality of the functions of work in life comes from the recent efforts of women to fill what some interpret as a void in their lives with the sense of identity derived from work. As some social critics have noted, the desire for all that work brings to the individual is at the foundation of the women's liberation movement.

There is also considerable evidence that work has the same meaning among the poor and among welfare recipients that it has for middle-class and employed individuals:

—A recent study for the Labor Department on the work orientations of welfare recipients found that "the poor of both races and sexes identify their self-esteem with work to the same extent as nonpoor persons do." The study found that although people on welfare are as committed to the work ethic as middle-class people, their attitudes differ in that they are not confident that they can succeed on a job. After experiencing failure, they are more likely to accept the dependence on welfare.[23]

—A recent study in South Carolina of 513 underprivileged workers found that the poor did not differ markedly from the middle class in the kind of satisfactions that they derived from work.[24]

—The Office of Economic Opportunity has sponsored a three-year study to assess the validity of the assumption that the working poor would stop working if they were guaranteed an annual income. *Preliminary* findings have shown little slackening in work effort among those urban families receiving a guaranteed income. In fact, hourly earnings appear to be higher for those in the experiment than for those in a control group. Although it is too early to assess the results of the experiment, there are signs that withdrawal from work effort is not as extensive as some had feared.[25]

In this regard, it must be realized that although *work* is central to the lives of most people, there is a small minority for whom a *job* is purely a means to a livelihood. To them a job is an activity that they would gladly forgo if a more acceptable option for putting bread on their table were available. What little evidence there is on this point indicates that for most such individuals the kinds of jobs that they see open to them do little to provide the sense of self-esteem, identity, or mastery that are the requisites for satisfying work. These individuals turn to other activities (music, hobbies, sports, crime) and other institutions (family, church, community) to find the psychological rewards that they do not find in their jobs. In effect, these activities, for these people, become their real work. This unusual phenomenon helps to explain the small amount of job withdrawal that occurs among welfare recipients. For example, welfare mothers may choose the personally fulfilling work of raising their children to the alternative of a low-level, unchallenging job—the only kind available to them.

The Change in Attitudes toward Work

Although social scientists have long disputed the precise contribution of the Protestant ethic to the genesis of capitalism, they generally agree that thrift, hard work, and a capacity for deferring gratification historically were traits widely distributed among Americans. Moreover, as part of the legitimacy of the economic system, individual members of our society were to be credited or blamed for their own circumstances, according to the degree of their prosperity.

But the ethic, or what has passed for it, appears to be under attack. Some futurists tell us that automation will make work unnecessary for most people, and that we may as well ignore

work and look to other matters, such as "creative leisure." More immediately, our attention is drawn to these alleged signs of work's obsolescence:
—The growth in the number of communes
—Numerous adolescents panhandling in such meccas as Georgetown, North Beach, and the Sunset Strip
—Various enterprises shifting to 4-day workweeks
—Welfare caseloads increasing
—Retirement occurring at ever earlier ages.

All of these are relatively benign signs; more malignant signs are found in reduced productivity and in the doubling of mandays per year lost from work through strikes. In some industries there apparently is a rise in absenteeism, sabotage, and turnover rates.[26]

Ironically, many of these symptoms have increased despite the general improvements in physical conditions and monetary rewards for work. In comparison with the dreary lot of most workers during the industrial revolution and, indeed, until quite recently, the workplace today is an Elysian field. Sweatshop conditions have all but disappeared. The extreme dangers of work appear to have declined in most industries. Women and children are seldom engaged in back-breaking drudgery. Arbitrary wage cuts and dismissals are relatively rare, and enlightened laws, personnel policies, and labor unions protect the worker in a variety of ways.

Quantitatively, the lives of workers away from work similarly have improved. Real income, standard of living, health status, and life expectancy have all risen markedly. Among most classes of workers, homes and cars are owned in abundance, and bank accounts continually grow. For those without work, there is social security, unemployment compensation, workman's compensation, and an income floor will very likely be established under welfare compensation. On the average, then, no workers have ever been as materially well-off as American workers are today. What, then, is wrong?

Social scientists are suggesting that the root of the problem is to be found in the changing needs, aspirations, and values of workers. For example, Abraham Maslow has suggested that the needs of human beings are hierarchical and, as each level is filled, the subsequent level becomes salient.[27] This order of needs is:

1. Physiological requirements (food, habitat, etc.)
2. Safety and security
3. Companionship and affection
4. Self-esteem and the esteem of others
5. Self-actualization (being able to realize one's potential to the full).

It may be argued that the very success of industry and organized labor in meeting the basic needs of workers has unintentionally spurred demands for esteemable and fulfilling jobs.

Frederick Herzberg suggests an alternative way of looking at the needs of workers—in terms of intrinsic and extrinsic factors.[28] Under this rubric, job satisfaction and dissatisfaction are not opposites but two separate dimensions. Extrinsic factors, such as inadequate pay, incompetent supervision, or dirty working conditions may lead to dissatisfaction, which may be reduced in turn by such "hygienic" measures as higher pay and "human relations" training for foremen. But such actions will not make workers satisfied. Satisfaction depends on the provision of intrinsic factors, such as achievement, accomplishment, responsibility, and challenging work. Satisfaction, then, is a function of the content of work; dissatisfaction, of the environment of work. Increases in productivity have been found to correlate in certain industries and occupations with increases in satisfaction, but not with decreases in dissatisfaction. Hence, hygienic improvements may make work tolerable, but will not necessarily raise motivation or productivity. The latter depends on making jobs more interesting and important.

A recent survey, which lends some support for this emphasis on job content, was undertaken by the Survey Research Center, University of Michigan, with support from the Department of

Labor. This unique and monumental study, to which we often refer in this report, is based on a representative sample of 1,533 American workers at all occupational levels. When these workers were asked how important they regarded some 25 aspects of work, they ranked in order of importance:

1. Interesting work
2. Enough help and equipment to get the job done
3. Enough information to get the job done
4. Enough authority to get the job done
5. Good pay
6. Opportunity to develop special abilities
7. Job security
8. Seeing the results of one's work.

What the workers want most, as more than 100 studies in the past 20 years show, is to become masters of their immediate environments and to feel that their work and they themselves are important—the twin ingredients of self-esteem.[29] Workers recognize that some of the dirty jobs can be transformed only into the merely tolerable, but the most oppressive features of work are felt to be avoidable: constant supervision and coercion, lack of variety, monotony, meaningless tasks, and isolation. An increasing number of workers want more autonomy in tackling their tasks, greater opportunity for increasing their skills, rewards that are directly connected to the intrinsic aspects of work, and greater participation in the design of work and the formulation of their tasks.

Who Is Dissatisfied?

When we cite the growing problem in the country of job dissatisfaction using the criteria laid out above, are we talking about 5% or 50% of the workers in the country? It is clear that classically alienating jobs (such as on the assembly-line) that allow the worker no control over the conditions of work and that seriously affect his mental and physical functioning off the job probably comprise less than 2% of the jobs in America.[30]

But a growing number of white-collar jobs have much in common with the jobs of autoworkers and steelworkers. Indeed, discontent with the intrinsic factors of work has spread even to those with managerial status. It is, however, almost as difficult to measure these feelings of discontent about work as it is to measure such other basic feelings as pride, love, or hate. Most of the leading experts on work in America have expressed disappointment over the unsophisticated techniques commonly used to measure work dissatisfaction.

The Gallup poll, for example, asks only "Is your work satisfying?" It is not surprising that they get from 80% to 90% positive responses (but even this crude measure shows a steady decrease in satisfaction over the last decade). When a similar question was asked of auto and assembly-line workers, 60% reported that their jobs were "interesting." Does this mean that such high percentages of blue-collar workers *are really satisfied* with their jobs? Most researchers say no. Since a substantial portion of blue-collar workers (1) report being satisfied with their jobs *but also indicate they wish to change them* and (2) report they would continue working even if they didn't have to *but only to fill time,* then this can only mean that these workers accept the necessity of work but expect little satisfaction from their specific jobs.[31]

Those workers who report that they are "satisfied" are really saying that they are not "dissatisfied" in Herzbergian terms— i.e., their pay and security are satisfactory, but this does not necessarily mean that their work is intrinsically rewarding. This distinction is illustrated by an interview sociologist George Strauss held with a blue-collar worker on a routine job. This worker told Strauss, in a rather offhand way, "I got a pretty good job." "What makes it such a good job?" Strauss responded. The worker answered:

Don't get me wrong. I didn't say it is a *good* job. It's an O.K. job—about as good a job as a guy like me might expect. The foreman leaves me alone and it pays well. But I would never call it a good job. It doesn't amount to much, but it's not bad.[32]

Robert Kahn suggests that the direct question of satisfaction strikes too closely to one's self-esteem to be answered simply:

For most workers it is a choice between no work connection (usually with severe attendant economic penalties and a conspicuous lack of meaningful alternative activities) and a work connection which is burdened with negative qualities (routine, compulsory scheduling, dependency, etc.). In these circumstances, the individual has no difficulty with the choice; he chooses work, pronounces himself moderately satisfied, and tells us more only if the questions become more searching. Then we learn that he can order jobs clearly in terms of their status or desirability, wants his son to be employed differently from himself, and, if given a choice, would seek a different occupation.[33]

More sophisticated measures of job satisfaction designed to probe the specific components of a job offer great contradictions to simple "Are you satisfied?" surveys. When it asked about specific working conditions, the Michigan survey found that great numbers of "satisfied" workers had major dissatisfactions with such factors as the quality of supervision and the chance to grow on a job. A 1970–71 survey of white, male, blue-collar workers found that less than one-half claimed that they were satisfied with their jobs most of the time. The proportion of positive responses varied according to the amount of variety, autonomy, and meaningful responsibility their jobs provided.[34]

Over the last two decades, one of the most reliable single indicators of job dissatisfaction has been the response to the question: "What type of work would you try to get into if you could start all over again?" Most significantly, of a cross section of white-collar workers (including professionals), only 43% would voluntarily choose the same work that they were doing, and only 24% of a cross section of blue-collar workers would choose the same kind of work if given another chance (see Table 1).[35] This question, some researchers feel, is a particularly sen-

Table 1. Percentages in Occupational Groups Who Would Choose Similar Work Again

Professional and Lower White-Collar Occupations	%	Working-Class Occupations	%
Urban university professors	93	Skilled printers	52
Mathematicians	91	Paper workers	42
Physicists	89	Skilled autoworkers	41
Biologists	89	Skilled steelworkers	41
Chemists	86	Textile workers	31
Firm lawyers	85	*Blue-collar workers, cross section*	*24*
Lawyers	83	Unskilled steelworkers	21
Journalists (Washington correspondents)	82	Unskilled autoworkers	16
Church university professors	77		
Solo lawyers	75		
White-collar workers, cross section	*43*		

sitive indicator because it causes respondents to take into account the intrinsic factors of the job and the very personal question of self-esteem. Those in jobs found to be least satisfying on other measures seldom would choose their present occupation again.

Another fairly accurate measure of job satisfaction is to ask the worker the question: "What would you do with the extra two hours if you had a 26-hour day?" Two out of three college professors and one out of four lawyers say they would use the extra time in a work-related activity. Strikingly, only one out of twenty nonprofessional workers would make use of the extra time in work activity.[36]

We are able, then, to differentiate between those jobs that are satisfying and those that are dissatisfying to the people who hold them. The prestige of an occupation is often an accurate predictor of the level of satisfaction found in a job (while the ranking of occupations by prestige does not correspond exactly with either salary or the amount of education needed to perform well on the job).[37] Moreover, prestige ranking of jobs is nearly identical with the ranking of jobs according to who would choose the same work again. Evidently, people know what work is satisfying and what work is not, even if they are unable to articulate the characteristics of each.

We also find that the jobs people find most satisfying contain most or all of the factors cited previously that workers find important in their jobs. The dissatisfying jobs contain only some or none of these factors. (Those jobs with highly dissatisfying aspects are found to correlate with social problems such as physical and mental illness, as we illustrate in Chapter 3.)

Demographic factors also play a part in the difference between satisfaction and dissatisfaction in the workplace. Young workers and blacks were found to be the most dissatisfied segments of the population in the University of Michigan Survey of Working Conditions. But even dissatisfaction among these groups was often found to correlate with specific kinds of jobs and job situations. For example, highly trained women in low-level jobs were often extremely dissatisfied, but women and men with the same training in the same jobs were equally satisfied.

Sources of Dissatisfaction
Based on what we know about the attitudes of workers toward their jobs, we can identify the following two factors as being major sources of job dissatisfaction: the anachronism of Taylorism and diminishing opportunities to be one's own boss.

The Anachronism of Taylorism Frederick Winslow Taylor, father of time and motion studies and author of *Principles of Scientific Management,* propagated a view of efficiency which, until recently, was markedly successful—so long as "success" was measured in terms of unit costs and output. Under his tutelage, work tasks were greatly simplified, fragmented, compartmentalized, and placed under continuous supervision. The worker's rewards depended on doing as he was told and increasing his output. Taylor's advice resulted in major, sometimes spectacular, increases in productivity.

Several events have occurred to make Taylorism anachronistic. Primarily, the workforce has changed considerably since his principles were instituted in the first quarter of this century. From a workforce with an average educational attainment of less than junior high school, containing a large contingent of immigrants of rural and peasant origin and resigned to cyclical unemployment, the workforce is now largely native-born, with more than a high school education on the average, and affluence-minded. And, traditional values that depended on authoritarian assertion alone for their survival have been challenged.

Simplified tasks for those who are not simple-minded, close supervision by those whose legitimacy rests only on a hierarchical structure, and jobs that have nothing but money to offer in an affluent age are simply rejected. For many of the new workers, the monotony of work and scale of organization and their inability to control the pace and style of work are cause for a resentment which they, unlike older workers, do not repress.

Attempts to reduce the harmful effects of Taylorism over the last two generations have not got at the nub of the problem. For example, the "human relations" school attempts to offset Taylor's primacy of the machine with "tender, loving care" for workers.[38] This school (which has many adherents in personnel offices today) ignores the technological and production factors involved in a business. This approach concentrates on the enterprise as a social system—the workers are to be treated better, but their jobs remain the same. Neither the satisfaction of workers nor their productivity is likely to improve greatly from the human relations approach. Alternatives to Taylorism, therefore, must arise from the assumption that it is insufficient to adjust either people to technology or technology to people. It is necessary to consider both the social needs of the workers and the task to be performed.[39] This viewpoint challenges much of what passes as efficiency in our industrial society.

Many industrial engineers feel that gains in productivity will come about mainly through the introduction of new technology. They feel that tapping the latent productivity of workers is a relatively unimportant part of the whole question of productivity. This is the attitude that was behind the construction of the General Motors auto plant in Lordstown, Ohio, the newest and most "efficient" auto plant in America. Early in 1972, workers there went out on strike over the pace of the line and the robot-like tasks that they were asked to perform. This event highlights the role of the human element in productivity: What does the employer gain by having a "perfectly efficient" assembly-line if his workers are out on strike because of the oppressive and dehumanized experience of working on the "perfect" line? As the costs of absenteeism, wildcat strikes, turnover, and industrial sabotage become an increasingly significant part of the cost of doing business, it is becoming clear that the current concept of industrial efficiency conveniently but mistakenly ignores the social half of the equation.

It should be noted that Taylorism and a misplaced conception of efficiency is not restricted to assembly-lines or, for that matter, to the manufacturing sector of the economy. The service sector is not exempt. For example, in the medical care industry, the phenomenal growth in employment over the past decade or so has occurred largely in lower-level occupations. This growth has been accompanied by an attempt to increase the efficiency of the upper-level occupations through the delegation of tasks down the ladder of skills. This undoubtedly results in a greater efficiency in the utilization of manpower, but it rigidifies tasks, reduces the range of skills utilized by most of the occupations, increases routinization, and opens the door to job dissatisfaction for a new generation of highly educated workers.

As we have seen, satisfying jobs are most often those that incorporate factors found in high-status jobs—autonomy, working on a "whole" problem, participation in decision making. But as Ivar Berg and others have noted, as a result of countless public and private policies and decisions that determine our occupational structure, growth in occupational opportunities has occurred largely in middle and lower levels. The automation revolution that was to increase the demand for skilled workers (while decreasing the need for humans to do the worst jobs of society) has not occurred. What we *have* been able to do is to create such jobs as teacher aides, medical technicians, and computer keypunch operators—not jobs with "professional" characteristics. Undoubtedly, these jobs have opened opportunities for many who would otherwise have had no chance to advance beyond much lower-skilled positions. But it is illusory to believe that technology is opening new high-level jobs that are replacing low-level jobs. Most new jobs offer little in the way of "career" mobility—lab technicians do not advance along a path and become doctors.

This problem of a fairly static occupational structure presents society with a formidable barrier to providing greater job satisfaction to those below the pinnacle of the job pyramid. Without a technological revolution there is little hope of flattening out this structure in order to give more workers higher-status jobs. It then becomes crucial to infuse middle- and lower-level jobs with professional characteristics, particularly if we plan to continue offering higher and higher degrees of education to young people on the assumption that their increased expectations can be met by the world of work.

Diminishing Opportunities to Be One's Own Boss Our economic, political, and cultural system has fostered the notion of independence and autonomy, a part of which is the belief that a hardworking person, even if he has little capital, can always make a go of it in business for himself. Or, to put it another way, if things get too bad in a dependent work situation, it has been felt that the individual could always strike out on his own.

This element of the American Dream is rapidly becoming myth, and disappearing with it is the possibility of realizing the character traits of independence and autonomy by going into business for oneself. The trend of the past 70 years or more, and particularly in recent years, has been a decrease in small independent enterprises and self-employment, and an increase in the domination of large corporations and government in the workforce. In the middle of the 19th century, less than half of all employed people were wage and salary workers.[40] By 1950 it was 80%, and by 1970, 90%. Self-employed persons dropped from 18% in 1950 to 9% in 1970. Individual proprietorships in service trades declined from 81% to 78% in only five years—from 1958 to 1963. From 1960 to 1970, government workers increased from 12% of the civilian labor force to more than 15%. Out of 3,534,000 industrial units employing 70% of the civilian labor force, 2% of the units accounted for 50.6% of the employees, and more than 27% of the employed were accounted for in 0.3% of the units.

Among a class of occupations notable for their autonomy—managers, officials, and proprietors (excluding farms)—self-employment fell from 50% in 1950 to 37% in 1960. On the farms, wage and salary workers increased as a percentage of all farm workers from 61% in 1950 to 80% in 1960. Even among authors, self-employment dropped from 62% to 38% in this period, while self-employed photographers declined from 41% to 34%. Although the percentage of self-employed lawyers has remained almost constant, in 1967 nearly half reported working in firms having 8 to 50 or more lawyers, suggesting some limitation on their autonomy and independence.

As these data attest, the trend is toward large corporations and bureaucracies which typically organize work in such a way as to minimize the independence of the workers and maximize control and predictability for the organization. Characterologically, the hierarchical organization requires workers to follow orders, which calls for submissive traits, while the selection of

managers calls for authoritarian and controlling traits. With
the shift from manufacturing to services—employment has gone
from about 50–50 in 1950 to 62–38 in favor of services in 1970—
the tyranny of the machine is perhaps being replaced by the
tyranny of the bureaucracy.

Yet, the more democratic and self-affirmative an individual
is, the less he will stand for boring, dehumanized, and authoritarian work. Under such conditions, the workers either protest
or give in, at some cost to their psychological well-being. Anger
that does not erupt may be frozen into schizoid depressed char-
acters who escape into general alienation, drugs, and fantasies.
More typically, dissatisfying working environments result in
the condition known as alienation.

Alienation exists when workers are unable to control their immediate work processes, to develop a sense of purpose and function which connects their jobs to the over-all organization of
production, to belong to integrated industrial communities,
and when they fail to become involved in the activity of work
as a mode of personal self-expression.[41]

Social scientists identify four ingredients of alienation: (1)
powerlessness (regarding ownership of the enterprise, general
management policies, employment conditions and the immediate work process), (2) meaninglessness (with respect to the
character of the product worked on as well as the scope of the
product or the production process), (3) isolation (the social aspect of work), and (4) self-estrangement ("depersonalized de-
tachment," including boredom, which can lead to "absence of
personal growth").[42] As thus broken down, alienation is inherent in pyramidal, bureaucratic management patterns and in
advanced, Taylorized technology, which divides and subdi-
vides work into minute, monotonous elements. The result of
alienation is often the withdrawal of the worker from community or political activity or the displacement of his frustrations
through participation in radical social or political movements.[43]

It seems fair to conclude that the combination of the changing social character of American workers, declining opportunities to establish independence through self-employment, and an anachronistic organization of work can create an explosive and pathogenic mix.

What Can Be Done—A "Social Efficiency" Model

One of the main burdens of this report will be to verify that work, health, welfare, family stability, education, and other matters of major concern do not reside in discrete compartments, but rather that we live in a closed system—"spaceship earth" to use Kenneth Boulding's phrase. These spheres of action are mutually influential, but one may be more dominant than the others. The empirical evidence and theoretical formulations presented in this report strongly suggest that, from the point of view of national policy, work plays a dominant role. This means that "trade-offs" might be made between work and these other concerns; i.e., the more that is done about work along the lines advocated in this report, the less that might have to be done about, say, medical care or public assistance or certain social programs for the aged.

It would be well to note, however, that acting on the trade-off potential will probably require a marked shift in perspective, particularly with regard to the lodgement of responsibility. If work is to become a lever for action, the responsibilities of employers, for example, would have to be greatly changed; they would no longer be considered as essentially producers of goods and services, but as actors who affect, and who in turn are affected by, the major institutions in society.

This shift in perspective may be highlighted through a contrast of industrial efficiency with "social efficiency." Other coinages would do equally well to illuminate the differences—for example, Willis Harman's "humanistic capitalism." [44] The contrast is between the narrow interest of producing goods and services and the broader interest of relating that production to other social concerns.

"Industrial efficiency" is here defined in its usual economic sense: the goal of an enterprise is to obtain the maximum output at a given level of costs (or a given level of output at a minimum cost). In optimizing costs and outputs, all substitutions ("trade-offs") are internal to the operation of the enterprise. Labor and capital—including intellectual, managerial, and the accumulation of skills, as well as physical capital—are substituted for one another to achieve efficiency for the firm, without regard to external effects.

"Social efficiency" draws on the economic notion of "externalities," which recognizes that the production of goods or services by a firm may result in costs or benefits that occur in society and which are not accounted for in the internal audit of any firm or all firms together. If the externalities are "diseconomies," the firm may be industrially efficient but socially inefficient. If the externalities result in social "economies," the firm may not be industrially efficient even though it is socially efficient. The social efficiency concept includes a variety of noneconomic social costs, such as the costs of social and political alienation. In the area of pollution control the concept has been used by the Federal Government in its attempts to have the industries responsible for pollution internalize some of the costs of cleaning the environment. The allocation of such social costs is a complex matter. In many cases, communities or societies choose to bear these costs in order that the industry may be able to continue to provide a valued service. But the need for sensitivity to the interrelations between social and industrial efficiency is increasingly being recognized by businessmen. A few far-sighted leaders even see that one depends on the other, and that businesses can sustain their long-run profitability by defraying many of the social as well as economic costs they incur.[45]

Some business leaders recognize that their firms capitalize on free or public goods and that it is their responsibility to replenish the public storehouse when they partake of its largesse. J. Irwin Miller of the Cummins Corporation says that "Every business is the beneficiary of services such as schools and government, and of enriching elements such as art and religion, which it did not pay for and without which it could not exist." [46] Other businessmen, such as Sidney Harman, President of Jervis Corporation, and Alfred J. Marrow, Chairman of the Board of the Harwood Companies, have expressed concern over the attitude of industry toward human capital. Harman writes:

In addressing the question of the employer's obligations to society, to stockholders and workers, [the businessman] must see them as intricately interrelated. One cannot, in effect, serve society at all if he does not serve its people. One cannot serve shareholders effectively if he does not act to make business itself an agent for human growth and fulfillment. For, unless the businessman-employer . . . recognizes this as a minimal obligation, he will in the long run (and more likely in the short term) participate in the destruction of the very instrument from which stockholders draw nourishment. [47]

Harman goes on to say that "work satisfaction—which is to say the attainment of a sense of purposefulness in his or her work, the achievement of a sense of personal worth and dignity —should be seen as a fundamental right of employees, and therefore a fundamental obligation of employers." Furthermore, "the consistent implementations of this view throughout the business community is the most reliable assurance of the preservation and constructive development of the free enterprise system." [48]

Extension of Corporate Responsibility

While there is growing evidence that a sense of corporate responsibility for the larger efficiency of society is emerging, there are a large number of areas in which the responsibility could be increased or lodged for the first time. Occupational health and safety is a prime example.

In 1969 workmen's compensation, covering 84.5 percent of the labor force, paid out a total of $2.5 billion—$1.5 billion for disability, $875 million for medical benefits, and $185 million for survivors benefits.[49] The $3.2 billion in insurance premiums paid by employers represents some "internalization" of the social disadvantages of hazardous employment but only a small portion and, obviously, not enough.

The inadequacy is to be found not only in the need for the recently enacted special legislation and funding for black lung disease—an example of a failure of industry to internalize costs —nor only in the small amount of compensation relative to earning capacity but also in the increasing injury-frequency rate, the rising average days of disability per case, and the increasing severity rate, which has been the lot of a majority of occupations. In 1968 a total of 14,311 people died in industrial accidents, about the same as the number of American fatalities in Vietnam that year.[50]

In the same year, 90,000 workers suffered *permanent impairment* from industrial accidents, and a total of 2,100,000 suffered total but temporary disability. . . . In 1969, [exposures to industrial pollutants in the workplace] caused one million new cases of occupational disease. Among the casualties were 3,600 dead and over 800,000 cases of burns, lung and eye damage, dermatitis, and brain damage.[51]

If the social diseconomies of hazardous employment were fully internalized by industry, one would expect the injury and disease rates to decline, on the assumption that it would be worthwhile to reduce the contribution of this factor to industrial inefficiency. It is not obvious how much industry should spend (either through legal enforcement of standards or out of a sense of responsibility) to reduce occupational hazards, but we cannot ignore the point that the failure to protect workers results in deaths, ruined lives, medical costs, public assistance, and other costs borne by individuals and society, not by industry.

We need only translate this social efficiency model to the less obvious problem that is a prime topic of this report—the effects of largescale, bureaucratic and assembly-line forms of work organization on the mental and physical well-being of workers.

Occasionally, a news story will report that a worker has gone berserk as a result of the conditions of his work and has killed a co-worker. Recently, a jury refused to convict an employee who killed two foremen and another worker in an auto plant on the grounds of temporary insanity, when testimony pointed up inhumane working conditions.[52] One may also read that an assembly-line worker in an automobile plant finds it necessary to consume large quantities of whiskey at lunch to face the relentless assembly-line in the afternoon. To what extent have modern production methods spawned alcoholism and violence? And to what extent would the revitalization of planning and decision making among employees lead to greater mental and physical well-being?

The redesign of work, as this report spells out in detail, *can* lower such business costs as absenteeism, tardiness, turnover, labor disputes, sabotage, and poor quality, all of which is to the advantage of employers and consumers. The evidence suggests that meeting the higher needs of workers can, perhaps, increase productivity from 5% to 40%, the latter figure including the "latent" productivity of workers that is currently untapped.[53] Indeed, the potential gains in productivity are so impressive, it is very likely that the redesign of jobs must be accompanied by an equivalent effort to create jobs, if the commitment of all concerned—particularly labor unions—is to be obtained.

Our final instance of the difference between industrial and social efficiency pertains to the unemployed person, who, in the existing accounting system, is an "inefficient resource." Whether it is because of changes in demand or in production methods, it is not efficient to retain an employee whose marginal product is of less value than his earnings and the capital costs supporting his work.

In humanistic and social terms, however, no one is "inefficient," and modern societies, recognizing this, find it worthwhile to provide some assistance when one is unemployed. But the assistance is generally very little, and the mental and physical suffering from unemployment quite large. The social efficiency model would assert that there are always jobs that need to be done in society, that the costs of unemployment are too high to be tolerated, and it is for people that employment exists, not the other way around.

For society, the main benefits from an increase in both the quantity and quality of jobs will be in avoiding some of the very large costs now incurred by the present way we do business. These costs are not fully tallied in the annual reports of our corporations and bureaucracies; they are the costs of such job-related pathologies as political alienation, violent aggression against others, alcoholism and drug abuse, mental depression, an assortment of physical illnesses, inadequate performance in schools, and a larger number of welfare families than there need be. These costs are borne by the citizen and by society; they must be included in any systematic accounting of the costs and benefits of work in America. A precedent for this has been established in environmental policy; the precedent needs to be extended to social policy.

2
PROBLEMS OF AMERICAN WORKERS

No one model can serve as representative of the problems of "the American worker." There are many workers, and the problems of the workplace impinge on different categories of workers in many different ways. In this chapter some of the demographic complexities of an inadequate quantity or quality of jobs are explored from the perspectives of the following groups: blue-collar and white-collar workers and managers, and young, minority groups, female and elderly workers.

Blue-Collar Blues
The "blue-collar blues" is probably one of the most misunderstood social phenomena of our time. Sam Zagoria, the director of the Labor-Management Relations Service, offers an explanation for the blues that transcends "hard-hat" or political stereotypes:

I suspect that much of the current voter unhappiness "with things as they are" is directed not only to the political decisions and domestic tensions about which candidates and office-holders are speaking, but also to the dreary way in which many people spend their working days. . . .[1]

Work problems spill over from the factory into other activities of life: one frustrated assembly-line worker will displace his job-generated aggression on family, neighbors, and strangers, while a fellow worker comes home so fatigued from his day's work that all he can do is collapse and watch television. The difference in reactions may only be a function of their ages, as this Studs Terkel interview with a steelworker illustrates:

You're at the tavern. About an hour or so?
Yeah. When I was single, I used to go into hillbilly bars, get in a lot of brawls. . . .

Why did you get in those brawls?

Just to explode. I just wanted to explode. . . .

You play with the kids . . . ?

. . . When I come home, know what I do for the first 20 minutes? Fake it. I put on a smile. I don't feel like it. I got a kid three-and-a-half years old. Sometimes she says, Daddy, where've you been? And I say, work. I could've told her I'd been in Disneyland. What's work to a three-year-old? I feel bad, I can't take it out on the kid. Kids are born innocent of everything but birth. You don't take it out on the wife either. This is why you go to the tavern. You want to release it there rather than do it at home. What does an actor do when he's got a bad movie? I got a bad movie every day.[2]

A study in British Columbia concluded that a restrictive and narrow work environment "is a burden not easily dropped at the mill gates." For example, workers who had socially isolated jobs tended to be unable to integrate into community life.[3] Other studies show that leisure cannot fully compensate for a dissatisfying work situation.[4]

There is now convincing evidence that some blue-collar workers are carrying their work frustrations home and displacing them in extremist social and political movements or in hostility toward the government. For other workers apathy is the reaction to the same set of social circumstances. The symptoms of the blue-collar blues are part of the popular sociology in America. The middlemass, the hard-hats, the silent majority, the forgotten Americans, the Archie Bunkers as they have been variously called are characterized as alienated from their society, aggressive against people unlike themselves, distrusting of others, and harboring an inadequate sense of personal or political efficacy. Yet, contrary to popular opinion, Stanley E. Seashore and Thad J. Barnowe found that the blues are not confined to any one cohort—sex, age, income status, collar color, or any combination of these traits.[5] Rather, the blues are associated with the possessor's conditions of life at work. But adequate and equitable pay, reasonable security, safety, comfort, and convenience on the job do not insure the worker against the blues. The potent factors that impinge on the worker's values, according to Seashore and Barnowe, are those that concern his self-respect, a chance to perform well in his work, a chance for personal achievement and growth in competence, and a chance to contribute something personal and unique to his work.

Further evidence that political and social attitudes and behavior are related to work experiences and expectations comes from a recent study of blue-collar union members by Harold Sheppard.[6] He found that where aspirations relating to work are not realized, it is not uncommon to find a degree of bitterness and alienation among workers that is reflected in a reduced sense of political efficacy. These "alienated" workers tend to participate less in elections and, when they do vote, tend to cast their ballots for extremist or "protest" candidates. These dissatisfied workers are far more likely than satisfied workers to believe that the lot of the average person has been getting worse. They are more authoritarian in their views (they tend to prefer strong leaders to democratically developed laws). The key variable in this study, as in the previously cited study, appears to be the nature of the tasks performed by the workers. For example, those workers with jobs that measure high on variety, autonomy, and use of skills were found to be low on measures of political and personal alienation.

An earlier study of 1,156 employed men revealed that the best independent predictors of work alienation are (1) a work situation and hierarchical organization that provide little discretion in pace and schedule, (2) a career that has been blocked and chaotic, and (3) a stage in the life cycle that puts the "squeeze" on the worker (large numbers of dependent children and low amounts of savings).[7]

These findings offer hope for positive action. Had it been, as most have felt, that the blues *were* strongly linked with such attributes as age, sex, class, collar color, race, or educational achievement, there would have been little opportunity for effective action to moderate the destructive elements of the blues. But fortunately, working conditions are far easier to change than demographic factors.

Furthermore, it appears that conditions in the workplace cannot be ignored when considering the requisite conditions for a politically healthy citizenry. As Robert Dahl states, if workers were to

discover that participation in the affairs of the enterprise . . . contributed to their own sense of competence and helped them to control an important part of their daily lives, then lassitude and indifference toward participation might change into interest and concern.[8]

The blue-collar blues, undoubtedly, have more than one wellspring of discontent. The economic squeeze, an inequitable tax system (for example, the proportion of earned income paid in social security and sales taxes is higher for blue-collar workers than for workers in higher income groups), the erosion of neighborhoods, and the decline in municipal services are real and tangible blue-collar grievances. But genuine alleviation of the blues is unlikely without changes in the quality of working life for middle-Americans. To accomplish these changes we must first identify clearly the *special* problems of workers. One of these work-related problems appears to be that the blue-collar worker sees his mobility and his children's mobility blocked.

Worker Mobility Many blue-collar workers do not believe that there is a great deal of opportunity to move up the ladder of success, and the lack of alternatives produces frustration. Robert Quinn has shown statistically that both job satisfaction and mental health are poorer when a worker feels "locked-in" to his job.[9] Workers who feel there is little opportunity for mobility within their work organization, or little control over their job assignments, or little probability of getting another job elsewhere, characteristically suffer from tension, job dissatisfaction, and mental health problems.

Workers also are no longer confident that education provides a key to advancement. Robert Schrank and Susan Stein have claimed that whites who are blue-collar workers: (1) see the attack on the relevance of schools as an attack on their and their children's chances to "make it"; (2) feel that their school is being used for experiments in desegregation and are bitter that through compensatory education blacks are leap-frogging steps to advancement that they are still required to take; and (3) are frustrated by the fact that employers have raised the credential requirements for better jobs faster than they can gain them.[10]

Moreover, the impact of technology has been acutely felt by the blue-collar worker—not necessarily because it puts him out of a job, but because it lowers his status and satisfaction from the job. Schrank and Stein highlight the interplay between education and technology in the lives of blue-collar workers:

Knowledge, not skill, is the critical factor in modern technology. For example, a craftsman who can square off a piece of steel with a hand file may be a true artisan; but his artisanship is useless on a numerically controlled machine tool which needs someone who understands a system.[11]

Another major change that has been linked to the blues is the new composition of the blue-collar labor force. Traditionally, the ranks were filled by new European immigrants as the children of the old immigrants moved into white-collar jobs. Now, with unskilled immigration from Europe at an ebb, the children of blue-collar workers (both men and women) are becoming a second (or third) generation of blue-collar workers. This is an important factor in the recent increase in the blues, for working-class culture (like that of the middle class) dictates that people should be constantly improving their standard of living —children should do better materially than their parents.[12] This does not mean that the blue-collar worker's goal is to become an upper-middle-class intellectual. Rather, it is a reflection of the fact that a setback—to a worse job, to a smaller house, or to an older car—is a serious threat to those who have lived with the possibility of unemployment and failure. To follow in Dad's footsteps into the factory, then, is only acceptable if things are clearly much better there than they were for Dad.

Young blue-collar workers also are better educated than their parents. In 1960, 26% of white and 14% of black craftsmen and operatives had completed four years of high school. By 1969, 41% of whites and 29% of blacks in those jobs had completed a secondary education.[13] When we recall that decisive factors in job dissatisfaction are monotony, decreased chances for learning, and little need for exercising judgment and place these alongside the fact that blue-collar workers are better educated than ever before, we begin to see one of the real causes of their blues. These better-educated workers, quite clearly, are not so easily satisfied as their forebears with the quality of most blue-collar jobs—a fact verified by the Survey of Working Conditions.

Society's View of the Manual Worker We must also recognize that manual work has become increasingly denigrated by the upper middle class of this nation. The problems of self-esteem inherent in these changing attitudes are further compounded by the impact of the communications media. For example, the images of blue-collar workers that are presented by the media (including school textbooks) are often negative. Workers are presented as "hard-hats" (racists or authoritarians) or as "fat cats" (lazy plumbers who work only twenty-hour weeks yet earn $400.00 a week). The view of the worker in the mass media is that he is the problem, not that he *has* problems.

Today, there is virtually no accurate dramatic representation —as there was in the 1930's—of men and women in working-class occupations. Instead, we have recently had the movie *Joe* and the television series about Archie Bunker. These stereotypes—ignoring the heterogeneity of blue-collar workers—do little to enhance the dignity of the worker or his job. For example, what does Archie do on the job? Is he ashamed of his job? Is that why he won't talk about it at home? Certainly, if he worked in an office we would see scenes of him at work. The negative view of blue-collar work on the show is reinforced by the fact that Archie's "socially enlightened" son-in-law is a future professional.

Research shows that less than one character in ten on television is a blue-collar worker, and these few are usually portrayed as crude people with undesirable social traits. Furthermore, portrayals tend to emphasize class stereotypes: lawyers are clever, while construction workers are louts. But it is not only the self-image of the worker that is being affected; television is conveying to children superficial and misleading information about work in society.[14] If children do, indeed, learn from television, they will "learn" that professionals lead lives of carefree leisure, interspersed with drama and excitement (never hard work), and that blue-collar workers are racist clods who use bad grammar and produce little of use for society.

The ramifications of the low societal view of the worker are extensive and related to the personal problems of workers: low self-esteem, alcoholism, and withdrawal from community affairs. Our interviews with blue-collar workers revealed an almost overwhelming sense of inferiority: the worker cannot talk proudly to his children about his job, and many workers feel that they must apologize for their status. Thus, the working-class home may be permeated with an atmosphere of failure—even of depressing self-degradation. This problem of esteem and identity is, perhaps, related to the recent rise in ethnic consciousness among the working class.

Statistical evidence indicates that the working class is composed heavily of Americans who identify themselves as "ethnics." In 1969, 46 million Americans identified themselves as members of some specific ethnic group; over 20 million of these people were in families earning between $5,000 and $10,000 a year.[15] The revival in ethnic identity has occurred mainly among second and third generation Polish, Italian, and Slavic workers in this income group. This "return" to ethnicity (the parents of these workers never abandoned their traditional roots) has occurred mainly in large, industrial, Northern cities —principally in Chicago, Detroit, Pittsburgh, Philadelphia, New York, and Boston. Significantly, working-class "ethnics" in these cities tend to hold jobs that are not intrinsically satisfying —jobs in heavy industry (steel, autos) which have low prestige, low autonomy, and little opportunity for growth. Thus, trapped in jobs that do not offer a high degree of self-esteem, many of these workers appear to have turned to their ethnic groups for a healthy self-concept. The clan, the tribe, or the ethnic group offers unquestioning acceptance and membership as it shields the individual from assaults on his self-esteem. In summary, the critical variable in ethnic discontent may be the nature of the jobs held by these workers.

White-Collar Privileges Blue-collar discontent is exacerbated by distinctions between blue-collar and white-collar privileges on the job. For example, the blue-collar worker must punch time clocks, making it difficult for him to arrange his work schedule to manage such personal chores as visiting the doctor, getting his car repaired, and visiting the school to discuss his children's problems. More basically, 27% of all workers have no paid vacations, 40% have no sick leave,[16] and perhaps 70% will never receive a private pension check (even though large percentages may be employed in firms with pension plans).[17] Virtually all of those workers who are without these benefits are found among the ranks of non-professionals.

A problem related to management privileges is the general feeling among workers that their bosses abuse their disciplinary prerogatives, and that their unions do not challenge such "abuses." They often claim that work rules, particularly in the auto industry, are similar to military discipline. Some younger, more educated workers are even beginning to question the constitutionality of punishment at work without due process.

For example, in some industries supervisors have the right to send offending workers home and dock their salaries for the time they were not permitted to work. Many such arbitrary dismissals occur when young, better-educated workers come into conflict with older, less-educated foremen, who rose to their job in a more authoritarian age. Other instances are due to unclear work rules. An autoworker explains his conflict with authority:

I'm a relief man and there's a lot of jobs I used to relieve that used to be easy, but now they're hard and sometimes you can't do everything, you know. And then the foreman comes up there and starts nagging you—you tell him you can't keep up with it. You can't keep up with it and he still keeps nagging you and nagging you. And they have a lot of dual supervision out there now, where you got one foreman, your foreman who's supposed to tell you what to do, and then they got another foreman who comes along and tells you what to do. And that's not right—it gets confused.

Perhaps the most consistent complaint reported to our task force has been the failure of bosses to listen to workers who wish to propose better ways of doing their jobs. Workers feel that their bosses demonstrate little respect for their intelligence. Supervisors are said to feel that the workers are incapable of thinking creatively about their jobs.

In summary, the cause of the blue-collar blues is not bigotry, the demand for more money, or a changing work ethic. An autoworker explains the real genesis of the blues:

If you were in a plant you'd see—everybody thinks that General Motors workers have it easy, but it's not that easy. Some jobs you go home after eight hours and you're tired, your back is sore and you're sweatin'. All the jobs ain't that easy. We make good money; yeah, the money is real good out there, but that ain't all of it—cause there's really a lot of bad jobs out there.

Schrank hypothesizes that blue-collar blues "result from rising expectations of status and mobility and the apparent inability of the system to deliver." [18] But we believe that the system can deliver. The proposals we make later in this report for portable pensions, continuing education and retraining for workers, and for the redesign of work tasks are proper responses to the real problems of blue-collar workers. To do otherwise treats the symptoms, not the causes, of the blues. Great care, then, must be taken to interpret wisely the signs of discontent among workers. Increased industrial sabotage and sudden wildcat strikes, like the one at Lordstown, portend something more fundamental than the desire for more money. Allegiance to extremist political movements may mean something other than hatred of those of another color.

White-Collar Woes

The auto industry is the *locus classicus* of dissatisfying work; the assembly-line, its quintessential embodiment. But what is striking is the extent to which the dissatisfaction of the assembly-line and blue-collar worker is mirrored in white-collar and even managerial positions. The office today, where work is segmented and authoritarian, is often a factory. For a growing number of jobs, there is little to distinguish them but the color of the worker's collar: computer keypunch operations and typing pools share much in common with the automobile assembly-line.

Secretaries, clerks, and bureaucrats were once grateful for having been spared the dehumanization of the factory. White-collar jobs were rare; they had higher status than blue-collar jobs. But today the clerk, and not the operative on the assembly-line, is the typical American worker, and such positions offer little in the way of prestige. Furthermore, the size of the organizations that employ the bulk of office workers has grown, imparting to the clerical worker the same impersonality that the blue-collar worker experiences in the factory. The organization acknowledges the presence of the worker only when he makes a mistake or fails to follow a rule, whether in factory or bureaucracy, whether under public or private control. As Simone Weil wrote:

For the bureaucratic machine, though composed of flesh, and well-fed flesh at that, is nonetheless as irresponsible and as soulless as are machines made of iron and steel.[19]

In a report on *The Quality of Working Life*, prepared for NATO, N. A. B. Wilson wrote:

Lack of positive feedback and feeling of connection between the individual worker and the centers where decisions affecting him are made are inevitable to some degree in any large organization, but there is every reason to believe that they are especial hazards in government departments.[20]

Traditionally, lower-level white-collar jobs in both government and industry were held by high school graduates. Today, an increasing number of these jobs go to those who have attended college. But the demand for higher academic credentials has not increased the prestige, status, pay, or difficulty of the job. For example, the average weekly pay for clerical workers in 1969 was $105.00 per week, while blue-collar production workers were taking home an average of $130.00 per week.[21] It is not surprising, then, that the Survey of Working Conditions found much of the greatest work dissatisfaction in the country among young, well-educated workers who were in low-paying, dull, routine, and fractionated clerical positions. Other signs of discontent among this group include turnover rates as high as 30% annually and a 46% increase in white-collar union membership between 1958 and 1968.[22] A 1969 study of 25,000 white-collar employees in eighty-eight major companies showed a decline in the percentage of positive responses concerning several key factors of job satisfaction since 1965. For example, there was a 34% decline in the belief that their company would act to do something about their individual problems.[23] These changing attitudes (and the failure of employers to react constructively to them) may be affecting the productivity of these workers: a survey conducted by a group of management consultants of a cross section of office employees found that they were producing at only 55% of their potential. Among the reasons cited for this was boredom with repetitive jobs.[24]

Loyalty to employer was once high among this group of workers who felt that they shared much in common with their bosses —collar color, tasks, place of work. Today, many white-collar workers have lost personal touch with decision makers, and, consequently, they feel estranged from the goals of the organizations in which they work. Management has exacerbated this problem by viewing white-collar workers as expendable: because their productivity is hard to measure and their functions often non-essential, they are seen as the easiest place to "cut fat" during low points in the business cycle. Today, low-level white-collar workers are more likely to be sacrificed for the sake of short-term profitability than are blue-collar workers.

Managerial Discontent

One finds evidence of increasing dissatisfaction with jobs even among such traditionally privileged groups as the nation's 4½ million middle managers. For example, where this group once represented a bulwark of company loyalty, today one out of three middle managers indicates some willingness to join a union. Another striking indicator of discontent is the apparently increasing number of middle-aged middle managers who are seeking a mid-career change.[25]

Why should there be job dissatisfaction among people who earn twenty thousand dollars a year? Some trained observers say that the new values of the counter-culture have had a noticeable effect even on these workers who clearly espouse mainstream views. As evidence, it is claimed that where it used to be considered a sign of dedication and admirable ambition for a manager to be seen carrying home a full attaché case, today it is seen only as compulsive behavior or evidence of "workaholism."

Instead of pointing to such cultural explanations, management scientists point to the inherent qualities of the jobs of middle managers as the prime source of their dissatisfaction. Characteristically, middle managers perceive that they lack influence on organization decision making, yet they must implement company policy—and often without sufficient authority or resources to effectively carry it out. They must then compete to gain the attention of top management for support for their particular projects or functions. This leads to tension, conflict, and unproductive and frustrating in-fighting in that spectrum on the organization chart with responsibility for planning, integrating, and controlling the entire managerial system. The manager's discontent thus spreads throughout the organization. For example, managers without power often establish a style that consists of applying inflexible rules and procedures—thus, they bureaucratize an institution and frustrate change down the line.

Frustration often causes managers to lose their commitments to their jobs and the companies they work for. A Gallup Poll in 1972 asked whether the respondents thought "they could produce more each day if they tried." While 57% of the total public responded that they could, the figure for professionals and businessmen was 70%, only slightly behind the 72% of 18–29-year-olds who felt themselves to be least extended on the job.

A general feeling of obsolescence appears to overtake middle managers when they reach their late 30's. Their careers appear to have reached a plateau, and they realize that life from here on will be along an inevitable decline. There is a marked increase in the death rate between the ages of 35 and 40 for employed men, apparently as a result of this so-called "mid-life crisis." [26] The causes of these feelings are often related to questions of technical competence, but much obsolescence is cultural or interpersonal: some older managers cannot cope with the values of younger subordinates; some cannot adjust their sights to radically new organizational goals; and some have become so identified with a faction in the organization that has lost favor over time that they become ineffective.[27]

The dollar costs of managerial obsolescence are hidden in poor or poorly timed decisions, in a lack of innovation or creativity, and in negative effects on the productivity of others. Businesses seem to reflect this lower productivity of older managers in the salaries they pay them: for each additional year of service with a firm, middle managers typically receive smaller annual increases.[28]

The social costs of managerial obsolescence can be seen in Tayloristic or other outmoded philosophies that these managers instill throughout their companies. Their styles of management lead to tension and, often, to subsequent physical and mental health costs for their subordinates. The personal costs of managerial obsolescence relate to the ways they must compensate for their feelings of inadequacy: such coping mechanisms as alcohol and extramarital affairs are frequently used.

If we use only extrinsic measures of satisfaction—pay, prestige, fringe benefits—managers appear not to have work problems. But the social, industrial, and personal costs related to their intrinsic dissatisfactions make proposals to facilitate mid-career change through portable pensions and retraining seem highly desirable.

Many managers, indeed, appear to wish to return to school in order to change careers, but many are locked into their present jobs through the security they fear they will lose: e.g., service perquisites and pensions. Those middle managers over 40 years of age feel that their opportunity for re-employment is slim, and younger managers cannot afford to quit their jobs —they must wait until their children are through with *their* schooling. Limited evidence about those middle-aged people who have returned to school full time indicates that many have had pensions or other outside resources.[29] Clearly, this places the manager who can afford a mid-career educational experience among a fortunate minority of his peers.

The Young Worker—Challenging the Work Ethic?

More than any other group, it appears that young people have taken the lead in demanding better working conditions. Out of a workforce of more than 85 million, 22½ million are under the age of 30. As noted earlier, these young workers are more affluent and better educated than their parents were at their age. Factually, that is nearly all that can be generalized about this group. But it is asserted by such authors as Kenneth Keniston, Theodore Roszak, Charles Reich, and others, that great numbers of young people in this age group are members of a counter-culture. The President's Commission on Campus Unrest wrote that this subculture "found its identity in a rejection of the work ethic, materialism, and conventional social norms and pieties." Many writers have stressed the alleged revolt against work, "a new 'anti-work ethic' . . . a new, deep-seated rejection by the young of the traditional American faith in hard work." [30] But empirical findings do not always support the impressionistic commentaries.

It is commonly agreed that there is a difference between the in-mode behavior of youth and their real attitudes. Many young people do wear beads, listen to rock music, and occasionally smoke pot, but few actually live in communes (and these few may be working very hard), and even fewer are so alienated that they are unwilling to play a productive role in society. Daniel Yankelovich conducted national attitude studies of college students from 1968 to 1971 and found that two-thirds of college students profess mainstream views in general.[31] But their feelings in particular about work (and private business) are even more affirmative:

—79% believe that commitment to a meaningful career is a very important part of a person's life.

—85% feel business is entitled to make a profit.

—75% believe it is morally wrong to collect welfare when you can work.

—Only 30% would welcome less emphasis on working hard.

While student feelings about work itself are generally high, Yankelovich found that attitudes towards authority are changing rapidly. In 1968 over half (56% of all students indicated that they did not mind the future prospect of being "bossed around" on the job. By 1971 only one out of three students (36%) saw themselves willingly submitting to such authority. Equally important, while 86% of these students still believe that society needs some legally based authority to prevent chaos, they nevertheless see a distinction between this necessity and an authoritarian work setting.

Rising Expectations Yankelovich also found a shift in student opinion on the issue that "hard work will always pay off" from a 69% affirmation in 1968 to a 39% affirmation in 1971. This certainly was, in part, indicative of the conditions in the job market for college graduates in 1971. But more basically, we believe, it highlights a paradox inherent in a populace with increasing educational achievement. Along with the mass media, education and its credentials are raising expectations faster than the economic system can meet them. Much of what is interpreted as anti-work attitudes on the part of youth, then, may be their appraisal of the kinds of jobs that are open to them.

The following case study of a young woman who is a recent college graduate illustrates the gap between expectations and reality:

I didn't go to school for four years to type. I'm bored; continuously humiliated. They sent me to Xerox school for three hours. . . . I realize that I sound cocky, but after you've been in the academic world, after you've had your own class (as a student teacher) and made your own plans, and someone tries to teach you to push a button—you get pretty mad. They even gave me a goldplated plaque to show I've learned how to use the machine.[32]

The problem is compounded by the number of students who are leaving school with advanced degrees, like the young Chicago lawyer in the following case:

You can't wait to get out and get a job that will let you do something that's really important. . . . You think you're one of the elite. Then you go to a place like the Loop and there are all these lawyers, accountants, etc., and you realize that you're just a lawyer. No, not even a lawyer—an employee; you have to check in at nine and leave at five. I had lots of those jobs— summers—where you punch in and punch out. You think it's going to be different but it isn't. You're in the rut like everybody else.[33]

Today's youth are expecting a great deal of intrinsic reward from work. Yankelovich found that students rank the opportunity to "make a contribution," "job challenge," and the chance to find "self-expression" at the top of the list of influences on their career choice. A 1960 survey of over 400,000 high school students was repeated for a representative sample in 1970, and the findings showed a marked shift from the students valuing job security and opportunity for promotion in 1960 to valuing "freedom to make my own decisions" and "work that seems important to me" in 1970.[34]

Many of these student findings were replicated in the Survey of Working Conditions sample of young workers. For example, it seems as true of young workers as it is of students that they expect a great deal of fulfillment from work. But the Survey findings show that young workers are not deriving a great deal of satisfaction from the work they are doing. Less than a quarter of young workers reply "very often" when asked the question, "How often do you feel you leave work with a good feeling that you have done something particularly well?"

Age Group	Percentage Answering "Very Often"
Under 20	23
21–29	25
30–44	38
45–64	43
65 and over	53

Other findings document that young workers place more importance on the value of interesting work and their ability to grow on the job than do their elders. They also place less importance than do older workers on such extrinsic factors as security and whether or not they are asked to do excessive amounts of work. But the Survey documents a significant gap between the expectations or values of the young workers and what they actually experience on the job. Young workers rate their jobs lower than do older workers on how well their jobs actually live up to the factors they most sought in work. For example, the young value challenging work highly but say that the work they are doing has a low level of challenge.

It has also been found that a much higher percentage of younger than older workers feel that management emphasizes the *quantity* more than the *quality* of their work. Furthermore, it is shown that this adversely affects the satisfaction of younger workers. Such findings contradict the viewpoint that there is a weakening of the "moral fiber" of youth.[35]

Many young union members are challenging some basic assumptions about "a fair day's work for a fair day's pay." In the past, unions concerned themselves with establishing what a fair day's pay would be, while the employer's prerogative was to determine what constitutes a fair day's work. Young workers are now challenging both unions and management by demanding a voice in the setting of both standards, as the following case illustrates:

Three young workers, aged twenty and twenty-one, were hired to clean offices at night. One evening the foreman caught one of the young janitors (who went to school during the day) doing his homework; another was reading the paper and the third was asleep with his feet up on a desk. The foreman exploded and gave them a written warning. The workers filed a grievance protesting the warnings: "We cleaned all the offices in five hours by really hustling and who the hell should get upset because we then did our own thing." One young worker said, "At school during study period I get my studies done in less than the hour and no one bugs me when I do other things for the rest of the time. We cleaned all those offices in five hours instead of eight. What more do they want?"

The union steward said he tried hard to understand what they were saying: "But the company has the right to expect eight hours work for eight hours pay. I finally got the kids to understand by taking them outside and telling them that if they got the work finished in five hours, then the company would either give them more work, or get rid of one of them. They're spacing it out nicely now and everyone's happy," he said, satisfied to have settled the grievance within the understood rules.[36]

The author of this study writes that the young workers were far from satisfied with the agreement. They wanted the union to establish what had to be done and how much they would be paid to do it, and then they wanted the same freedom that professionals have to decide how to operate within the time and work frame allotted.

In summary, we interpret these various findings not as demonstrating a shift away from valuing work *per se* among young people, but as a shift away from their willingness to take on meaningless work in authoritarian settings that offers only extrinsic rewards. We agree with Willis Harman that:

The shape of the future will no more be patterned after the hippie movement and the Youth Revolution than the Industrial Age could have been inferred from the "New Age" values of the Anabaptists.[37]

New Values A mistake is made, however, if one believes that the new attitudes toward authority and the meaning of work are limited to hippies. Judson Gooding writes that young managers, both graduates of business schools and executive trainees, "reflect the passionate concerns of youth in the 1970's—for individuality, openness, humanism, concern and change—and they are determined to be heard." [38]

Some young people are rejecting the corporate or bureaucratic worlds, while not rejecting work or the concept of work or profit. Gooding tells of one young former executive who quit his job with a major corporation because

You felt like a small cog. Working there was dehumanizing and the struggle to get to the top didn't seem worth it. They made no effort to encourage your participation. The decisions were made in those rooms with closed doors. . . . The serious error they made with me was not giving me a glimpse of the big picture from time to time, so I could go back to my little detail, understanding how it related to the whole.[39]

This young man has now organized his own small business and designed his own job. As the publisher of a counter-culture newspaper, he might be considered a radical in his beliefs and life style, yet he says "profit is not an evil." Of course, many young workers do question the *use* of profits, especially those profits that they feel are made at the expense of society or the environment. Some businesses themselves are adopting this same attitude.

It may be useful to analyze the views of today's youth not in terms of their parents' values but in terms of the beliefs of their grandparents. Today's youth believe in independence, freedom, and risk—in short, they may have the entrepreneurial spirit of early capitalism. Certainly they are more attracted to small and growing companies, to small businesses and to handicrafts, than to the bureaucracy, be it privately or publicly owned. (The declining opportunity for such small-scale endeavors [documented in Chapter 1] probably contributes to both the job dissatisfaction of the young and their apparent lack of commitment to the kinds of jobs that are available.) On the other hand, their parents share a managerial ethic that reflects the need for security, order, and dependence that is born of hard times. Of course, this is being a bit unfair to the older generation and a bit over-generous with our youth, but it serves to get us away from the simplistic thinking that the "Protestant ethic has been abandoned." Who in America ever had the Protestant ethic and when? Did we have it in the thirties? Did the poor people or even middle-class people ever have it? It is argued by Sebastian deGrazia that the Protestant ethic was never more than a myth engendered by the owner and managerial classes to motivate the lower working class—a myth which the latter never fully accepted.[40] Clearly, it is difficult to measure the past allegiance of a populace to an ideology.

But we *can* measure the impact of the present work environment on youth's motivation to work. For example, the Survey of Working Conditions found that youth seem to have a lower attachment to work than their elders on the same job. There are several reasons other than a change in the work ethic why this might be so. *First,* as we have already posited, young people have high expectations generated by their greater education. *Second,* their greater affluence makes them less tolerant of unrewarding jobs. *Third,* many new workers, particularly women, are voluntary workers. They are more demanding because they don't *have* to take a job. *Fourth,* all authority in our society is being challenged—professional athletes challenge owners, journalists challenge editors, consumers challenge manufacturers, the moral authority of religion, nation, and elders is challenged. *Fifth,* many former students are demanding what they achieved in part on their campuses a few years ago—a voice in setting the goals of the organization. The lecture has been *passé* for several years on many campuses—in colloquia and in seminars students challenge teachers. Managers are now facing the products of this progressive education. (One wonders what will happen when the children of today's open classroom, who have been taught to set their own goals and plan their own schedules, enter the workforce.)[41] *Sixth,* young blue-collar workers, who have grown up in an environment in which equality is called for in all institutions, are demanding the same rights and expressing the same values as university graduates. *Seventh,* there is growing professionalism among many young white-collar workers. They now have loyalty to their peer group or to their task or discipline, where once they had loyalty to their work organization.

In sum, it does not appear that young workers have a lower commitment to work than their elders. The problem lies in the interaction between work itself and the changing social character of today's generation, and in the failure of decision makers in business, labor, and government to recognize this fact.

The young worker is in revolt not against work but against the authoritarian system developed by industrial engineers who felt that "the worker was stupid, overly emotional . . . insecure and afraid of responsibility." [42] This viewpoint is summed up in Frederick Taylor's classic dictum to the worker:

For success, then, let me give one simple piece of advice beyond all others. Every day, year in and year out, each man should ask himself, over and over again, two questions. First, "What is the name of the man I am now working for?" and having answered this definitely, then, "What does this man want me to do, right now?"

The simplistic authoritarianism in this statement would appear ludicrous to the young worker who is not the uneducated and irresponsible person on whom Taylor's system was premised. Yet, many in industry continue to support a system of motivation that was created in an era when people were willing to be motivated by the stick. As an alternative to this approach, many personnel managers have offered the carrot as a motivator, only to find that young people also fail to respond to this approach.

From our reading of what youth wants, it appears that under current policies, employers may not be able to motivate young workers at all. Instead, employers must create conditions in which the worker can motivate himself. This concept is not as strange as it seems. From biographies of artists, athletes, and successful businessmen, one finds invariably that these people set goals for *themselves*. The most rewarding race is probably one that one runs against oneself. Young people seem to realize this. They talk less positively than do their elders about competition with others. But they do talk about self-actualization and other "private" values. Yankelovich found that 40% of students—an increasing percentage—do not believe that "competition encourages excellence," and 80% would welcome more emphasis in the society on self-expression.

Compared to previous generations, the young person of today wants to measure his improvement against a standard he sets for himself. (Clearly, there is much more inner-direction than David Riesman would have predicted two decades ago.) The problem with the way work is organized today is that it will not allow the worker to realize his own goals. Because of the legacy of Taylorism, organizations set a fixed standard for the worker, but they often do not tell him clearly why that standard was set or how it was set. More often than not, the standard is inappropriate for the worker. And, in a strange contradiction to the philosophy of efficient management, the organization seldom gives the worker the wherewithal to achieve the standard. It is as if the runner did not know where the finish line was; the rules make it a race that no worker can win.

It is problematic whether the intolerance among young workers of such poor management signals temporary or enduring changes in the work ethic. More important is how management and society will reckon with the new emphasis that the workplace should lose its authoritarian aura and become a setting for satisfying and self-actualizing activity.

The Minority Worker

Minority workers and their families are serious casualties of the work system in our society. One out of three minority workers is unemployed, irregularly employed, or has given up looking for a job. Another third of minority workers do have jobs—full time, year-round jobs—but these are mainly laboring jobs and jobs in the service trades which often pay less than a living wage.[43]

In the logic of "first things first," the minority worker's most immediate need is for a job that pays enough to support himself and his family. For many such workers, the goal of a quality job that offers a range of intrinsic satisfactions is seen as a luxury that they cannot yet afford, and many look for jobs—the only ones they are likely to get—that they know beforehand they will hate. In effect, minority workers are the unwilling monopolists of the worst jobs that our society has to offer. Yet, even these jobs are despised not so much because the worker can't take satisfaction from the work itself but because he can't earn a minimally decent living by doing them.

A few statistics can help state the problem in simple money terms: the median income of all adult males in the U.S. in 1969 was $6,429; the median income for minority males in that same year was $3,991. For all women, the median income was $2,132; for minority women, $1,084. Finally, 33.6 percent of all males had a money income of less than $4,000 in 1969, but 50 percent of minority males received less than $4,000 in that year.

Not all poor people, of course, are black, Chicano, Puerto Rican, or Indian, nor are all minority persons poor. The point here is that minority workers are, to a striking degree, disproportionately unemployed or working at bad jobs. This disproportion reflects the persistent, systematic discrimination and closed off opportunities that racial minority persons experience in work, education, and other major institutions in our society.

One might expect that the third of minority workers in middle-level blue-collar, white-collar, and professional jobs would find their jobs as rewarding as their white counterparts do, but this does not seem to be the case. The most dissatisfied group of American workers, for example, is found among young black people in white-collar jobs. The Survey of Working Conditions reveals that 37% of blacks under age 20 express negative attitudes about their jobs. Through age 44, blacks are about twice as likely as whites to be dissatisfied with their current work. Beyond that age, the percentage of dissatisfied blacks drops to below the level for whites. But older blacks are twice as dissatisfied with their lives in general as they are with their jobs (most other groups are about as satisfied with one as they are with the other). This suggests that older black people—who often have experienced years of employment discrimination—are unique in that they view the issue of job satisfaction primarily in terms of employment vs. no employment—a sad commentary on the long-range effects of racial injustice.

Another important finding of the Survey was that, unlike for whites, satisfaction does not increase for blacks until their incomes surpass $10,000 a year. Blacks with incomes below this level apparently feel that small increments in income do not offer them sufficiently greater ability to consume. This is probably a reflection of the fact that the minority dollar at that level of income does not buy the same amount of housing, education, or consumer goods that the dollars of whites and wealthy minority group members buy. (This finding may also provide a key to why very small monetary incentives to work provided by welfare programs often fail to motivate workers who are at the margin of poverty.)

The Survey also found that minority workers, like whites, are dissatisfied with meaningless, routine, and authoritarian work tasks and environments. But for many employed blacks, problems of discrimination take precedence over many of these issues. (And, often, blacks express concern with these issues in terms of discrimination.) Undertrained black workers who find themselves in highly competitive "white" work environments scarcely have the luxury of searching for intrinsic work rewards. They are worried about security and survival in what they undoubtedly feel is a hostile and threatening work situation. The Survey findings support this interpretation. They reveal that 22% of black workers under age 44 complain of racial discrimination on the job while only 5% of older blacks report such problems. Furthermore, only 12% of blacks in blue-collar jobs say they experience discrimination, as opposed to 29% among blacks in white-collar jobs.

Thus, perceptions of racial discrimination are most prevalent among those blacks who are young, educated, and in white-collar jobs. These are young people who have seen the rules of society turned around in their favor within their own lives. They now find themselves in environments in which only people with considerable self-confidence and experience find themselves comfortable. These young workers, like their employers, were unprepared for the radical shift in the opportunity structure in business. The psychiatric case study presented below illustrates the peculiar difficulties that blacks may experience when they enter into occupations once reserved for whites:

Let us finally tell you about John. Some years ago he sought psychiatric help because he was facing court action. In an outburst of temper he had injured a fellow worker and was being sued. . . . His crippling symptom, however, had to do with work, and, in a larger sense, with success. It all came to focus on a job he obtained while in treatment. He joined an executive training program with a group of eager young men who were to compete against one another for a few positions that led rapidly up the management ladder. . . . He entered the scene full of confidence and as he compared himself with the others he saw that he had many advantages. He performed brilliantly in the classroom. On occasion he felt dismay over what seemed to be a pervasive confidence in his white middle-class competitors. . . . At about this time the training schedule called for a week of specialized study in another city and John's entire class was flown to that city and given comfortable hotel accommodations. . . . John returned from the trip shaken. . . . The crux of the problem seemed to lie in the luxurious surroundings. . . . And perhaps the most troubling aspect of the whole situation was the ease with which John's white colleagues seemed to accept this bounty as the most natural thing in the world. . . . He was troubled and wanted to establish the "proper" relationship with other Negroes who had jobs inferior to his own. . . . He felt uneasy with white employees at a level below his own. . . . On one occasion an immediate superior suggested that he take care of his dress. . . . This hurt him deeply. . . . While the training program was complex and comprehensive, the essential skill to be mastered and demonstrated was the capacity for supervision. . . . When this became clear John was troubled by the difficulty he had in being firm with subordinates. . . . At about this time his supervisor called him in and told him his continuing deficiency was serious and was likely to jeopardize his success in the program. John felt trapped and tried desperately to do better, but to no avail. His depression deepened, his efficiency dropped, and he was finally dismissed as a failure.[44]

This case history could be offered in a *class* rather than a *race* context, since many problems of human adjustment have to do with shifts in socio-economic roles. But the problem of adjustment is exacerbated by conflicting white and black standards of language, dress, demeanor, and conduct. Employers often use white standards to judge employees without recognizing this conflict. Indeed, it is alleged by some blacks that even workers serving black customers in enterprises owned by whites must meet standards of whites rather than blacks. Young blacks raise the question of whether employers have a responsibility to recognize the legitimacy of black life styles and attitudes regarding employment matters. To complicate the issue, young minority group leaders sometimes argue that for employers and the society to assume a "responsibility" for them smacks of what they call a "plantation mentality." They would prefer to speak of the "rights" of minority workers. Indeed, even this may be too "liberal" a term for them. Increasingly, they speak of "community requirements and demands" with respect to employment and advancement.[45]

These developments underscore the point that for many people, equality, as Max Ways has written, "is a steep and endless stair." [46] The work problems of young blacks are perceived as problems of equality. Therefore, the problems are not easily quantified and not easily rectified. Because of this, white employers (and, often, white co-workers) are becoming increasingly frustrated (and intolerant) as black demands accelerate almost in proportion to employers' concessions.

Equality, Ways says, "reflects the desire of individuals to emulate the good life as exemplified by others, to catch up, to improve, to excel, to contribute, to count (and be counted) as responsible actors in their time." Viewed in this respect, the problems of young minority workers are closely related to the issues of participation and self-actualization that affect all workers, regardless of race or ethnic background.

Clearly, the issue that stands behind black attitudes about

discrimination in general is that they feel that they have been denied full and equal participation in American society. They have had little control over the institutions that affect their lives—community, political, educational, or economic. The current design of work—the one place where most blacks have intimate contact with whites—reinforces their feelings of discrimination. Therefore, the redesign of work tasks to increase worker participation in the decisions that directly affect the worker may be *particularly responsive* to the needs of minority group members.

Likewise, the removal of authoritarian work settings will be especially important to minority workers who see insensitive and order-barking white "bosses" as representatives of a social order designed to keep them in the lower strata. Such innovations as non-hierarchical (or autonomous) work groups might demonstrate to minority workers that they are respected as equals. Sullen and hostile minority workers can never be cajoled or threatened into cooperative attitudes in the workplace. They will only become fully productive when the signs of discrimination (as they define them) have been removed.

Employers who learn to deal with the rising and changing demands of minorities (which sometimes merely means not being put off by insulting rhetoric) will contribute to their own welfare and to the welfare of the society in the long run. As Ways says, we must realize that equality is not a zero-sum game. Each player's gain need not be matched exactly by another's loss, for "again and again, the sum of gains has exceeded the sums of the losses." One of the gains of a congenial work environment that demonstrates respect and trust for all workers is likely to be an increase in the productive contributions of minority workers.

Perspectives on Women and Work
Housekeeping may still be the main occupation of American women, but it is no longer the only occupation or source of

identity for most of them. In the past, a woman's sense of identity and main source of satisfaction centered on the husband's job, the home, and the family. Today, there are alternatives opening to increasing numbers of the female population. In addition to the fact that half of all women between the ages of 18 and 64 are presently in the labor force, Department of Labor studies have shown that 9 out of 10 women will work outside the home at some time in their lives.[47] Increasingly, women of all ages are year-round, full-time members of the labor force. For many of these women, the traditional role played by work in the home is being supplemented or supplanted by work in the labor force. The following comment is probably not atypical for a working woman today:

. . . I had no confidence in myself, except at my job. I kept on feeling, if only I could find some missing element, I could enjoy cleaning house. But the whole thing is structured so that a woman loses her identity, so that she puts herself aside for another person. Men don't benefit either, but they don't lose so much. It was no problem for my husband. He didn't need to get his identity from our marriage. He got it from his job.[48]

The women's movement has focused considerable attention on the role of work in life, and because of the kinds of dissatisfying jobs they have held traditionally, we can reasonably expect women to be speaking out more forcefully on the quality of working life.

What is the quality of working life for women in the labor force? The job of secretary is perhaps symbolic of the status of female employment in this country, both qualitatively and quantitatively. There are 9 million secretaries and they compose nearly one-third of the nation's female workforce. Judy Klemesrud has written that the secretary is often stereotyped as a "gum-chewing sex kitten; husband hunter; miniskirted ding-a-ling; slow-witted pencil pusher; office go-fer ['go-fer coffee,' etc.]; reliable old shoe." [49] Certainly, many secretaries have very poor jobs by the accepted standards of job satisfaction. Typists, in particular, have low status, little autonomy, little opportunity for growth, and receive low pay. In many instances (in typing pools, for example), the typist is viewed as little more than an appendage to the machine she operates. But the problems of women and work extend far beyond just this one often unrewarding job.

Much of the work that women currently do outside their homes deflates their self-images. The majority of the worst white-collar jobs probably are held by women: keypunch operators, telephone company operators, and clerical workers. Women are also over-represented on assembly-lines—the worst jobs in the economy. Yet, as the Survey of Working Conditions showed, women tend to derive the same satisfaction as men do from the intrinsic rewards of work—when they are available. The Survey also found, however, that women are nearly twice as likely as men to express negative attitudes toward their present jobs. The cause of this dissatisfaction seems to lie in the discrepancy between women's high expectations about work and the actual low social and economic statuses of their jobs. Education is another important variable. A recent study of *The Quality of Life* shows that college educated women are most happy if they have jobs, and less happy if they don't (presumably because they tend to have more interesting jobs); married women without college educations are not necessarily less happy if they don't have jobs (presumably because of the less interesting jobs that are available to them).[50]

Keeping these factors in mind, we can turn to a closer examination of work in the lives of women. The most important fact is that almost all women are working unless they are disabled. Some work in the market for pay; others work in the home; and many do both. In what follows, we will first look at the social and economic factors relating to job satisfaction for women in the market and then briefly examine home work.

Women in the Labor Force It is necessary to understand some of the psychological obstacles that have thwarted women in their attempts to be successful, effective, and satisfied participants in their work. One of the major barriers to the full utilization of women in the labor force has been the perpetuation of myths and fallacious generalizations about women as a group. Most of these myths are based on traditional concepts about women which have long ceased to have any validity or relevance. The factual basis for many of these myths has been challenged by statistical measures.

For example, marriage and the attendant child bearing and rearing are often seen as preventing a woman from working or as having unproductive consequences for the job itself due to excessive absenteeism or a high turnover rate. According to national statistics, of the female workforce, which numbered 31.5 million in 1970, four out of ten women were mothers.[51] Of these working mothers, 36 percent have children under the age of six. A Public Health Service survey of work time lost due to illness or injury revealed that women lost on the average 5.6 days as compared to 5.3 for men. The available statistics on labor turnover indicate that net differences for men and women were also small. In 1968, the monthly quit rates averaged 2.2 percent for males and 2.6 for females in manufacturing industries while median years on current jobs were equal to 4.8 for males and 2.4 for females.[52] While it is true that many women leave work for childbirth, this absence is temporary for the majority of them. And, despite the break in employment, the average woman worker has a worklife expectancy of 25 years. The single woman worker averages 45 years in the labor force, as compared with 43 years for the male.[53]

Where an individual employer's statistics reflect significantly higher turnover rates or absenteeism, it may be because he restricts his employment of women to clerical and other low-status jobs. Shorter job tenure for women can clearly be related to the employment of women at lower levels of the occupational scale where they have little prospect for advancement or job satisfaction.

Prospects for advancement for women employees may be further curtailed because of the belief that neither women nor men work well for women supervisors. A Department of Labor survey indicates that at least three-fourths of both male and female respondents (all executives) who had worked for women held favorable views of women supervisors. Nonetheless, few firms are willing to invest in executive training programs for their female employees. As a result, women's earnings do not increase as they gain additional experience, and the male-female earnings gap widens with age. Even more surprising is the fact that this kind of flat "age-earnings profile" is almost as characteristic of career-oriented women who work continuously as it is for those with more limited work experience. Apparently, these women suffer by association with other women or are subjected to "statistical discrimination" as females.

Sex-Typing One of the most pervasive and consequential of all cultural attitudes relating to sex concerns occupational sex-typing. Occupational sex-typing occurs when a large majority of those in an occupation are of one sex, and when there is an associated normative expectation that this is how things should be. Characteristics necessary for success in a sex-typed occupation become those associated with either a male or female role stereotype. Thus, occupations for women are found closely linked to their homemaking role; others to their socialization as men's helpmates. Conversely, occupations from which women are excluded tend to be those that involve "non-feminine" pursuits or those that necessitate supervision of other employees. The result of these exclusionary practices is to crowd women into a limited number of jobs where the pressures of excess supply lowers wages below the level that would otherwise prevail. Women become secretaries, schoolteachers, waitresses, and nurses, while men become plumbers, doctors, engineers, and school administrators. Once such a division of labor becomes established, it tends to be self-perpetuating since each sex is socialized, trained, and counseled into certain jobs and not into others.

The particular division of labor that emerges has little social or economic rationale. What is "man's work" in one period or place may become "woman's work" under different circumstances. For example, schoolteaching, telephone operating, and clerical work were once male occupations in the United States. More recently, the occupations of bank teller and school crossing guard have been feminized. In the Soviet Union, 79 percent of the doctors, 37 percent of the lawyers, 32 percent of the engineers, and 76 percent of the economists are female.[54] Thus, cross-cultural and historical materials suggest that the present occupational structure does not reflect basic and unchanging differences in temperament or ability between the sexes. More important, a rather extensive body of evidence shows that the present division of labor is not the result of differences in the quality or the demographic composition of the male and female labor force. Nor are there important differences between working men and women where schooling, age, race, and geographical distributions are concerned.[55]

Economic Disparities With these social considerations in mind, we can turn to several economic factors relating to job satisfaction for women. These factors include wage disparities, lack of incentives for participation in the labor force, and unemployment problems of women.

There is some evidence that differences in earnings of men and women are quite large. In 1955, the average female employee earned 64 percent of the wages paid to a similarly employed man; and by 1970, she took home only 59 percent as much. This wage disparity is reflected in a more tangible sense in the figures for saleswork in the United States for 1970. In the sales field, women averaged $4,188 versus $9,790 earned by similarly employed salesmen.[56] (A good part of this discrepancy is due to differences in proportion of year worked. For exam-

ple, only 25 percent of women sales workers were employed
full-year, full-time in 1969, as compared to 68 percent of male
sales workers.)

While strides to correct pay discrepancies have been made
through equal pay legislation, many economists dismiss the significance of this approach, pointing out that discrimination
against women more often takes the form of job segregation
rather than unequal pay; that is, women are being penalized
not so much by being underpaid as by being underutilized.
While this is the case more often than not, courts that have defined equal work as that which is "substantially" equal have
ruled that $441½ million in back wages are due to over 108,000
employees under the Equal Pay Act of 1963.[57]

Government is quite appropriately reluctant to intervene in
matters involving family life. Consequently, those responsible
for public policy have often shied away from taking a stand on
the pros and cons of women working. Yet the issue has a way
of coming in the back door, and it is doubtful that there is such
a thing as a truly neutral policy. For example, the lack of availability of adequate day care facilities has had the effect of preventing many women who would wish to enter the labor force
from doing so. At present, only 2% of the children of working
mothers are in group care institutions (day care centers, nursery
schools, and after-school centers). It is likely that many more
women would enter the labor force if suitable, inexpensive
child care facilities were available. But government subsidies
could tend to create a bias in favor of institutionalized as opposed to other types of care. This is a problem because it is not
at all clear what the long-range effects are on a child raised in a
day care setting without the influence of either parent. In
Sweden, for example, the government is considering ways in
which reductions in working hours could best be distributed
over the working week so that husbands as well as wives could
participate more fully in child care and other household tasks.[58]

In addition to such disincentives for participation, another area of Federal policy that is of concern to women is female unemployment. Significantly, 11% of all families in the U.S. in 1967 were headed by females, the majority of whom were in the labor force.[59] The unemployment rate of this group was substantially higher than the rate for married men. It is sometimes suggested or implied that unemployment among women is less serious than it is among men—these figures for mother-headed households belie such assumptions. It is true that many married women are "secondary workers" in the sense that their income is additional to, and much smaller than, their husband's. Yet 86 percent of all working wives had husbands earning less than $10,000 per annum. In 1966, 61 percent had husbands earning less than $7,000. Most women work, then, for economic reasons, not just for "pin money." [60] They work to secure additional income to provide their families with a car, home, or college educations that could not otherwise be afforded. The average woman worker is a secretary who increases family income by about 25%, and this permits many lower-middle-class families to achieve middle-class status, something the husband could not achieve for his family on his own. Sociologically as well as economically, this is an important fact: It means that women in white-collar jobs are quite often married to men who are in blue-collar jobs. The effect of this status differential within the family should not be overlooked. It helps to explain why many men oppose women working. For blue-collar men, far more than white-collar men, retain strong beliefs about the "division of labor" between the sexes. A wife who works at a higher-paid job than her blue-collar husband damages his self-esteem because he feels he has failed as a breadwinner. Research shows that both partners are lower in marriage happiness if the wife works out of necessity rather than if she works by choice. In addition, it has been found that among male blue-collar workers, discontent with life is highest for those whose wives were also working.[61] One way out of this unhappy dilemma is to work toward the elimination of sex, class, and role stereotypes which damage the self-esteem of both men and women in the working class.

Women's status as "secondary workers" is largely the result of their roles as mothers and their lower earnings. Ironically, if there were less sex bias in employment opportunities, women's income would less frequently be "the marginal income," and there would probably be greater concern about their unemployment rates, in spite of the fact that self-supporting women, female family-heads, and families dependent on the wife's earnings would be in a much less precarious position than is now the case.

In light of these considerations, unemployment among women deserves more serious attention. Women face substantially higher unemployment rates than men. (The respective rates were 4.7 and 2.8 in 1969 and 6.9 and 5.3 in 1971.) Significantly, economists have shown that the greater the dispersion of unemployment rates in an economy, the more difficult it is to achieve acceptable trade-offs between inflation and unemployment. Thus, any policy that reduced this dispersion (even if it did not change the average unemployment rate) would decrease the rate of inflation associated with that level of unemployment. Also, the division of jobs into male and female categories reduces the efficiency of making placements and thereby raises the levels of unemployment and unfilled jobs.

Working at Home Although more and more women are seeking paid employment, the majority of the female population of working age is still engaged in "keeping house." It has been estimated that working women spend an average of 40 hours per week on housework which, when added to their market work, means that they probably end up doing a much higher proportion of society's total work (paid and unpaid) during a given year than men.[62]

Juanita Kreps calculates that the 1960 GNP would have increased by $105 billion, or by over one-sixth, if all homemaking wives (aged 18 and over) without preschool children had been employed outside the home.[63] Although she does not claim that these women would make any greater productive contribution in the market than they do in the home, she does suggest that our failure to include the value of housewives' services in the gross national income may have important consequences for the social status attached to this occupation. There are two consequences of this situation. *First,* women may choose market over nonmarket work because they—and others—undervalue the latter, and this may lead to a misallocation of resources between the two activities. *Second,* women with little or no alternative source of income may be forced to work even when society might benefit more from their nonmarket activities. Thus, subsidies to AFDC mothers could well be justified as payments for nonmarket work rather than as a dole in lieu of "work."

In summary, it is clear women have consistently been relegated to the lower-paying, lower-status jobs in the money economy. Their actual contribution to the economy is far below what could reasonably be expected on the basis of their education, abilities, and work experience. The occupational status of women is the major symptom of an opportunity structure that is much more limiting for women than for men. And, work in the home is not considered to be "real work" by society.

How can these situations be remedied? Equal employment opportunity legislation may be of significance, especially when it involves affirmative action programs that require employers to take the initiative in recruiting and promoting women in all types of work, prohibit sex segregating ads, and concentrate on eliminating discriminatory patterns and practices. However, additional programs must be designed to cope with institutional sexism, not just individual prejudice. Many of our present laws and court procedures help protect women against overt acts of exclusion, but they are of little use in eliminating customary patterns of behavior and cultural stereotypes that limit opportunities for all but the most aggressive of a discriminated-against group.

A serious concern over the job satisfaction of women workers indicates the need: (1) to change the cultural stereotypes about the character of females, (2) to achieve mobility and earnings parity between the sexes, (3) to substantially advance the opportunities for voluntary participation of women in the labor force, (4) to eliminate traditional factors that denigrate women who work by choice in the money economy without building new pressures that denigrate women who freely choose work in the home, and (5) to redesign the jobs of women and men to make them more intrinsically rewarding.

Older Workers and Retirement

In 1900, two-thirds of American men who were 65 years of age and older were working. By 1971, the figure had dropped to one-fourth, with a smaller proportion on a year-round, full-time basis. For most of the members of this age group today, we expect and often require them to retire.

To some extent, humane considerations have been important in this uncoupling of the older person from the workforce. Because much of the labor in the early and middle stages of the industrial revolution consisted of heavy, physical effort over a long workday and workweek, relief through retirement became a desirable goal. The same humaneness is to be found today in the efforts to secure relief from the psychological burden of routine, monotonous, and fragmented jobs. In this view, retirement is one of several escapes from work; short workdays and workweeks, and longer or more numerous holidays are others.

But other factors appear to have played a much stronger and pervasive part in the reduction of employment opportunities for older Americans:

1. The Great Depression drastically reduced the total demand for employable persons. During this period, retirement, through

Social Security benefits, became a conventional tool for dealing with our unemployment problem by eliminating part of the population from the competition for scarce jobs. In recent years, when unemployment has never fallen below 3.5% of the civilian labor force, pension plans have become a primary means for distributing an inadequate amount of work.

2. The number of elderly has expanded, along with their percentage of the population. Between 1940 and 1970, the number of people 65 years of age and older increased from 9 million to 20 million, and from 6.8% to 9.9% of the population. In earlier years, high death rates kept their numbers and percentage down.

3. Attitudes toward the past—and the elderly are the living repositories of the past—changed markedly, downgrading the contributions and perceived value of the aged. "Industrial society," J. H. Plumb writes, "unlike the commercial, craft, and agrarian societies which it replaces, does not need the past. Its intellectual and emotional orientation is towards change rather than conservation, towards exploitation and consumption. The new methods, new processes, new forms of living of scientific and industrial society have no sanction in the past and no roots in it." [64] This emphasis on novelty, concomitant with the rapid pace at which change has been introduced, as Alvin Toffler notes in *Future Shock*, has led to a "throw-away" culture. The aged are one of our "throw-aways."

4. The industrial revolution required workers to be highly mobile and not to be bound to any specific locale or set of traditions. Housing and transportation policies were joined to that need, thereby giving impetus to the nuclearization of the American family and the demise of the three-generation household. The elderly and their problems could then be subsumed under what Philip Slater calls our "Toilet Assumption," which is "the notion that unwanted matter, unwanted difficulties, unwanted complexities and obstacles will disappear if they are removed from our immediate field of vision. . . . We throw the aged and psychotics into institutional holes where they cannot

be seen. . . . Our approach to social problems is to decrease their visibility. . . . When these discarded problems rise to the surface again . . . we react as if a sewer had backed up." [65] In large measure, then, we stopped caring. When the sewer backed up, we assuaged our guilt with a few piecemeal, inadequate bureaucratic responses. Perhaps the most interesting social maneuver we have undertaken has been to enforce a certain degree of filial responsibility through payroll taxes for Social Security. Although benefits for the elderly are a function of what they and their employers have contributed, they are only loosely so; the system definitely entails a significant redistribution of funds from "their children" to the elderly.

5. We have come to associate aging *per se* as an unqualified sign of decreasing work and training capacity, without regard for the heterogeneity of the 60-plus age group and in ignorance of new and special work arrangements and retraining techniques.

Because we have been little concerned with (or blind to) the effects of these changes in our treatment of and attitudes toward the elderly, we have not bothered to collect very much systematic information about the effects. We have ignored their contribution to the present level of our economy, and we value the economic contributions of the retired elderly at nearly zero. Only their political value in proportion to their numbers has risen; hence, the large increases in Social Security, Medicare, and several favorable tax breaks in recent years. These non-work measures undoubtedly relieve the economic hardship of growing old in a society where filial responsibility is largely a matter of governmental decree. But none substitutes for the basic nutrient of work—increasingly important because of the decline in strong family relationships—namely, the visible assurance that one is needed. It is somewhat absurd to spend billions in biomedical research to enable people to live longer, while simultaneously making that living more onerous, financially as well as psychologically. The least that could be done is to make "retirement" an option, provide substitute activities, and remove obstacles to part-time employment.

What the future holds in store for the elderly is not obvious. Without an economic catastrophe, we are unlikely to return to the three-generation household. But we are undergoing an agonizing reassessment of the value of technology and economic growth in conjunction with "quality of life" issues. Should technology and its incessant preoccupation with novelty be devalued, and conservation rise in value, the aged may benefit. Should the interest in "job satisfaction" take hold and spread widely and rapidly, the relationship between such satisfaction and longevity (plus the evident desire to reduce population growth through a reduction in births) would increase the proportion of elderly people in our population beyond current projections. If this occurs, the need to keep people in the labor force beyond the current "normal" age of retirement will become even more acute.

But of all these forces, the future of one is most crucial—the total demand for workers. So long as total demand oscillates in the range of the last two decades, the 65 and older cohort will be at a competitive disadvantage and will continue to be denied the economic and psychological rewards of work. So much is predicated on the expansion in demand for workers, not only for the older members of our society but for others, that without an extraordinary change in employment policy, the possibilities of employment for the elderly are slim. It does not seem possible for hopes to be realized unless policy moves toward making the total demand for workers equivalent to the total demand for jobs.

Retirement Retirement at age 65 (now optional at age 62) is an artifact of Social Security laws. Over time, however, this specific age has acquired certain conveniences, which has led to its adoption as a "normal" retirement age because:
—It enables employers to dispense with the services of older

workers gracefully. The administrative difficulties of selectively firing older, often "faithful," workers are thereby avoided.

—It enables older workers to salvage more of their self-respect when they are members of a class that is cut loose by compulsion from the workforce than they would if they were individually removed. Retirement, therefore, is socially acceptable.

—It enables younger workers to look forward to advancement and to the perquisites enjoyed by older workers in a system that shows preferment to seniority. Thus, retirement presumably removes some of the obstacles to "upward mobility."

Despite the advantages of each of these, they are conveniences only—conveniences that ossify the structure of work as it has emerged from the industrial revolution. They do not automatically mean that the present retirement system is beneficial for all concerned.

The lack of satisfaction with work—and the concurrent need to distribute a total amount of work among a larger number of people eligible for work—has led to a trend of ever-earlier retirement.[66] The United Auto Workers have gained a provision in which workers with 30 years of work and who have reached an age of 58 may retire. Confirming observations on the relative dissatisfactions of unskilled versus skilled labor, nearly twice as many unskilled than skilled chose early retirement. At General Motors, out of 20,000 eligible, 13.5% chose to retire, 16% among the unskilled and 9% among the skilled. Among steelworkers similar results were reported.[67]

Among those who have retired, one finds that a sizable minority—one-third in a 1965 Harris poll—find their retirement satisfactions below expectations. Among the dissatisfied retirees, financial problems loomed as the greatest source of dissatisfaction (40%), while more than 20% were unhappy about the loss of a work role. In another study, reluctant retirees were much more dissatisfied with the loss of their work role than those who had retired willingly.[68] Moreover, a large number of the reluctant retirees consisted of those men and women who had become discouraged looking for work and, at age 62, grasped the only straw available to them—reduced Social Security benefits. The lack of available work, age discrimination, and the fact that older workers sometimes are "pension liabilities," had contributed to their inability to find work.

The thrust toward "early" retirement calls into doubt the very meaning of "retirement." For one thing, the earlier the retirement, the less likely it is that the worker will be content with pasturage, and the more likely that "change of occupation" will be one of the meanings of "retirement." For example, early "retired" steelworkers are opening citrus groves in Florida and cheese factories in Wisconsin. Certainly, a man who entered the armed services at age 18 and "retires" at age 38 is not about to occupy himself with shuffleboard in St. Petersburg, Florida, with 80-year-old playmates. And recent analysis of census data indicates that older men increasingly do not and will not want to retire at age 65.[69] However, independent income acquired from a pension, plus the availability of work, can combine to increase the mobility of "retired" workers, and, potentially at least, enhance their satisfaction with life.

Pension Plans The rub is, of course, can they in fact acquire a deferred, non-trivial income, and will there be jobs available to which they can turn? The latter largely depends, as noted earlier, on national employment policies; the former depends on the realizable benefits of pension plans.

Social Security pensions (OASDI) provide the major underpinning for deferred income among most workers. In recent decades, however, private pension plans have grown markedly. The main reasons for this growth appear to be: the desire to supplement income from Social Security; wage freezes in World War II that transferred demands from present income to future income; and the more flexible provisions of private pensions, especially with respect to early retirement, than in Social Security. Today, the assets of private pension plans are worth about $150 billion.

The rapid growth in private pension "coverage" has, however, tapered off in the last decade, and the rate of increase in the number of people employed has exceeded the rate of new additions to pension plans.[70] Hence, it is unlikely that current policies and trends will lead in the near future to the participation of most workers in such plans.

The major problems workers are having with private pensions are:

1. Most workers are not "covered" by private pension plans; only about 35% are participating now.[71]

2. Most workers who are theoretically "covered" will not receive any benefits, and some of the remainder will receive reduced benefits because of the mismatch between their work experience (e.g., years in the same job) and the requirements of their plans. More than 70% will very likely forfeit their benefits.[72]

3. Some workers are victimized by such sinister practices as being fired just before they are eligible to receive benefits or through hanky-panky played with pension funds in mergers, as well as by mismanagement, bankruptcies, and the like.[73]

4. Most pension plans that give workers rights to benefits prior to their retirement require 11 or more years of continuous employment with the same employer, in addition to meeting certain age requirements. But data on job tenure show that fewer than 50% of working men have a tenure of 10 or more years until they are over the age of 45, while no more than 62% of any age group works 10 years or more for the same employer. For women, only in the age group 65–69 do we find slightly more than 50% working for 10 or more years continuously for the same employer. In other words, private pension plans are so constructed that most workers will *not* benefit from them.

5. The types of jobs that women and minorities hold, and the

shorter duration of their employment on the average for any particular employer, means that their access to private pension plans is less, and their forfeiture rate greater, than the average for white male employees.

6. The forfeiture of private pension benefits is largely a function of the fact that most workers cannot accumulate their pension plan "credits"—i.e., they do not work long enough for one employer to obtain a right in part or all of the plan's benefits (the rights are not "vested" in them); and they cannot take their "credits" from job to job, as they do under Social Security—i.e., their plans are not "portable." There are exceptions to the latter, most notably in the pension plan for teachers (TIAA) and in certain of the building trades.

There are a host of other problems in both private and public (governmental) pensions, but we cannot concern ourselves with them here. Suffice it to say that disentangling all the problems of pensions is no mean task.

All in all, what the enumerated problems boil down to is that a minority of workers are able to participate in private pension plans; a minority of those who do participate will actually receive any or full benefits; women and minorities are especially discriminated against; and, as workers near the tenure and age requirements of most pension plans, they are faced with a powerful incentive to remain in their jobs, which tends to reduce their mobility and the overall efficiency of the economy.

The combination of a movement toward early retirement, the use of early retirement to change occupations, and the relatively small percentage of the workforce that can avail itself of this opportunity foreshadow largescale demands for changes in the pension system of the Nation. Should jobs become more plentiful, and the demands for job satisfaction affirmed, then employers will not be able to retain older workers by threatening them with a loss of pension rights—that would be intolerable to the workers. Moreover, the employers will be able to achieve their objective—of low turnover—through job satisfaction rather than through a feared loss of economic security. Much earlier vesting and the ability to carry pension "credits" from job to job will undoubtedly be demanded by workers, the first to increase economic security and the second to increase mobility. Together with early retirement, earlier vesting and portability would increase the number of people who could supplement earned income from another occupation.

The achievement of such objectives will not be easy. The main problem with increasing the number of workers who would receive benefits through vesting and portability is that benefits might be reduced to trivial levels, or costs might be driven up to intolerable levels. This issue—a complex one— revolves around the distribution of income over a lifetime (how much to set aside for later use, by forced or voluntary means), and the distribution of work in our society.

But earlier vesting and portability would clearly reduce inequities in the existing private pension plans and enhance the worker's ability to change occupations—to be freed from a job that keeps him only because it holds out a promise of economic security. Perhaps the financing problem mentioned above could be resolved by greatly enlarging profit sharing (see Chapter 6), by devoting a significant portion of the worker's share in the profits to deferred income, and altering the tax laws to permit individuals other than the self-employed to deduct contributions to their pension plans. An alternative to making these marked improvements in private pensions would be to eliminate the need for private pensions by liberalizing the benefits and retirement provisions of Social Security—a position that has many proponents. The pros and cons are much too elaborate to be detailed here.

From the point of view of this report, the objectives—earlier vesting and portability—are attractive because: (1) they would help shift the emphasis in jobs to their satisfaction as a means of retaining employees, by removing the threat of losing a pension; (2) they would improve the negotiating position of older workers, either where they work or elsewhere; and (3) they would reduce the likelihood, perhaps eliminate it, that anyone would be condemned to a really unsatisfying job for a lifetime. Removing the impediments to vesting and portability would, finally, help open the course through which a new conception of retirement—"changing occupations"—may flow.

3
WORK AND HEALTH

Public concern for health in the United States is demonstrated by the following: (1) the $70 billion-plus annual expenditure on medical care, (2) the recent legislation calling for a large expansion in the training of physicians and other medical care personnel, (3) greatly increased expenditures for cancer research, and (4) the existence of a half-dozen proposals for national health insurance on the Congressional agenda. There is one major fallacy with these efforts: health and medical care are not synonymous. While it may be a worthwhile objective in itself to improve the quality and distribution of medical care, the confusion of medical care with health detracts attention from the separable and more important goal of improving health. Indeed, the evidence suggests that if improving health is truly a national goal, we should make a decided shift in our attention away from medical care institutions. This report focuses on work, but the environment, housing, nutrition, and the uglification of our cities and roadways are clearly other places to look for means to improve health.

Improvements in work hold out opportunities for *avoiding* physical and mental illness and thereby avoiding medical care bills—one of the most inflationary of all bills in the American economy. The brief data presented in the first chapter of this report, on occupational health and safety, illustrate the point. There we referred to the hundreds of thousands of avoidable work-related illnesses and injuries. Prevention of these illnesses and injuries would obviously reduce demand for medical services, which is a reasonable alternative to the prevailing strategy of increasing the supply of such services. But even if this economic relationship were not obvious, preserving the health of workers would be a worthwhile objective in itself.

We turn now to a brief summary of the opportunities that reside in work for improving physical and mental health.

Work and Longevity

In an impressive 15-year study of aging, the strongest predictor of longevity was work satisfaction.[1] The second best predictor was overall "happiness." These two socio-psychological measures predicted longevity better than a rating by an examining physician of physical functioning, or a measure of the use of tobacco, or genetic inheritance. Controlling these other variables statistically did not alter the dominant role of work satisfaction.

Another link between work and longevity is provided by an examination of the Abkhasian people of the Soviet Union that was undertaken by anthropologist Sula Benet.[2] In 1954, the last year for which figures are available, 2.5% of the Abkhasians were 90 years of age or older, compared with 0.1% of all Russians, and 0.4% of Americans. This society displays, along with other traditional societies, a close social system and the increasing prestige of Abkhasians with age. They also have, as some other societies do, healthy diets. But a major distinguishing characteristic is lifelong work. Abkhasians at the age of 100 or more still put in as much as 4 hours a day on their farms. Benet writes:

Both the Soviet medical profession and the Abkhasians agree that their work habits have a great deal to do with their longevity. The doctors say that the way Abkhasians work helps the vital organs function optimally. The Abkhasians say, "without rest, a man cannot work; without work, the rest does not give you any benefit."

The opposite of the Abkhasian system is what we frequently find in the United States: otherwise healthy elderly Americans adopt a "sick role," a culturally sanctioned reason for admittance to a nursing home, when the real reason is family rejection.[3] Instead of a respected work role, we provide our older citizens with a sick role that encourages psychosomatic illnesses and excessive use of the medical care system—which might better be called in this instance the "tender loving care" system.

Recent research in Italy has established a link between adverse working conditions and the aging process itself.[4] Although similar studies have not been undertaken in the United States, the Italian findings that poor working conditions appear to affect the "manner" in which people age are consistent with other things we know about work and aging. In this connection, we might also discuss the absurdity of investing millions of dollars on physiological and chemical research aimed at retarding the "aging process" while simultaneously encouraging the early retirement of workers. Unlike the Abkhasians, we have failed to pick up the challenge of structuring work duration to mesh with the needs, desires, and capacities of older persons. The effects of such a failure are often tragic, as the following case study illustrates:

"Mr. Winter" single-handedly ran an operation that nobody else in his company fully understood, nor in fact cared to understand. As Mr. Winter reached his 64th birthday, a bright and talented younger man was assigned as an apprentice to learn the complex set of activities so that at the end of the year, he could take over the operation and the old master could benefit from a well deserved retirement. Mr. Winter objected, claiming that he did not want to retire, but the company had rules. Not long after retirement a substantial change in Mr. Winter took place. He began to withdraw from people and to lose his zest for life. Within a year after his retirement this once lively and productive businessman was hospitalized, diagnosed as having a senile psychosis. Friends from work and even family soon stopped coming to visit as they could evoke no response. Mr. Winter was a vegetable.

About two years after the apprentice had stepped up to his new position of responsibility he suddenly died. The company found itself in a serious predicament. The function that was vacated was essential to company operations, but which no one else in the company could effectively perform. A decision was made to approach Mr. Winter and see if he could pull himself together enough to carry on the job and train somebody to take over. Four of his closest co-workers were sent to the hospital. After hours of trying, one of the men finally broke through. The idea of going back to work brought the first sparkle in Mr. Winter's eyes in 2 years. Within a few days, this "vegetable" was operating at full steam, interacting with people as he had years before.[5]

Why is job satisfaction perhaps one of the best ways of extending the length of life? Other factors are undoubtedly important—diet, exercise, medical care, and genetic inheritance. But research findings suggest that these factors may account for only about 25% of the risk factors in heart disease, the major cause of death. That is, if cholesterol, blood pressure, smoking, glucose level, serum uric acid, and so forth, were perfectly controlled, only about one-fourth of coronary heart disease could be controlled.[6] Although research on this problem has not led to conclusive answers, it appears that work role, work conditions, and other social factors may contribute heavily to this "unexplained" 75% of risk factors. As Harry Levinson writes, such a finding may be difficult to accept:

Despite having learned the power of that which is not readily visible, physicians as a profession have not caught up altogether with other powerful non-visible, toxic agents, namely, feelings. It seems extremely difficult to grasp the idea that feelings are the primary participants of behavior and a major influence in health and sickness.[7]

Heart Disease

Given the fact that heart disease accounts for about half of all deaths, and that socio-psychological factors may account for much of the risk, the question has arisen—and has been treated at length: What factors in work are associated with a high risk of heart disease? Risk refers to above-average mortality and abnormal blood pressure, cholesterol, blood sugar, body weight, and the like.[8] The high risk factors that have been identified are as follows:

Job dissatisfaction, represented by tedious work, lack of recognition, poor relations with co-workers, and poor working conditions.[9]

Low self-esteem, in both white-collar and blue-collar work-

ers, and particularly observed when jobs were lost by the closing of factories.[10]

Occupational stress, components of which include extraordinary work overloads, responsibility, and conflict or ambiguity in occupational roles. The effects of stress in relation to
heart disease have been uncovered among professors,[11] among
tax accountants as income tax deadlines approached,[12] and
among medical students on the day before examinations.[13] The
stress of work overload appears to result from the feeling that
one does not have enough resources, time, or ability and, hence,
may fail.[14] Responsibility, especially for other people rather
than for things, has been pinpointed as a risk factor among
managers, scientists, and engineers in NASA, as well as among
executives.[15] Retrospective studies of heart disease patients also
found this factor to be highly significant.[16] Certain occupations, such as air traffic control and railroad train dispatch-
ing, share the extraordinary stress of having to make life-and-
death decisions minute after minute, with considerable tolls in
heart mortality.[17] Stress was indicated in a variety of blue-
collar and white-collar jobs,[18] as well as among several categories of practice in fields of medicine, dentistry, and law.[19]

Excessively rapid and continuous change in employment.[20]

Incongruity between job status and other aspects of life, such
as having high educational attainment but low job status.[21]

Certain personality characteristics, in particular, excessive
drive, aggressiveness, ambitiousness, competitiveness, and a
sense of urgency about time.[22] This factor has been found to
increase risk among blue-collar workers and NASA professionals.[23] Personality traits *alone* do not account for increased
risk of heart disease, but the important point is that jobs affect
personality, and certain kinds of jobs affect certain kinds of
personalities differently. Moreover, there is no conclusive evidence that people with these personality characteristics select
themselves into stressful positions and that, therefore, noth-

ing can be done about their stress and its consequences.[24]

Lack of stability, security, and support in the job environment has been documented in several recent studies.[25] It has also been found that a low risk of heart disease occurs in situations where stability, security, and support were present among NASA professionals,[26] industrial workers,[27] and Japanese workers.[28]

Work and Other Physical Illnesses

In addition to heart disease, several other illnesses have been found to be highly associated with occupational stress. The most convincing evidence pertains to peptic ulcers[29] and both arthritis[30] and rheumatoid arthritis.[31] Links also have been suggested for stroke and gout (a form of arthritis).

In uncovering the relationships between physical illness and work problems, investigators also note psychological effects as well. For example, in the study of individuals with high educational achievement but low job status, anger, irritation, anxiety, tiredness, depression, and low self-esteem were also found.[32] We turn now to a somewhat more detailed examination of the relationship between work and mental health.

Work and Mental Health

Employers complain about apathetic workers. Workers express the frustrations and dissatisfactions of their lives and jobs. Managers report sleeplessness, anxiety, and tension. Trained analysts of our industrial world describe the alienation of blue-collar workers, their hostility toward others and toward authority, as well as their lack of self-respect. These are all comments on the mental health of American workers.

"Mental health" is a broad concept. It can be narrowed if we say an individual is mentally healthy if he has a variety of sources of gratification; he is not self-centered, yet he understands and accepts his assets and limitations; he sets realistic

goals; and he is a productive member of society and partici-
pates in the world around him.[33] In short, the mentally healthy
person feels he is leading a rewarding life and esteems himself.

In studies such as those conducted by the University of
Michigan's Institute for Social Research, a variety of mental
health problems have been related to the absence of job satisfaction. These include: psychosomatic illnesses, low self-esteem,
anxiety, worry, tension, and impaired interpersonal relations.
The factors correlating with these problems seem to be: low
status, little autonomy, rapid technological change, isolation
on the job, role conflict, role ambiguity, responsibility for man-
aging people, shift work, and threats to self-esteem inherent in
the appraisal system.[34]

Other correlations, which have been established in numerous studies, are: low socio-economic status with high rates of
psychiatric hospitalization and symptomatology; lengthy unemployment periods with high rates of suicide and psychiatric
hospitalization; and a positive association between job satisfaction and mental health. These correlations, it should be
noted, do not yield to unambiguous interpretation; occupation
frequently cannot be isolated from such other variables as education and income. One exception appears to be the conclusive evidence of a causal link between physically hazardous
conditions of work, as encountered by soldiers and mine workers, and symptoms of mental illness.[35]

It has also been found that workers in low-skilled and unskilled jobs have poorer mental health than do workers in
skilled jobs. This is particularly true with respect to such indices of poor mental health as little satisfaction with life and
job, but less so in relation to psychiatric signs and symptoms.
The findings also show that workers in these low-level jobs
adapt by limiting their aspirations and their expectations and
that, in effect, the greatest mental health deficit suffered by
these workers is lack of involvement in the job and, consequently, lack of self-fulfillment.

Mental Health and Industrial Workers Arthur Kornhauser's well-documented twenty-year-old study of blue-collar workers, *Mental Health of the Industrial Worker,* is generally regarded today as an underestimate of the mental health problems of automobile (assembly-line) workers, especially with respect to the alienation of young workers.[36] Yet, in his sample of 407 autoworkers, approximately 40% had some symptoms of mental health problems, and the key correlation was between job satisfaction and mental health. Kornhauser's findings have been generally corroborated by subsequent studies.

While it is clear from his study that mental health has many roots—advantages of education, favorable economic conditions, and the like—separable and distinct occupational effects were found when these other factors were held constant. His principal findings were:

—Job satisfaction varied consistently with the skill level of jobs held. Higher-level blue-collar workers had better mental health than non-skilled workers.

—Job dissatisfaction related to the characteristics of jobs— dull, repetitive, unchallenging, low-paying jobs rated lowest in satisfaction. Absenteeism correlated loosely with job dissatisfaction.

—Work was the most central measurable institution in the lives of the workers, above family, leisure, and social activities, but only 25% of the workers would choose the same kind of job if they had to do it again.

—Feelings of helplessness, withdrawal, alienation and pessimism were widespread. For example: 50% of assembly-line workers felt that they had little influence over the future course of their lives (compared with only 17% of non-factory workers).

—Workers with lowest mental health and job satisfaction scores were often escapist or passive in their non-work activities: they watched television; did not vote; and did not participate in community organizations.

—Wages, security and physical conditions of work were not as accurate predictors of mental health as challenge of the job and its intrinsic interest

—Self-esteem correlated strongly with job satisfaction and mental health.

Kornhauser concludes:

. . . Poorer mental health occurs whenever conditions of work and life lead to continuing frustration by failing to offer means for perceived progress toward attainment of strongly desired goals which have become indispensable elements of the individual's self-identity as a worthwhile person. Persistent failure and frustration bring lowered self-esteem and dissatisfaction with life, often accompanied by anxieties, social alienation and withdrawal, a narrowing of goals and curtailing of aspirations —in short . . . poor mental health.

Coping, or Adjustment Downward Failure to adjust to other personalities and to one's environment as a definition of mental illness is to be rejected out of hand. An apathetic worker, for example, is not necessarily mentally ill. Where mobility is blocked, where jobs are dehumanized, where rewards are slight, failing to strive hard at the job can hardly be a criterion of mental illness. Madness may lie in adjusting to the pathologies of organizations.[37] A person who becomes an automaton in an automated factory or office may have adjusted perfectly, but he hardly enjoys good mental health.

The best description of coping through limiting one's aspirations comes from Eli Chinoy's classic study of automobile workers.[38] Many of these workers were found to have very few ambitions, even regarding the rather realistic goal of becoming a foreman. Their idea of a better job was merely one that was off the assembly-line but still in a low, blue-collar level in the same plant. Some may have fantasized about leaving the factory and opening their own gas stations, but they never took any realistic steps in this direction. Only in their hopes that their children would get white-collar jobs could one measure any strong expression of their aspirations.

In another study, of women employed by the Bell Telephone Company, those who were considered to be "healthy," by such measures as compliance with job demands, days absent from work, and the ratings of company psychiatrists, were often un-married, lived routine, dull, and withdrawn existences, and re-fused to get involved with other people.[39]

Because of the almost limitless adaptability of some workers, very repetitive and routine work can appear satisfying.[40] That is, some workers apparently prefer mechanically paced, highly structured jobs and claim some satisfaction in their very rigid-ity and mindless (but predictable) triviality. Kornhauser, how-ever, has observed that: "The unsatisfactory mental health of working people consists in no small measure of their dwarfed desires and deadened initiative, reduction of their goals, and restriction of their efforts to a point where life is relatively empty and only half meaningful." [41] In the end, for workers like these, there are only two options: to maintain high expec-tations from work, and thereby suffer constant frustration, or limit their expectations, which produces a drab existence.

Special Means of Coping ALCOHOLISM, DRUG ABUSE, AND SUICIDE
Alan McLean writes that "workers with personality disorders, including alcoholism and drug abuse, may find that their psy-chiatric disorders stem partially from job insecurity, unpleas-ant working conditions or hazardous work." [42] Although little quantitative research has been done to support this statement, many doctors and social scientists corroborate it from their own clinical observations. For example, stress has long been linked to alcoholism among executives. Our interviews with blue-collar workers in heavy industry revealed a number who found it necessary to drink large quantities of alcohol during their lunch to enable them to withstand the pressure or overwhelm-ing boredom of their tasks.

Our interviews with younger workers on similar jobs uncov-ered a surprising amount of drug use on the job, particularly among assembly-line workers and long-haul truck drivers. A recent study by the New York Narcotics Addiction Control Commission showed that drug use varied significantly by type of occupation.[43] In another study, of a UAW local affiliated with a plant employing 3,400 people, 15% of the workers were estimated to be addicted to heroin.[44]

Like drug abuse, alcoholism probably has no single cause. However, several occupational risk factors appear to lead to excessive drinking.[45] Non-supportive jobs in which the worker gets little feedback on his performance appear to cause the kind of anxiety that may lead to or aggravate alcoholism. Work "addiction," occupational obsolescence, role stress, and unstructured environments (for certain personality types) appear to be other important risk factors for both alcoholism and drug addiction.

While the Federal Government fails to gather suicide statistics by occupation of the victim, we do know that the suicide rate is higher among white men than among black men and higher among men than women. If the tendency to commit suicide is not a race-linked or sex-linked genetic factor (as it most probably is not), then it is possible that the differences in suicide rates are a function of the roles played by people in society.

Tentative support for this hypothesis is provided by a study which found that women doctors and chemists had extremely high suicide rates: for women chemists, the rate was nearly five times higher than the rate among white women in general.[46] One might attempt to account for these rates through the chemists' and doctors' access to and knowledge of lethal chemicals, but other studies indicate that professionals who are competitive, compulsive, individualistic, and ambitious tend to have a high risk of suicide. In this respect one might note the rising rate of suicide among blacks at the same time that many are moving into occupational roles similar to those held by whites. And finally, other evidence links cyclical fluctuations in the unemployment rate to suicide rates and psychiatric hospitalization.

Although *causal links* between alcoholism, drug abuse, or suicide and working conditions have not been firmly established (and, because of inadequate measuring devices, may never be established), there is considerable evidence concerning the *therapeutic value* of meaningful work for these and other mental health problems.

For example, several experiments designed to rehabilitate drug addicts are underway in New York. Most important for all concerned will be the attitude of businessmen toward drug abusers. Especially, they must recognize both the value of work as therapy and their responsibility for reducing the social costs of drug abuse. In a recent newspaper article, Howard Samuels, a member of New York City's Narcotics Control Commission, is quoted as saying:

Most drug-treatment programs lack what many addicts need most—sufficient vocational training, job development and placement, rehabilitative support when they get jobs. Almost no existing drug treatment programs are able to cope adequately with the job needs of addicts.[47]

In the same account, W. Wayne Stewart, medical director of the Sun Oil Company, said:

Industry increasingly has become aware that firing drug addicts isn't the long-run answer because firing them simply shifts the burden to some other company or to the nation's welfare rolls. . . . Because half of all addicts are so hooked they can't quit, it would be better if industry and government would try to give them jobs to improve their economic stability and social adjustment. . . .[48]

It is probably fair to say that all the evidence available to date is *suggestive* rather than conclusive; yet the recalcitrance of alcoholism, drug abuse, and suicide to abate when treated with non-work alternatives indicates that if changes in work were only a remotely possible solution they should be pursued

vigorously. For while it is patently difficult to change habits
and attitudes directly, work can be altered relatively easily.
VIOLENCE Violence is universally recognized as one of the most
frightening social problems the Nation faces. Sabotage—violence done to inanimate objects—is rising in some industries.
Erich Fromm suggests that the source of violent aggression is
to be found in what he calls the "bored" character of modern
man which is a by-product of "the structure and functioning
of contemporary industrial society." He goes on to say:

It is by now widely recognized that most manual work is boring
because of its monotony and repetitiveness; much white-collar
work is boring because of its bureaucratic character, which
leaves little responsibility and initiative to the individual.

Leisure, too, has become boring, he suggests, because

. . . it follows by and large the consumption pattern and is in
fact managed by industry, which sells boredom-compensating
commodities. . . . Among the answers to the question of how
violence—and drug consumption—can be reduced it seems to
me that perhaps one of the most important ones is to reduce
boredom in work and in leisure.[49]

The roots of sabotage, a frequent aspect of industrial violence, are illustrated by this comment of a steelworker: "Sometimes, out of pure meanness, when I make something, I put a
little dent in it. I like to do something to make it really unique.
Hit it with a hammer; deliberately to see if it'll get by, just so
I can say I did it." [50] In a production world where everything
is alike, sabotage may be a distortion of the guild craftsman's
signature, a way of asserting individuality in a homogeneous
world—the only way for the worker to say, "That's mine." It
may also be a way of striking back against the hostile, inanimate objects that control the worker's time, muscles, and brain.
Breaking a machine in order to get some rest may be a sane
thing to do.
But, alternatively, the design of work can be changed, rehu-

manized, and stripped of those conditions that produce violent reactions.

DELINQUENCY, CAUSES AND CURES While the causes of delinquency are undoubtedly as complex as the causes of drug abuse and alcoholism, a current project at the National Institutes of Mental Health suggests that work problems and orientations of parents can contribute to the delinquency of their children, and much other evidence links unemployment and underemployment with delinquency.[51]

On the rehabilitative side, another small but imaginative NIMH program dealing with juvenile delinquents integrates the concepts of providing services at the workplace and using work as a means of rehabilitation. For ten years, 20 boys, 10 delinquents in an experimental group and 10 in a control group, have been the subject of study. The experimental group was found rewarding work, and the work became a focus for other social services including psychotherapy, remedial education, and counseling. This group showed a lower rate of delinquency than the control group. The researchers explain that work is the key variable in the differences between the two groups:

Employment, which is therapeutic in itself, was used to provide a focus in reality for the psychotherapeutic and re-educative endeavors. For anti-social adolescents, work can play a crucial role not only because it facilitates identity formation, provides an avenue for the channeling of aggressive and sexual energies, and alleviates material needs, but also because it can be used as a fulcrum for therapeutic intervention.[52]

In the first five-year follow-up to the study, unemployment was correlated with arrests for both groups. But more important was the *kind* of employment: ". . . employment by itself does not seem to serve as a deterrent to crime if this employment has no meaning, no status, and no opportunities for learning and personal growth." [53]

Work has been used as a form of rehabilitation for centuries —but not always successfully. Apparently, many failures occur because meaningless work has been prescribed. Its very uselessness has lowered the self-esteem of the mental patient, welfare recipient, prisoner, or physically handicapped person. Instead of being the means by which self-confidence was improved, inadequate work struck a further blow at the pride and self-respect of the person who needed help. For example, prisoners have traditionally made license plates and prison garb—neither of which requires the kinds of skills that are transferrable to the outside world, and neither of which does anything but reinforce the view that society sees prisoners as expendable and worthless. Likewise, work has been used ineffectively as a form of rehabilitation in mental hospitals because of "institutional peonage" in which patients do low-status or meaningless work for no pay or a pittance.[54] The patient's sense of worthlessness is thus reinforced in this way; his self-esteem is further eroded.

Work may be the best therapy possible for juvenile delinquents, mental patients, prisoners, drug addicts, and alcoholics, but unless job satisfaction is made possible as a part of such therapy, work will only compound their difficulties.

A Note on Costs A case study concerning a paper bag manufacturing plant will serve to illustrate the potentially high costs to workers and employers of job environments that adversely affect mental health. The workers in the plant described were, in general, poorly educated, low-skilled machine operators:

Management was suspicious of its employees, feeling that "they are always trying to get away with something." The factory floor was noisy, dingy, hot in summer, cold in winter. Rules were plentiful and strictly enforced. Suspicion and open dislike of management for workers and workers for management was evident. Two years ago, a factory worker died of a heart attack while working at his job. As the news got around the plant, several women employees became ill and fainted. A few weeks later, noxious odors leaked into the plant through sewage pipes and a few employees were overcome and had to leave work. Although the odor was quickly eliminated, employees began complaining of dizziness, nausea, malaise, headaches, and other problems. A team from the Public Health Service was called in, but no toxic agents could be discovered, and medical doctors could find nothing physically wrong with any of the workers after thorough examinations and laboratory tests. A representative of the National Institute of Occupational Safety and Health was then called in, and concluded from the evidence that it was a case of industrial hysteria, a physical reaction to the psychological stresses of the job. He offered suggestions for remedying the situation, but no action was taken. A year later, the plant was burned to the ground. Arson was suspected.[55]

What is particularly significant about this admittedly extreme example is that only a small investment might have offset the dire consequences of management's inaction. By using available job redesign techniques for reducing anxiety in the plant, the workers could have been spared mental and physical anguish, and both they and the company could have avoided the extreme costs.

Unfortunately, these job redesign techniques (which we describe in detail in the next chapter) have not been used on a wide scale. They require tailoring to meet specific problems, but their potential value has been demonstrated. But before these techniques can be put into practice, we must make a commitment to improving the mental health of workers as a good in itself and accept the desirability of reducing medical costs through preventive measures in the workplace.

Conclusion

Throughout this chapter we have assumed that workers are sufficiently healthy in the first instance to show a decline in health as a result of their jobs. We have ignored, mainly because of the lack of data, the level of health a person must have in order to work at all, or to work as much as he would like to, or in jobs which he may only secretly aspire to. Quite rightly, these matters cannot be ignored. They deal with nutrition and caloric intake, with one or another debilitating conditions, chronic and acute, and with physical imperfections correctible by so-called cosmetic surgery. Certainly, in this latter instance, the person whose mirror daily assails his self-esteem will be hard put to derive self-esteem from a job he really does not want, while he is denied the job he wants because he lacks the requisite physical attributes.

If we look upon work as a means of avoiding certain mental and physical health problems, we must also look upon our health specialists and others in our society as a means of enabling people to work. All parts of society are, after all, mutually interactive—a central point of this report.

4
THE REDESIGN OF JOBS

The concepts of work developed in this report provide a useful vantage point from which to review national policies and attitudes influencing the world of work. Through the perspective of work, our purpose in the next three chapters is to identify shortcomings in policies and attitudes on these policies and open them for a reconsideration of alternatives.

We cannot, of course, analyze the government's role in relation to the institution of work without including the questions of equity that we raised in the chapter on workers, or the questions of Federal policy in employment, health, education, welfare, and manpower that are all intricately interrelated to the institution of work. As complicated as this analysis must be, then, it nevertheless offers the opportunity for a systematic evaluation of many national issues.

It is exactly because work is complexly linked to so many of the major domestic issues of the nation that it becomes an invaluable tool for analysis. The institution of work can be used to trace the ramifications of social action. One can see what the likely consequences of a change in one part of the social system will be for other parts of the system.

A singularly important feature of such an analysis is that it allows us to measure the costs and benefits of trade-offs between national investments in one area and national investments in another. We do not propose to develop such an intricate accounting system here. Nor is it the purpose of this report to present legislative or administrative proposals. Rather, we wish to offer a framework in which specific questions might be analyzed and policy developed.

But inherent in our analyses of current work-related national programs and policies is the suggestion that there *is* a better way to do things. Of course, there are many "better ways," and the choice between these alternatives is, as it should be in a democratic society, a political choice. It would be presumptuous of us, then, to suggest that any one route to change is the right route, or that any one alternative *must* be pursued. Consequently, we shall limit our discussion here to a few alternative responses to national problems in order to indicate (1) the range of options that are open to policy makers, and (2) the promise of a work-oriented policy analysis.

Recapitulation of the Problem

In the preceding chapters, the economic, social, and personal consequences of work dissatisfaction have been elaborated. The main conclusion is that the very high personal and social costs of unsatisfying work *should* be avoided through the redesign of work. The burden of this chapter is to show that not only can work be redesigned to make it more satisfying but that significant increases in productivity can also be obtained. In other words, workers can be healthier, happier in their work, and better contributors to family and community life than they are now, without a loss of goods and services, and without inflating prices.

To recapitulate, the following factors are, with high probability, determinants of satisfaction and dissatisfaction at work:[1]

Occupation and status: The higher the status of an occupation, the more satisfied are the people who engage in it. Researchers reason that the major variables are prestige, control over conditions of one's own work, cohesiveness of one's work group, and ego gratification from the challenge and variety of the work itself.

Job content: Intrinsic factors such as challenge appear to affect satisfaction and dissatisfaction most substantially. The aspects of job content that appear most consistent in their negative effects are fractionation, repetition and lack of control, or, in positive terms, variety and autonomy. Workers in all occupations rate self-determination highest among the elements that define an ideal job. Content of work is generally more important than being promoted.

Supervision: High worker satisfaction is associated with considerate and thoughtful behavior among employers. Satisfaction is also associated with supervisory behavior that shares decision making with subordinates. The delegation of authority (participative management) has positive effects.

Peer relationships: Most people are more satisfied to work as members of a group than in isolation. Workers prefer jobs that permit interaction and are more likely to quit jobs that prevent congenial peer relationships.

Wages: High pay and high satisfaction with work tend to go together. However, it is difficult to ascertain the extent to which high wages in themselves produce sustained high levels of satisfaction, and the extent to which the higher levels of satisfaction that are typical of higher paid jobs reflect the variety, substantive interest, and autonomy that are also typical of such jobs. Moreover, even among high-paid workers, variations in job control make a difference in the degree of job satisfaction. But in a culture in which wages constitute the major source of income for most workers, wages undoubtedly determine a portion of job satisfaction. Certainly, a level of wages that will support an adequate standard of living is of primary importance. Beyond that point, workers tend to measure their wages in terms of "equity"—i.e., in relationship to the contributions that their fellow workers are making to the enterprise, and the salaries they are receiving.

Mobility: More than three-quarters of all workers queried by the Survey of Working Conditions said that it was important or somewhat important to them that their chances for promotion should be good. Also, large percentages of workers strongly resent being trapped in a job.

Working conditions: Bad physical conditions (long hours, temperature, ventilation, noise, etc.) can make any job unbear-

able. Involuntary night shift work also causes low job satisfaction—probably because it interferes with other valued activities
such as marriage, child rearing, and friendships.

Job security: Older workers, in particular, find that security
of employment is a prerequisite for other sources of satisfaction.

It follows that if autonomy, participation, challenge, security, pay, mobility, comfort, and the opportunity for interaction with co-workers are increased, the satisfaction of workers
with their jobs should increase. We turn now to consider what
has been done about several of the most important matters.
(The question of mobility will be dealt with in Chapter 5.)

Solutions: Reforms and Innovations in the Workplace

Most of the work redesign effort has confined itself to small
work groups. Little of it has embraced the wider implications
of the systems viewpoint and involved a plant or a corporation
as a whole. The major exception to this trend is a General
Foods manufacturing plant that was designed to incorporate
features that would provide a high quality of working life, en-
list unusual human involvement, and achieve high productivity. Management built this plant because the employees in an
existing plant manifested many severe symptoms of alienation.
Because of their indifference and inattention, the continuous
process type of technology used in the plant was susceptible to
frequent shutdowns, to product waste, and to costly recycling.
There were serious acts of sabotage and violence. Employees
worked effectively for only a few hours a day and strongly re-
sisted changes that would have resulted in a fuller utilization of
manpower.

Management enlisted the advice and cooperation of workers
and consultants from business schools, and together they designed a plant along the following lines:

Autonomous work groups: Self-management work teams
were formed and given collective responsibility for larger seg-

ments of the production process. The teams are composed of from eight to twelve members—large enough to cover a full set of tasks, and small enough to allow effective face-to-face meetings for decision making and coordination. The teams decide who will do what tasks, and most members learn to do each other's jobs, both for the sake of variety and to be able to cover for a sick or absent co-worker.

Integrated support functions: Activities typically performed by maintenance, quality control, custodial, industrial engineering, and personnel units were built into the operating team's responsibilities. The teams accepted both first and final responsibility for performing quality tests and ensuring that they maintained quality standards.

Challenging job assignments: An attempt was made to design every set of tasks in a way that would include functions requiring higher human abilities and responsibilities. The basic technology employed in the plant had been designed to eliminate dull or routine jobs insofar as possible. Still, some nonchallenging but basic tasks remained. The team member responsible for these operations is given other tasks that are mentally more demanding. The housekeeping activities were included in every assignment—despite the fact that they contributed nothing to enriching the work—in order to avoid having members of the plant community who did nothing but cleaning.

Job mobility and rewards for learning: The aim was to make all sets of tasks equally challenging although each set would comprise unique skill demands. Consistent with this aim was a single job classification for all operators, with pay increases geared to mastering an increasing proportion of jobs, first within the team and then in the total plant. Thus, team members were rewarded for learning more and more aspects of the total manufacturing system. Because there were no limits to how many team members could qualify for higher pay brackets, employees were encouraged to teach each other.

Facilitative leadership: In lieu of "supervisors" whose responsibilities are to plan, direct, and control the work of subordinates, a "team leader" position was created with the responsibility to facilitate team development and decision making. It is envisioned that in time the team leader position might not be required.

Managerial decision information for operators: The design of the new plant called for providing operators with economic information and managerial decision rules. This enables production decisions ordinarily made at the second level of supervision to be made at the operator level.

Self-government for the plant community: Management refrained from specifying in advance any plant rules; rather, it was committed to let the rules evolve from collective experience.

Congruent physical and social context: Differential status symbols that characterize traditional work organizations were minimized in the new plant—for example, by a parking lot open to all regardless of position, single office-plant entrance, and common decor throughout office, cafeteria, and locker room. The technology and architecture were designed to facilitate rather than discourage the congregating of team members during working hours. The assumption was that these *ad hoc* meetings often would be enjoyable human exchanges as well as opportunities to coordinate work and to learn about each other's job.

Using standard principles, industrial engineers had indicated that 110 workers would be needed to man the plant. But when the team concept (rather than individual assignments) was applied, and when support activities were integrated into team responsibilities, the result was a manning level of less than 70 workers. While this 40% smaller work force is impressive, it is not the major economic benefit, because labor costs per unit are not a large percentage of the cost of goods sold in this particular business. The major economic benefit has come from such factors as improved yields, minimized waste and avoidance of shutdowns.[2] Significantly, these are productivity items that are related to *technology* but are especially sensitive to the *work attitudes* of operators.

What is particularly encouraging is the impact of this unique worksetting on employees' extra-plant activities. For example, many workers have been unusually active in civic affairs—apparently, significantly more so than is typical of the workers in other plants in the same corporation or in the same community.[3] It has long been observed that workers in dull, isolated, or routine jobs seldom participate in community affairs, but this is the first instance where it has been shown that the redesign of work can have positive effects on community participation.

This General Foods plant is not a unique example, although the extent of the redesign is unusual. Several other cases illustrate the positive results of job redesign. Some clearly show the need for extensive planning *before* implementation should be attempted. For example, the first major experiment in Norway was carried out in the metal-working industry, a critical but unproductive sector of the Norwegian economy. A dilapidated wire-drawing plant was chosen for the experiment on the grounds that if improvements could be realized there, they could be achieved anywhere. But productivity increased so much due to job redesign that the experiment was suspended: the unskilled workers in the experiment had begun to take home pay packets in excess of the most skilled workers in the firm, thus engendering bitterness.[4] Following are some other successful examples of the redesign of both blue- and white-collar jobs:

At the *Banker's Trust Company,* many typists had repetitious jobs that entailed recording stock transfer data. Production was low, quality was poor, attitudes slack; absenteeism and turnover were high. The workers decided to try to redesign their own work tasks. Among other changes, they eliminated the work of a checker, and of a special group that made corrections by assuming these responsibilities themselves. This change permits a $360,000 annual savings, and the social problems have been largely eliminated. Similar results have been reported at *Traveler's Insurance* with keypunch operators.[5]

On a *Corning Glass* assembly line, women workers formerly assembled hot plates for laboratory use. Now, each worker assembles a whole plate. Employees put their initials on each final product to allow identification with the work and to reference customer complaints. They also are given the opportunity to schedule their work as a group, and to design work flow improvements. Quality checks previously made by a separate group are conducted by the workers themselves. In six months following the change, rejects dropped from 23% to 1%, and absenteeism from 8% to 1%. During this same time, productivity increased. Also, the reputation of this division as an undesirable place to work was reversed. Other job change projects have been conducted at Corning with more complex instruments.[6]

Until 1967, *Texas Instruments* contracted for its cleaning and janitorial services. But the firm's engineers evaluated the plant as only "65 percent clean." Apparently, the contractor's ability to do the job well was aggravated by a quarterly turnover rate of 100 percent. Preceded by careful planning and training, the following actions were taken in a test involving 120 maintenance personnel:

—Cleaning service teams of 19 people were organized and were given a voice in the planning, problem solving, and goal setting for their own jobs.

—They were thoroughly trained in the job requirements and techniques, and were provided with adequate equipment to do the job.

—They were held accountable for the overall job. The means of getting the job done were left to them. It was also the teams' responsibility to act independently to devise its own strategies, plans, and schedules to meet the objective.

—They were taught how to measure their own performance and were given the freedom to do so, both as individuals and as teams.

These were the outcomes:

—The cleanliness level rating improved from 65 percent to 85 percent.

—Personnel required for cleaning dropped from 120 to 71.

—Quarterly turnover dropped from 100 percent to 9.8 percent.

—From the fourth quarter of 1967 until the fourth quarter of 1969, costs savings for the entire site averaged $103,000 per annum.[7]

Motorola Inc. has restructured an assembly operation so that each employee involved in the experiment, instead of working on one or two components of the total product, now puts together the entire combination of eighty different components. Each employee is personally responsible for the quality of his receivers. His name appears on each of his units, and he must personally repair any unit that does not meet testing requirements. Early results from the experiment indicate that the technique of individual assembly requires 25 percent more workers, as well as a more detailed training program. However, these greater costs are just about offset by higher productivity, by the need for less inspection, by lower repair costs, by improved quality, and by reduced employee turnover and absentee rates.[8]

Norway's *Norsk Hydro* fertilizer company was experiencing steadily tougher competition and decreasing profits. Management also considered that their relationship with labor was unsatisfactory. In response to this situation, the company selected a fertilizer processing plant with about fifty employees for a job-redesign effort. The idea behind the experiment was that every worker should be able to get help from others when he needed it. To achieve this, the following organizational changes were made:

—Shifts were organized into flexible subgroups, each responsible for production in an assigned work area. Individual workers were not given specific jobs.

—The organization was built up without supervisors.

—Each worker was given the opportunity to learn all the tasks within his subgroup through job rotation and mutual aid.

—It was left to the worker to decide how quickly and how much he wanted to increase his competence, thus leaving little chance for too much or too little variation in a job.

—A bonus system was installed that paid the workers according to factors they themselves could influence, such as quantity produced, cost, loss of materials, and working hours. Since the bonus included all workers in the 50-man plant, it was aimed at stimulating cooperation.

—Basic wages were paid according to the number of jobs in the plant that a worker was *able* to do rather than the actual work he did.

The human outcomes of this participative work restructuring were measured by asking the workers involved whether their jobs were satisfying or not satisfying in general, and specifically with regard to variety, learning, responsibility, and security. The questions were asked while the workers were still on their previous jobs and, again, on their new jobs after the experiment had been underway for one year. The percentage of workers expressing satisfaction increased from 58 to 100 on general satisfaction, from 45 to 85 on variety, from 33 to 96 on learning, from 42 to 96 on responsibility, and from 39 to 73 on security. The economic result was that production costs per ton steadily decreased by about 30% during the first six months of the project and absenteeism in the experimental factory was 4% against 7% for a "control" factory and 7.5% for the firm as a whole. Norsk Hydro has since begun to extend participative management throughout the company.[9]

In the appendix to this report, there is a summary of an additional 30 examples of efforts to redesign work.

It has been estimated that some 3,000 American workers have been involved in *extensive* redesign efforts. Because of the small number, one is tempted to call them "experiments." But precisely because the workers participate in the redesign of the work, and each of the resulting sets of working conditions must vary with the workers' choices, one can only conclude that the redesign of work would be experimental until the last workplace was restructured. Although these are general principles that apply to all job restructuring situations, each workplace must "experiment," must determine its own specific design.

This is not to say that no general principles whatsover can be derived from the redesign that has occurred. To the contrary, these examples have in common the participation of workers (1) in decision making, and (2) in many cases, profit sharing. A few comments are in order on both of these.

Participative Management In the redesigned worksettings mentioned above, one finds the workers participating in decisions on:
—Their own production methods
—The internal distribution of tasks
—Questions of recruitment
—Questions regarding internal leadership
—What additional tasks to take on
—When they will work
Not all of the work groups make all of these decisions, but the list provides the range within which the workers are participating in the management of the business or industry. Participative management does *not* mean participation through representatives, for, as experience has shown, that kind of participation may foster alienation through the inevitable gap between expected and actual responsiveness of the representatives. Nor does this kind of participation mean placing workers or union representatives on the board of directors of a corporation. Where workers have so served (in Norway, for example),

neither participation by the rank and file nor productivity has increased, and worker alienation has not decreased.[10]

Participative management means, as the examples above illustrate, that workers are enabled to control the aspects of work intimately affecting their lives. It permits the worker to achieve and maintain a sense of personal worth and importance, to grow, to motivate himself, and to receive recognition and approval for what he does. It gives the worker a meaningful voice in decisions in one place where the effects of his voice can be immediately experienced. In a broader sense, it resolves a contradiction in our Nation—between democracy in society and authoritarianism in the workplace.

Not all of a company's decisions, of course, are turned over to the workers when they participate in management. Upper-level managers continue to run the company, handle major financial transactions, and coordinate all the functions. Although they are no longer involved in planning the details of every operation in the company, they serve as expert consultants to the teams of workers. Some managerial jobs, however, do tend to be eliminated such as some of the lower- and middle-management positions as well as foremen in authority-less intercalary positions. But these jobs are frequently unsatisfying (foreman jobs go begging in the auto industry) and unproductive. Without retraining opportunities for individuals in these jobs, however, either they would be put out of work or, with the threat of that possibility, oppose the redesign of work.

The concept of work design needs also to be applied to management, where participation can also usefully be increased. The work of managers needs to be redesigned not only because it is unlikely for authoritarian managers to support the humanization of work for lower-level workers, but also for their own physical and mental health.

Two factors stand out as contributing to mental and physical health problems of managers: (1) territorial conflict and ambiguity regarding responsibility, and (2) having insufficient resources with which to complete their tasks.[11] Some steps are already being taken to provide greater job satisfaction for management, including the decentralization of authority to middle and lower managers, and the formation of teams of managers to solve specific, non-recurrent problems—both are actions that increase participation. Such innovations increase the autonomy of managers, the variety of their work, and the opportunity for their self-actualization. While it is not clear that all techniques for participation can be applied equally to managers and to lower-level workers, at least one successful redesign—for aerospace engineers—has been accomplished along these lines in California.[12]

The main conclusion to be drawn from the above is simply this: It is feasible to redesign work up and down the line, from upper-level managers to lower-level workers, with the objective of greatly increasing participation in workplace decisions, increasing variety, and making more effective use of worker potentials. And, through the attainment of this objective on a wide scale, not only should there be large gains in the physical and mental well-being of workers, but other social benefits—such as participation in community affairs—should also accrue. There are, to be sure, costs and obstacles: in particular, certain problems are likely to develop when the traditional prerogatives of middle managers, as well as their jobs, are threatened. Other problems will be taken up later, and solutions to these obstacles will be suggested.

Participation in Profits Participation in profits is needed to avoid having workers feel that participative management is merely a refined Tayloristic technique for improving productivity at their expense. The redesign of work tasks through participation will increase productivity, but some experience has indicated that without profit sharing workers may feel that they have been manipulated, and productivity may slip back to former levels. Profit sharing is also the most direct response to the problem of equitable wage increases for employees: the contribution of the worker can be tied directly to his salary increases.

Profit sharing also responds to another problem—that of inflation generated by rising salaries not tied to productivity. Negotiated contracts during 1969–70 awarded compensation increases to labor in the range of 7 to 15 percent, while our national productivity was increasing by only 0.5 percent in 1969 and 0.9 percent in 1970.[13] Profit sharing could be of some help in reducing these inflationary tendencies of our economy by tying wage increases in particular industries more closely to productivity increases.

When these increases are paid to the worker in the form of stock ownership ("deferred profit sharing"), they are of considerable economic and psychological benefit. But "direct profit sharing"—a contracted portion of profits above a decent wage—is a particularly valuable motivator because it closes the income gap between employer and employee without taking from one to give to the other, and because it does away with a special privilege that separates workers from managers.

Either by design or default, a fragmented approach to motivation has evolved in American business. Executives have been rewarded through salary, profit-sensitive bonuses, and stock options; salaried personnel through salary, status, and fringe benefits (largely unrelated to performance); and hourly employees by wages. Corporate pyramids are thereby carefully stratified, with horizontal modes for motivating each stratum. This drives an additional artificial wedge between classes of workers and adds to the hostility, alienation, lack of cohesion, and loss of identification with the firm that plagues our corporations.

In 1971 the Profit Sharing Research Foundation studied a group of the largest department store chains in the United States.[14] They divided the chains into those with profit-sharing plans and those without, and compared them on both operating ratios and growth measures over a period of 18 years. On all significant measures, the profit-sharing group of companies outperformed the non-profit-sharing group by substantial and widening percentages, as shown in Table 2.

While it is impossible to isolate effects of profit sharing from other factors that affect profitability, the managers of these companies nevertheless assert that profit sharing has contributed importantly to their efficiency and growth.[15] The following case study illustrates the point:

The *Lincoln Electric Company* nearly four decades ago established a unique system of incentive management to motivate employees to high levels of performance. Central to the plan was a profit sharing program. After deducting taxes and reserves to be plowed back into the business, and after paying stockholders an annual dividend of about 6 percent, Lincoln distributes 100 percent of the remainder of profits to employees in

Table 2. Performance Comparisons between Profit-Sharing and Non-Profit-Sharing Companies

	Profit-Sharing Companies	Non-Profit-Sharing Companies
Ratios (1969)		
Net income to net worth	12.78%	8.00%
Net income to sales	3.62%	2.70%
Indices (1969)	*1952 = 100*	
Sales	358.4	266.0
Net worth	376.1	256.7
Earnings per common share	410.5	218.8
Dividends per common share	293.7	175.3
Market price per common share	782.1	397.6
Other Measures		
Approximate company earnings per employee (1969)	$1,165	$647
Growth of the invested dollar (1952–1969)	$9.89	$5.61

the form of profit sharing contributions. All employees share in these incentive earnings.

1969 year-end profit sharing totaled $16,544,000, divided among the company's 1,973 employees. The profit sharing contribution amounted to 100 percent to 105 percent of annual pay for the average worker.

Allocation of the profit sharing contribution is made to individual employees based on a merit rating program that measures the employee's actual performance on the job. The rating determines his cash profit sharing, and his opportunities for promotion. All promotions are made from within the organization, and strictly on merit; seniority does not count.

Today, Lincoln's welding machines and electrodes are sold at about 1934 prices—the year when the first profit sharing incentive bonus was paid. During this same period, all cost elements going into Lincoln's products (such as labor rates, cost of copper and steel) increased three-to-six fold or more. Yet prices have been held stable because of the employees' individual and collective efforts to cut costs and increase productivity.

Concomitant with profit sharing, Lincoln Electric Company offers its employees complementary inducements to cut costs while turning out quality products. One particularly important inducement is continuity of employment and security against layoffs. The company guarantees at least thirty-two hours of work fifty weeks a year for each employee after two years of service. (No specific rate of pay is guaranteed; the employee must be willing to accept transfer from one job to another, and work overtime during periods of peak demand.)

In line with its policy of rewarding the individual in proportion to his contribution to the company, most production employees are paid on straight piece work. Basic wage rates are set by a committee of supervisors using a job evaluation procedure that measures each position according to the demands it makes upon the worker. The basic wage structure is competitive with other companies.

Among other methods of motivating employees to achieve high productivity are a stock purchase plan, an "advisory board" of elected employee representatives who suggest changes and policies in operations to management, and a system of organizing work that lets many plant employees function almost as independent subcontractors in their own jobs, performing a complete assembly operation at a specified piecework price and accepting responsibility for quality. This "factory within a factory" system not only eliminates some assembly-line type work, but also reduces the need for supervisors.[16]

Some unions believe that profit sharing will lead to unemployment as workers "work themselves out of a job." But the increased efficiency of companies with profit sharing does not appear to lead to unemployment. Characteristically, profit-sharing companies do about a 25% better job of enlarging their markets and creating jobs than do less efficient non-profit-sharing companies.[17]

Although the record of profit sharing is generally positive, it does not automatically insure greater productivity. To be truly effective it must be tied to participative management. Some other general guidelines seem to prevail that are necessary for long-term success:

Profit sharing must be clearly in addition to adequate base pay and fringes. Where this is not the case, workers interpret it as a substitute for wage and fringe increases which—because it is more complicated in its mechanisms—is more subject to manipulation by the employer.

Profit sharing must be tied to the "productivity" of the worker or his small group and not to the "profitability" of the entire firm. Profitability relates to increases in the net financial worth of a firm—a condition that is most often not affected by the efforts of an individual worker. Productivity is the physical output per worker—a condition that is often controllable by the worker. In some industries, it is difficult to measure individual worker productivity. For example, where the pace of a worker is controllable by the pace of a machine, his productivity is not under his control. However, management experts have been able to develop proxy measures that work quite well under these circumstances.

Payments must be sensitive to small group productivity. Consider the worker employed by a 100,000-employee corporation who works on the shop-floor with a team of 13 other workers. His share in the portion of profits allocated to the plan is about one-hundred thousandth of that share (adjusted to his income). It is unlikely that this worker will connect his own efforts, ingenuity, ideas, and willingness to participate—or the efforts of his immediate group—to the amount of his share in the profits. (Obversely, if he and his group devoted themselves full-time to sabotage, perhaps they could reduce their annual share in the profits by a few dollars each.) The implementation of this principle will require a redefinition of productivity to account for indirect costs such as turnover, absenteeism, and other costly symptoms of the "withdrawal-from-work" syndrome along with the development of sound techniques for measuring small-group productivity.

Return must be immediate and based on productivity. Again, take an extreme case and imagine a worker whose efforts are rewarded by a share in profits paid annually. Even if his share in these profits is significantly affected by the productivity of his group, the reward may be too far in the future to affect his performance and that of his group. Ideally, the distribution of profits should follow closely the period of productivity.

The plans must be contractual. Arrangements that can be arbitrarily rescinded are seen as paternalistic and, therefore, unsuited to the current and future labor force.

The argument can then be summed up: Both human goals (autonomy and interdependence) and economic goals (increased productivity) can be achieved through the sharing by workers in both the responsibilities of production and the profits earned through production. Most workers will willingly assume responsibility for a wider range of decisions (and by so doing to increase productivity and profits) if they are also allowed to share in the results.

Neither profit-sharing arrangements alone nor responsibility-sharing arrangements alone are likely to make significant differences in themselves. Profit sharing without responsibility sharing does not increase the size of the profit to be distributed. Responsibility sharing without profit sharing is basically exploitative and is usually rejected by workers.

Obstacles to the Redesign of Jobs

So far, we have seen that the redesign of work is feasible, that a careful alteration of jobs can lead to participation in responsibility and profits, and that the precise nature and extent of participation is a matter for experimentation within each workplace.

If the advantages of redesigning work are as compelling as the examples used here suggest, what need is there to advocate it or, for that matter, write about it? Why not simply get out of the way to avoid being crushed in the stampede? The answer is, of course, "it isn't as easy as it looks."

The reluctance of employers to move swiftly appears to stem from the following:

1. There is no end to personnel theories, administrative panaceas for revitalizing work organizations, and consultants claiming arcane knowledge of alchemical transformations. Single remedies (e.g., "job enrichment," "job rotation," "management by objectives") abound for the ills of work. Such efforts have failed because there is no single source of job dissatisfaction. In brief, the bad experiences of employers in the past have led them to ask: whom can I trust?

2. Some employers, trusting or not, simply do not know how to proceed. They don't know how to redesign work themselves; they don't know to whom they can turn; they may not even know where to begin to look for assistance.

3. For some employers, the experimental information gained to date is in firms different from theirs, and they would prefer to have directly applicable information before making a move.

4. Some employers may be willing to make changes but lack risk capital for transitional costs. In the short-run, these costs may not be trivial. Our Motorola example shows that the firm had to train the employees how to assemble all components into a final product, and had to hire additional workers in order to maintain a critical scale of operations. Unit production costs eventually ended up the same as those on the abandoned

assembly-line, but that eventuality was not known at the start.

5. In some industries there is opposition from trade unions to the notion of job redesign.

We do not know how extensive these problems are, nor which are crucial. We shall suggest shortly a *procedure* for getting at these problems—a procedure which experience suggests could prove most helpful. But we recognize, in the final analysis, that the reluctance of employers to act will never be overcome by arguments based simply on improving the welfare of workers. Employers for the most part see their responsibility in terms of profits. In their view, their obligations are to shareholders, not to workers. It is imperative, then, that employers be made aware of the fact that *thorough* efforts to redesign work—not simply "job enrichment" or "job rotation"—have resulted in increases in productivity from 5 to 40%. In no instance of which we have evidence has a *major* effort to increase employee participation resulted in a long-term decline in productivity. Based upon an analysis of the job redesign efforts outlined in the appendix of this report, it appears that the size of increase in productivity is, in general, a function of the thoroughness of the effort (holding the nature of the industry and its technology constant). Thus, employers who make *genuine* efforts to redesign work most often will be responding directly to their obligations to shareholders.

The Role of the Trade Unions

Clearly, the prime responsibility for improving the quality of working life rests with employers. But as Taylorism could not have succeeded without the acquiescence of the trade unions, the reversal of the effects of these efforts will likewise require an active and responsible union role.

After a phase of initial hostility, the American Labor movement saw many of the techniques of scientific management as a fundamental revolution in American industry, holding great promise for advancing the economic well-being of the worker.

Indeed, both industry and labor have benefited greatly from the fruits of increased productivity derived from industrial efficiency.

In part because of this success, labor has continued to emphasize extrinsic rewards for workers. But the union strategy of only bargaining for extrinsic rewards has begun to show signs of wear. Worker discontent with this traditional role of unions has left many union leaders bewildered and frustrated. Jerry Wurf, President of the Federation of State, County and Municipal Employees (AFL-CIO) says that "the greatest labor leader avocation these days is to gripe about the lack of their members' appreciation for all that they are doing for them." [18] There is considerable evidence that (1) alienated workers are less loyal to their unions than are non-alienated workers and (2) workers in jobs with little intrinsic satisfactions are least favorably inclined toward unions regardless of their age.[19] Young workers who are rebelling against the drudgery of routine jobs are also rebelling against what they feel is "unresponsive" and "irrelevant" union leadership.

There are several reasons why unions have been slow, even slower than management, to come to grips with the problems created by scientific management. Some union officials feel that they have been misled by managerial changes in the past, and that job redesign is yet another scheme to reduce the size of the workforce through wringing every ounce of productivity out of the worker. Another explanation is offered by Albert Epstein of the Machinists and Aerospace Workers, who says that "if the trade unions have not dealt energetically with this question, it is because they were absorbed with other issues which seemed more important to them." But Epstein adds that "there is nothing inherent in the trade union structure which must necessarily prevent it from taking up the question. . . ." [20]

It is true that unions have limited their concern to questions dealing with protection for all jobs in a company or an industry, and consequently, they have little experience with questions of specific job design. The answer to their problem may lie in developing cooperative efforts to carry out the redesign of work. But the first union question is that of a commitment. As Irving Bluestone of the U.A.W. writes, "Just as management is beginning to ponder the new problems of discontent and frustration in the work force, so must unions join in finding new ways to meet these problems." [21] If new ways are to be charted and accepted, the trade union movement must be among the initiators of new demands for the humanization of work. At the very least, such an initiative would improve their members' evaluations of their unions. And, if dissatisfying jobs lead to high turnover, it is difficult to see how unions can develop any long-term attachment among temporary members.

The Role of the Government in Job Redesign

Management, unions, and workers, in the final analysis, are the only ones who know the right way to build their product or perform their service. However, government does have a legitimate role to play in encouraging these parties to redesign work tasks—especially since the failure to do so is adding to the tax burden of all Americans through increased social costs.

For example, to ignore the trade-off potential between increasing the satisfaction of work and paying ever-more and ever-higher medical bills is to choose spending over investing. More significantly, it may also be the equivalent of persisting in a "no-win" policy concerning the health of Americans. We have sufficient information about the relationship between work and heart disease, longevity, mental illness, and other health problems to warrant governmental action. That jobs can be made more satisfying and that this will lead to healthier and more productive workers and citizens is no longer in doubt. What remains is to find a way to overcome the reluctance of employers and unions to act.

International experience in Scandinavia suggests that government can act as a catalyst to encourage and aid union and management efforts to redesign work. In Norway, the government, employers, and labor unions jointly sponsor an organization—the Norwegian National Participation Council—that encourages experimentation in the design of work (such as the Norsk Hydro experiment mentioned above). They have also formed a Parliamentary Commission to work with labor and management to encourage the redesign of jobs.[22] Similar efforts have taken place in Sweden and have helped to create the climate that led to changes on the automobile assembly-line at the SAAB and Volvo corporations.

It would appear to be worthwhile to emulate these Scandinavian experiences. They might be adapted to the American system through the formation of a public corporation with the following kinds of functions:

—To compile and certify a roster of qualified consultants to assist employers with the technical problems in altering work

—To provide a resource to which management and labor can turn for advice and assistance

—To provide an environment in which researchers from various disciplines who are working on job redesign can meet with employers, unions, and workers to pool their experience and findings.

There may also be a need for some financial capital in order to fund improvements in work conditions. The Federal Government, as one of the principal purchasers of medical care, might consider trade-offs between health care and work redesign purchases. Alternatively, it could provide tax incentives, loans, or grants to employers who are impeded by financial obstacles.

Research and Training A variety of training, demonstration, research, and experimentation options also exist. For example, the government might consider funding programs to retrain the tens of thousands of managers and industrial engineers who were taught the "efficiency expert" concepts of Frederick

Taylor and the inadequate approaches of the "human relations" school. While this is a project primarily for our business and engineering schools to undertake in conjunction with employers and employer associations, the government might consider financial incentives to encourage the process.

Demonstration grants might also be awarded to address the considerable technical problems involved in redesigning some of the worst jobs in the economy—e.g., those on the assembly-line. Also, several areas of research deserve added attention and support from the Federal Government—as well as from others. The kinds of populations, for example, included in research on occupational stress and disease need to be broadened. The great bulk of existing research deals with white male, and/or white-collar workers in specific organizations. More attention needs to be paid to blue-collar workers, specific age groups, women, blacks, and Mexican-Americans. Also, nationwide sampling efforts such as the U.S. Department of Labor's Survey of Working Conditions should be expanded.

Research on the working woman, in particular, should be expanded, not only because more women are working, nor only because their growing insistence on equality will change the kinds of work they traditionally perform, but most importantly because the difference in longevity between men and women suggests that occupation plays a central role in the genesis of disease and premature death. The most striking fact about the distribution of coronary heart disease in America is the degree to which it afflicts middle-aged white men and spares young and middle-aged white women. Throughout the period of peak occupational endeavor (ages 25–64) the male mortality rate from coronary disease among whites is from 2.75 to 6.50 times greater than the female rate. The unique hormonal makeup of women prior to menopause (the usual "explanation" for the difference in coronaries) has recently been discounted on the grounds that there is no noticeable increase in female death rates following the onset of menopause.[23] Clearly, this is an example of the kind of vital research that could be done. An expansion in research is also needed to sharpen the diagnostic procedures used to identify sources of stress and satisfaction in the work situation and in the person.

All of these training and research efforts could be funded under existing authority lodged in the Departments of Labor, Commerce, and Health, Education, and Welfare. The challenge is not necessarily to develop new legislation but to reorder priorities within these Departments. Some of the research, training, and demonstration money currently allocated to other issue areas could be transferred to this effort, where greater benefits would be likely than from existing expenditures.

But we should realize that simply funding more purely academic research is not the answer to the problems of America's workers. Research will not lead to the discovery of some formula that simultaneously maximizes productivity and satisfaction. Instead, as we have said, the redesign of each job constitutes a unique experiment—one that can be facilitated through knowledge of certain principles, techniques, and past experiences—but one that essentially requires the cooperation of workers, managers, and unions in a frequently complex trial and error process. Thus, what is needed more than pure research is (1) the translation of available research into "actionable" methods, and (2) a commitment and willingness to try new forms of work. In the long run, such a commitment would reflect the desire to become an experimenting society—not merely in the sense of trying new things, but in terms of trial and careful evaluation under circumstances that we can afford and measure. This is as much the opposite of sweeping, unevaluated fad and reform as it is the opposite of rock-bound resistance.

Experimentation Such an experimental approach is novel only in its application to problems of social policy. In other sectors of life it is as familiar as the design and trial of a pilot plant. It waits to be tried with respect to the social arrangements of work as well as to the technical. Outside the realm of work, examples of such experiments have begun to appear. The experiments with income maintenance may settle ancient ideological battles about what people will do when the threat of poverty is removed: will they become more or less active in the search for employment? The experiment with educational vouchers, to be spent by parents for the educational arrangements of their choice, may help discover ways of increasing parental influence without at the same time increasing inter-group conflict. Such a commitment to experimentation was also behind the effort to establish a National Institute of Education, and, particularly, the Foundation for Higher Education, which clearly recognized the difference between operational experimentation and scholarly research.

Industry has begun to experiment with work design in a promising but tentative fashion. Xerox has permitted a small number of their executives to spend a year working in public service agencies. One might see this developing into an experiment in institutional rotation, in which a manager spends a year at a major corporation, another in city government, and another at a university interspersed throughout his working life. Not only would the worker benefit from the variety but the institutions would benefit from a broadening of their perspectives. Lufthansa has experimented with *"Gleitzeit,"* or gliding work time, which means that a work place is open for business between, say 7 a.m. and 7 p.m., and workers can choose any time to start work and go home at any time—as long as they work for a total of 40 hours in a week. Lufthansa developed the concept mainly to alleviate peak hour traffic conditions, but found that the benefits to worker freedom and flexibility were greater in the long run. They also experienced a 3% to 5% increase in productivity.[24]

A general experimental goal for America might be to incorporate those functions of variety and autonomy that make for job satisfaction among independent professionals into the jobs of lower-level workers. For example, professionals can work at home if it is convenient. But a great deal of other work can be done this way—for example, product design and planning, market research, computer programming.[25]

Robert Kahn has suggested an experiment to suffuse even lower-level jobs with the flexibility of professional jobs.[26] He would break down the work day into units (modules) that represent the smallest allocation of time on a given task that is sufficient to be economically and psychologically meaningful. Workers could allocate their time as they saw fit—working a two-hour module on one task, the next two hours on another task, etc. The modules would provide variety and a chance to learn other tasks. They would also facilitate the scheduling of one's work to meet personal needs (child care, schooling) and would open up needed part-time employment. One could also accumulate work credits in order to earn a sabbatical. Kahn posits that the benefits from the experiment might be the improved self-esteem, self-development, and mental and physical health of the worker, and higher productivity for the organization. To what extent the costs of the experiment would reduce or offset the gains could only be determined by trial and evaluation.

The major issue, however, is not the work module or any other single idea, but the problem of society to which it is an attempted response—dissatisfying work. That problem can be solved by the process of innovation, trial, and evaluation—in other words, by action—and by no other means.

We have had too much of assumption and stereotype. Management has accepted too long, for example, the assumption that every increment of fractionation in a job represented a potential increment of production. Unions have assumed too long that they could prevent workers from being exposed to unreasonable hazards or physical strains, but not from being bored to death. And the larger society has assumed too long that there was no such thing as social-psychological pollution— that the effects of montonous or meaningless jobs could be sloughed-off as the workers went through the plant gates to home and community.

An experimenting society would approach the humanization of work by replacing such assumptions with facts, and by learning such facts through the familiar and unavoidable process of trial and evaluation. In this process industry, unions, and government could collaborate to the benefit of all.

The options for governmental action, then, are numerous. They range from establishing trade-offs between medical expenditures and funding work redesign experiments, to establishing a public corporation to encourage work redesign, to a major commitment to become an experimenting society. Large-scale experimentation in the redesign of work could well begin within the Federal Government itself. The range of options and the opportunities for trade-offs are clearly great.

5
WORK, EDUCATION, AND JOB MOBILITY

In the preceding chapter we discussed several options for improving work satisfaction through the redesign of jobs. Although job redesign is the major tool with which we might make work more satisfying, it does not respond fully to several of the structural problems we have identified in the world of work. For example, job redesign is not particularly responsive to the problems of worker mobility nor to the problems of unrealizable work expectations that are raised through the credentialling process of the schools. Rather, it appears that *educational policy* may be the most appropriate lever on these particular problems of job dissatisfaction. This relationship between work and education is not obvious, especially if it is approached from an analytical framework that segments social policy into discrete categories. We argued earlier that medical care is not synonymous with health; here we argue that schooling is not synonymous with education. By viewing education policy from this broader perspective, the subtle interrelationships between work and education become more evident, the trade-off potentials between various programs in these sectors become clearer, and the opportunity for building a coherent social policy may be enhanced.

As noted at the end of the chapter on health, changes in work design can substitute for medical care, and medical care can also complement and support improvements in work. Similarly, work and education have their complementary as well as their substitutability (trade-off) aspects. In the following section we shall discuss one such complementary relationship between job training and work, and then go on in the remaining sections to look at some other linkages between work and education.

Worker Retraining
Many of the prime sources of job dissatisfaction that we have identified relate to the worker's perception of being trapped in

his present job or status. Often, workers feel locked-in to their jobs or status as a result of sex, race, or age discrimination, as a result of financial constraints such as unportable pensions, as a result of being in a "dead-end" job, as a result of lacking the skills needed for advancement, and as a result of feeling that they have no options available to them other than the *status quo*. Workers who feel locked-in to their jobs quite often have symptoms of mental and even physical ill health. In addition, the productivity of these workers is quite probably lower than it would be if they felt they had the opportunity for mobility. From the societal point of view, workers with such problems are less likely than satisfied workers to participate constructively as citizens. In one study of blue-collar workers 40 and older, alienation was found to be highest among those workers who possess high achievement values but whose jobs were rated low in terms of variety, autonomy, and meaningful responsibility.[1] A particularly significant factor emerged from this study: it was found that those workers who have high alienation scores also score high on the desire to change their jobs. Nearly 40% of the over-40 workers in the study have thought seriously about making an effort to enter a different occupation, *and* would enter an education program to acquire new skills if such a program were available that promised a reasonable living allowance. The intrinsic content of their jobs—not income—distinguished these second-career candidates from the non-candidates.

Mid-Career Change Much has been made of the aerospace executive who quits his job to go back to school to become a doctor or the accountant who becomes a schoolteacher. But quantitative studies of worker attitudes have shown that the desire for self-actualization is a leading goal of many workers who are not executives or professionals. Both white- and blue-collar workers want to be able to grow on the job, want to be continually learning and facing new challenges. As we have suggested, mobility for many workers can be enhanced by making private pensions portable. For others, who are blocked by the consequences of sex or race discrimination, mobility can be facilitated by affirmative action programs. For many workers, however, particularly blue-collar and non-professional white-collar workers, the prime block to mobility is the lack of an opportunity for mid-career retraining and, often, the lack of funds to pay for such an experience. For these workers the financial obstacle is the greatest: if they go back to school they will lose their income but will still have to meet their families' bills plus the added costs of their education.

Mid-career change is often advocated as a solution to many of the problems of today's workers. We have increasing evidence of what has been called the "mid-career crisis" that leads to the desire for a "second career." Several societal developments seem to be at the heart of this phenomenon. The first of these is the increasing rate of change in our society—technological, economic, and cultural—that modern man finds so unsettling. Related to this "future shock" is the fact that commitment to one life-long occupation is no longer as feasible as it was in the past: "Once a coal miner, always a coal miner" is no longer a valid description in an age when the mine is quite likely to close down. A second factor is quite simply that workers are living longer; a forty-year working life is a great amount of time to devote to one career. Third, the general increase in expectations and in general education has left many workers with high aspirations in low-level jobs. For such workers a career change can be an avenue to mobility, self-actualization, and job satisfaction.

There are sound economic as well as social reasons that argue for an opportunity for mid-career retraining. If the economy were static, the number of workers needed in each skill category would not change. Early in his working experience each person would make a career choice and progress upward in responsibility and salary until reaching retirement. But there is no such economy. The real economy is dynamic. Every year, old products and old production techniques are rendered obsolete. Employees are replaced by machines or are laid-off by companies whose products become less competitive. Where products can be imported from countries with lower labor costs, American industry ceases producing these goods and shifts to high technology industries with exportable products. Changes in national priorities, such as the shift from a war-time to a peacetime economy, change the need for certain skill categories. New priorities such as increases in health care, increased efforts to clean up the environment, and the rebuilding of the cities all would create demands for people with skills different from the current mix. These changes are rapid: the economy's need for a particular skill can double or be reduced by half in twenty years —about half the length of an average career. Within an industry growing at an average rate, there are about five new openings for every hundred workers each year—about half due to retirement and half to industry growth.[2] In non-growing or declining industries these openings are virtually non-existent. Thus, by mid-career, an individual's chances for promotion can be very slight. This often results in career stagnation or pressure for early retirement.

One of the consequences of such stagnation is a serious inflationary effect on both slow- and fast-growing industries. In a slow-growing industry, employees age in their jobs, their pay increases due to seniority, but they are not promoted to more responsible positions. In rapidly declining industries, many long-term employees are retained in jobs because of union agreement long after their jobs are no longer needed.

Additionally, the lack of mobility *from* these slow-growing or declining industries leaves labor scarcities in the rapidly growing industries. Consequently, premium wages have to be paid to attract employees from the decaying industries or from other firms within the growing industry. In addition, some needed positions are not filled or are filled by inexperienced persons, thus decreasing the efficiency of the growing industry. Both of these circumstances contribute to inflation.

Career immobility can be a major source of inflationary pressure even at times of high unemployment if the unemployed do not have the skills to compete for the jobs that are open. Furthermore, due to the internal wage structure of any industry, increased demands due to labor shortage at any skill level will increase inflationary wage pressures throughout the entire company, not just at the skill level for which there is a shortage.

In addition to increasing inflation, career immobility may cause the economy to respond too slowly to changing needs. While it is difficult to estimate the extent that changes are delayed, the effect in economic terms may be very large. Since the relative size of industries typically changes by fifty percent in about 20 years, even a one-year delay in industry response to changing national needs could have a major effect on the economy's ability to adjust effectively to technological advances, to changes in national priorities, and to changes in international trade markets.

In devising a response to the problems of immobility, Herbert Striner has recently suggested that we should conceive of worker retraining as a "national capital investment." [3] He describes the new educational and training programs of West Germany in which more than a quarter of a million German workers go back to school annually to increase their productivity, effectiveness, and job satisfaction. Striner implies that this program helps to create conditions that permit a low unemployment rate to be accompanied with acceptable levels of inflation. Similar programs in Denmark, France, and Sweden also show exceptional social and economic benefits for the society and the individual worker.

In the United States there are several ways one could implement a program to increase worker mobility. For heuristic purposes, we present two alternative models here. The first could be a basic "Worker Self-Renewal Program" that would provide training and a living allowance for a small number of workers who wish to move from declining industries or job categories into growing industries or higher skill levels (and would be made available to other workers only if there were a surplus of funds). This minimum effort would be designed to have the optimum effect on inflation; it would also have some positive effects on unemployment. The second type of Worker Self-Renewal Program would be closer to a true "sabbatical" program in that it would offer workers financial support to take off as much as a year for anything from skill upgrading to a liberal arts experience. It would be open to all workers and would be, perhaps, six times as expensive as the smaller program. It would have a much larger effect on unemployment and would bring social benefits to a much wider segment of the population.

Basic Worker Self-Renewal Program To combat inflation, the basic program would concentrate on workers in skill categories that are growing at less than the average national rate of 2.2%.[4] It would be directed to people in their mid- or late-careers and not at entry-level positions. In order to achieve an optimum effect on inflation, it would be necessary to remove workers from slow-growing industries to create vacancies in these industries at a rate equivalent to the average vacancy rate for all industries. Workers would be removed from these industries for purposes of retraining. After they are retrained they would increase competition for openings in the fast-growing industries to a rate equivalent to that of an average industry. In other words, by increasing mobility from slow-growing industries competition for jobs in all industries, in effect, might be "equalized." If too many workers were retrained under this proposal, unnecessary worker scarcity would be created in the declining industries. If too few were retrained, unnecessary scarcity would remain in the rapidly growing industries. Either case would result in a smaller reduction of the rate of inflation than if the optimum number of workers were trained.

In order to determine the desirable program participation

rate needed to achieve this balance, we analyzed the growth rates of over 200 skill categories as projected by the Department of Labor.[5] It was found that approximately 500,000 workers per year (about 0.5% of the work force) would have to be retrained to have the desired effect on inflation. About one-half of these workers would come from low-skilled or unskilled job categories; the other half would be semi-skilled or skilled workers. A similar analysis was undertaken by the Urban Institute, with similar results.[6]

The renewal program would likely induce a large number of workers in mid-skill categories to be trained for jobs at higher skills, thus leaving behind openings for previously unskilled workers or participants in Manpower Training Programs. Moving employed workers up the skill ladder a small step at a time is far more likely to be successful than manpower programs that attempt to train unskilled workers for low-skilled positions that do not exist. In addition, by making vacancies available at low- to middle-skill levels, it should ameliorate the placement problems of manpower training program graduates—which tend to be quite serious in periods of slow to moderate economic growth.

Striner has estimated that the cost of mid-career retraining would be about $2,000 per person. Assuming that each worker receives a living allowance of 70% of his normal salary for a year's training (approximately $5,600 on the average), the total cost of a Worker Self-Renewal Program for 500,000 trainees would be from $3 billion to $4 billion annually. Approximately $1 billion of the cost would be for training and the remainder would be for the workers' stipends.

Striner suggests that retraining programs could be financed by a fund that combined the financing for retraining with unemployment compensation programs. Using Striner's assumptions, in order to meet the cost of 500,000 workers participating per year, a 0.75% payroll tax on all wages up to $9,000 would need to be added to present unemployment insurance taxes.

(The present cost of unemployment insurance comes to 1.2% of payrolls, using a $9,000 wage base; the average combined federal-state cost runs about 2.2% on the present taxable wage base of $4,200.) This increase would be shared equally by employer and employee.

As an alternative source of financing, it could be argued that all or part of the $3 to $4 billion could be paid from the almost $30 billion being spent annually on higher education by the states and the federal government. This would be equitable because workers have contributed to these programs through taxes but have had little chance to benefit from the expenditures.

The overall effect on the economy of a program of this dimension should be positive. Although there would be a reduction in the Gross National Product of $3 to $5 billion resulting from the loss of output of the workers who are in retraining, this apparent loss to the economy should immediately be covered by filling the vacated positions from the ranks of the unemployed. Economists argue that roughly half of the jobs that will be created by removing workers for retraining will be filled by those officially counted in unemployment statistics, while the other half will come from those who are unemployed but not counted in unemployment statistics because they are "out of the labor force." [7] To whatever degree old positions are not filled because they were unneeded in the first place, there would be no actual reduction in output. Thus, the net effect of the program would be a reduction in the unemployment rate by about 0.25%, with no appreciable change in output.

Additionally, there will be an effect on the GNP of about $1 billion annually due to the cost of training. However, this training will substitute, to a large extent, for similar but less effective efforts that are undertaken by current industrial, manpower training, or higher education programs. Subcontracting these efforts, the net negative effect on the GNP thus would be expected to amount to less than the $1 billion total. The remaining deficit should be overcome by three other factors that are harder to measure but are clearly of a larger magnitude than this substitution effect. First, there would be savings to the economy from the elimination of unnecessary jobs. Second, the workers' productivity will increase due to their retraining. And third, the reduction in inflation that will result from the program would allow a more vigorous job creation policy to be pursued, thereby increasing the GNP through increasing the labor force participation rate. Further analysis is needed to accurately assess these benefits, but they would most likely exceed the $1 billion figure for training costs. For example, a reduction of unemployment by less than 0.1% would alone make up the difference.

A Universal Worker Self-Renewal Program A universal program could provide all workers with the opportunity for a six-month sabbatical every seven years or a one-year sabbatical every fourteen years. The survey results cited above offer a rough indication that probably less than half of those workers qualified would take advantage of such a program. This would mean that about three million workers would be enrolled in the program at any given time. Assuming the same stipend and training costs of the basic program, the universal Worker Self-Renewal Program would cost about $22 billion per year.

Such a program would have a more significant effect on the lives of all working Americans in that it would make lifelong education a reality. It would also represent a breakthrough in redistributing work time versus leisure time over the lifespan of most Americans. Furthermore, there is also some reason to believe that, with increasing awareness of the benefits of continuing education, a universal Worker Self-Renewal Program would create a positive incentive for students to forgo the "lock-step" in education. With a sabbatical program, students might be likely to take smaller doses of education in their early adulthood, in anticipation of using the opportunity for additional education when they are more interested in doing so or when the need for retraining arises. Although the primary social justification for both the basic and universal programs is that they would provide opportunity for career mobility to those workers who are dissatisfied because they are "locked-in" their jobs, the *economic* rationale for the basic program differs from the *economic* rationale for a universal program. The basic program is designed to have an optimum effect on the inflation-unemployment relationship. As such, the basic program can serve to facilitate other, important programs (most particularly, job creation) that are currently hamstrung because they are tied to the problem of inflation. The decision to expand to a universal program would include factors other than this essential, economic one. A basic program should be viewed as a kind of necessary, economic tool, while a universal program should be viewed as one of many possible responses to national needs—similar in intent to other educational and social programs. One would, of course, design a universal program to include the necessary counter-inflationary measures inherent in the basic program, but it is essential to stress that expanding the size of the retraining program would have little additional effect on the inflation-unemployment problem. The economic benefits of a universal retraining program would be derived in ways other than through a further dampening of inflation.

If one assumes that 3% of the workforce would be out of the labor force at any one time, this would represent a considerable drain on the GNP as a result of decreased worker output. However, all the productive jobs that are vacated by trainees should be filled from the ranks of the unemployed. The actual numerical effect this would have on the unemployment rate is difficult to estimate because the extent to which the program would substitute for training that would have been done anyway, and the extent to which the program would stimulate earlier entry into the workforce by young people postponing their educations, cannot be accurately predicted. Such effects should not be construed as undesirable: they would balance the effect of the program on the GNP. Also, it would make it possible to spread present expenditures for job training and higher education over a worker's career and make them more readily available to those workers who really need them when their need is greatest.

In the short run, however, early entry into the workforce and substitutions for present training will account for only part of the 3 million jobs that are affected. If it is assumed that, initially, such substitutions would account for only 1 million of the jobs, the rest of the jobs would be filled by one million unemployed workers and another one million workers who are technically out of the workforce. Also, many workers would choose to participate in the program at a time when they otherwise would have been unemployed. This would have the effect of lowering the unemployment rate at a given program level. This level of program participation could be keyed to the economy in such a way that more workers would participate when unemployment rates would have been higher. In this way, fluctuations in the unemployment rate would, to some extent, be smoothed out.

To the degree that the program would not be a substitute for existing higher education, manpower training, or industry training efforts, there would be an impact on the GNP equivalent to the additional costs of training for the program. Assuming that 1 million workers would have been trained in these other programs, the remaining $2/3$ of the training costs would amount to about 0.4% of the GNP. To analyze the impact of the universal program on the economy, the effect of this additional training cost would have to be weighed against the benefits to be derived from the elimination of unnecessary jobs through increased mobility, from the increased productivity of retrained workers and from more efficient use of education expenditures to meet training needs. While no detailed analysis is available, a rough estimate would indicate that these benefits would far exceed the cost to the GNP of training.

In the long run, this program could be designed not to entail an increase in total spending for education and training. The goal of the program would be to modify existing forms of education and training efforts in order that the worker could benefit from these at more appropriate times in his career and in forms more appropriate to his needs. Eventually, the funds for the program could come entirely from substitutes for some of the approximately $20–30 billion spent annually on industry training,[8] for some of the $27 billion annual expenditures on higher education, and for most of the $1 billion spent annually on manpower training.[9]

This approach to analyzing the costs of the program suggests that a promising method for financing might be to establish a mechanism to tap funds from the recipients of savings and benefits from the program. Particularly, savings to businesses from reduced training costs, and savings to government programs from reduced expenditures in higher education, welfare, manpower training, and vocational education programs could be estimated and directly transferred to a Renewal fund. It is not clear what an appropriate share would be from each sector, but one effective mechanism to generate the substitution effect would be to give workers vouchers that they could then use as they saw fit in industrial training or in colleges or universities. In this way, transferred funds could be returned to the sources where savings occurred. A non-regressive tax on the salaries of workers could be designed to supplement the fund, because they will benefit from such things as additional earning years because of deferred education and increased salaries because of higher levels of skill training.

In considering financing alternatives for Worker Renewal, it would be necessary to ensure that the mechanisms are consistent with the principal goals of the program. For example, it is highly unlikely that the mobility goals of the program would be met if contributions were voluntary on the part of either industry or workers. The workers most in need of training are in the declining industries that can least afford to sponsor such a program, and the workers in these industries probably can least afford the training costs. The under-employed, in particular, would be virtually eliminated from participation if the system were based on voluntary contributions.

It has been suggested that it might be desirable to permit people to borrow against their social security or other vested or portable retirement benefits to finance their sabbaticals. The main problem with this method is that it undercuts the meaning and value of a pension. In effect, one would have to make the tough decision to mortgage his future if he chose to take some of his social security benefits at an earlier age in the form of a sabbatical; although, as mentioned in an earlier chapter, "early retirement," or the receipt of pension income relatively early in life provides a base of security enabling the pensioner to shift his occupation. But for people other than those in the military, these benefits generally come too late to qualify as "mid-career." However, it may be worthwhile to provide the following kind of option for a worker: either early retirement without a sabbatical, or a later retirement with a sabbatical.

Another method of financing would be to tailor Federal student aid to the needs of older students by making large grants for the shorter periods of educational experience that workers will use: for example, young students might take a thousand dollars a year for four years while older workers might need four thousand for one year.

Conclusion We have analyzed only the tangible economic effects of the Worker Self-Renewal Program, but it is clear that the intangible human benefits might be vastly more significant. Needless to say, the benefits of the opportunity for employment presented to the unemployed and the "hidden unemployed" would be substantial. More directly, those workers who have not been able to actualize their career goals would have a meaningful second chance in life. Even those workers who do not actually take advantage of the program are likely to have some comfort in the knowledge of the additional option. It is also reasonable to deduce that as workers gain greater mobility and freedom of choice with respect to jobs, there may be a shortage in supply of workers for certain undesirable work. Consequently, the employers will be under great pressure to restructure those jobs in order to attract the workers they need.

In conclusion, the above analysis indicates that a Universal Worker Self-Renewal Program may well justify itself on grounds of economic efficiency. When the broader considerations of social efficiency are also taken into account, the case for it becomes even more compelling.

Education

In our exploration of the interrelationships between work and education, the following shortcomings became evident:

1. The market value of education has driven out its other values. One consequence of this has been to require, needlessly, ever-higher credentials for the same work.
2. Jobs have failed to change in step with the increased educational attainments and concomitant aspirations of the new workforce.
3. Vocational education in the high schools has failed to give students useful skills or place them in satisfying jobs.
4. We have largely neglected the educational needs of older workers.
5. The schools themselves are a workplace, influenced by, and influencing, other workplaces. As such, the schools would benefit from a redesign of their work.
6. The high schools have not yet discovered a proper role for themselves to play in "career education."

The "Value" of Education For some years, Americans have assumed that increasingly higher levels of education are crucial to an individual's chances for "getting ahead"—e.g., finding and keeping a good job, making more money, obtaining the respect of others. National policies—such as the G.I. Bill of Rights, and the National Defense Education Act (which emphasized scientific and technical skills)—have all been incentives to advanced educational attainment. Similarly, the expansion of professional and white-collar occupations has created a demand for workers with higher levels of education. But this interest in "attainment" has been focused on the credentials of education —high school diploma, baccalaureate, and graduate degrees— rather than on the learning. The plethora of economic articles that have appeared in recent decades, demonstrating the economic value of ever-higher education, undoubtedly abetted this emphasis on credentials. Moreover, credentialism spread well beyond the white-collar sector; high school diplomas became a prerequisite for most apprenticeships, and even for entry-level, semi-skilled jobs.

Yet, the economy itself has not been changing rapidly enough to require or to absorb the spectacular increase in the educational level of the workforce. The expansion of professional, technical, and clerical jobs absorbed only 15% of the new educated workers; the remaining 85% accepted jobs previously performed by individuals with fewer credentials.[10]

While new industries have appeared in recent decades that need a well-educated workforce, most employers simply raised educational requirements without changing the nature of the jobs. There are probably a number of reasons for their actions, ranging from using credentials as a means of excluding the "undesirable," to hiring people "like one's self" to increase personal comfort. One important reason has been the belief that the more highly educated worker is likely to be more productive, more trainable, and have more self-discipline than the person with less education. However, for a large number of jobs, education and job performance appear to be inversely related. The less educated tend to remain with an employer longer and be more productive than those workers with ten or more years of education. The more highly educated workers become bored with unchallenging work and express their dissatisfaction in lower productivity and higher turnover rates.[11]

If matters continue as they are, the disparity between the supply and demand of educated workers is likely to be exacerbated in the next decade. About ten million college graduates are forecasted to enter the job market in that period, while only four million graduates will leave the workforce through retirement or death. This means that there will be 2½ college graduates competing for every "choice" job, not to mention the additional 350,000 Ph.D.'s who will be looking for work.[12] The problem would be greatly ameliorated if the highly touted "automation revolution" occurs and shifts the occupational structure of the nation in such a way as to greatly increase the demand for upper-level jobs without expanding low- and middle-level jobs. Continued growth in the economy would also create millions of new jobs, but growth alone will not change the occupational structure of the economy. Without major changes in the quantity and quality of work, one consequence of this oversupply of graduates will be a large class of underemployed college graduates, disillusioned with work and resentful of the poor returns on their investment in collegiate education. Although the value of a college education is *not* solely measurable in terms of its usefulness in the marketplace, the dominant interest, constantly reinforced in America, is in its marketability. Indeed, the decline in the market value of higher education may endanger the American commitment to education, precisely because its non-market aspects have been ignored or grossly undervalued.

The very fact that we think about "career education" and talk about the value of schooling in terms of an investment that will yield future earnings indicates not only how important work has become in our thinking, but how other motivating forces have been de-emphasized. Formal education, for example, was once conceived of much more as a "preparation for life," whether or not it led to a specific job. In other nations and cultures, the non-economic values of education have been considered predominant. For example, not long ago in rural Ireland, each child learned "his or her part in the farm economy, not as vocational preparation, but as a making ready for marriage." [13]

Today, we think of career education as an end in itself, for the personal reward of earning an income for oneself, not as a preparation for life, marriage, citizenship, or any other social function. We cannot turn back to a peasant economy, of course, but the crucial point here is that we have put too much emphasis on the credentials of education. We have encouraged unreal expectations and, quite possibly, have caused a great degree of frustration among our youths who have not been able to realize the "payoff" they had anticipated.

The high school "drop-out" is an interesting case in point: conventional wisdom may be incorrect with respect to the bleak future ahead for high school drop-outs and the value of a high school diploma as a credential for employment. In one study, drop-outs had higher unemployment rates than high school graduates—29% versus 13%—but differences in ability and family background accounted for this gap more than did the lack of a diploma. That is, "dropping out may contribute to unemployment, but it is also a conveniently-measured symptom of more basic causes of unemployment." [14]

Once employed, drop-outs were found to earn no less than employed high school graduates, even when job seniority was controlled (when uncontrolled, the drop-outs averaged higher weekly wages). Furthermore, although drop-outs tended to have somewhat lower status jobs, they generally had higher levels of job satisfaction than did the graduates.[15]

To sum up the foregoing: educational requirements for jobs have increased, but there is little correlation between educational achievement and job performance; college graduates are not faring as well on the job market as they used to; and high school drop-outs are not faring as poorly as expected. These findings suggest that the value of increasing levels of education (credentials) as a means of finding rewarding work has been grossly over-estimated. This does not mean that education should be valued less, for its non-market values have been ignored. But what this does mean is: (a) the validity of using education predominantly to raise income is growing more and more questionable; (b) requiring more credentials to perform an unchanged job lowers performance and reduces job satisfaction; and (c) the design of work is lagging considerably behind the changes that have occurred among the workers, including their educational attainments.

Vocational Education While the subject of drop-outs provides us with a special case for examining the relationship between credentials and several job-related factors, the subject of vocational education provides us with a general case for examining the efforts of schools to relate directly to the world of work.

The objective of vocational education has been to provide high school graduates with marketable job skills. But in an extensive study of vocational education it was found that

> many students, at all school levels, were able to enjoy higher wages by moving out of their field of training as they entered the labor market. . . . The relationship of the job to the field of training appears to have no significance in influencing the level of employment, wages, and earnings following graduation.[16]

Among high school vocational graduates, more than half took first jobs in fields unrelated to their training, in contrast with only 25% of those who acquired specific skills in technical schools or community colleges after graduation from high school. With respect to the level of jobs taken by vocational graduates, there appears to be a disquieting, high proportion of vocational trainees in unskilled and semi-skilled jobs. A national sample of high school vocational graduates showed a fairly high proportion in such jobs three years after graduation, far more, it should be noted, than the graduates of post-high school vocational programs.[17]

Another study, recommending a reduced role for vocational curricula in the high school, found high school vocational education inattentive to the unskilled nature of entry jobs, the competing sources of labor, and the desire of employers to do their own training when it is needed.[18] Furthermore, it is not clear whether or not vocational training at the high school level pays off in higher wages. However, junior college graduates consistently start higher and continue to have a wage advantage over vocational high school and post-high school technical school graduates.[19]

It is sometimes argued that high school graduates with vocational training experience fewer and briefer spells of unemployment than those with only a regular high school education. But a national, longitudinal survey found that vocational graduates did not have better unemployment records than academic graduates. Among all vocational graduates, those from high school had higher unemployment rates than those taking junior college and other post-secondary vocational courses.[20] Of course, this may be a reflection of employer reliance on credentials as much as it is recognition of reduced competence of the students.

From the evaluations of vocational education, then, it appears that a very expensive form of education—costing perhaps 50–75% more than other high school curricula[21]—has a very low utility. Only a small proportion of entry-level jobs for high school graduates require the specific training and skills offered by vocational education; vocational graduates more often than not take jobs for which they were not trained; their unemployment records are not better than other high school graduates, except those in the general curriculum; and their pay isn't better. Most of the literature on vocational training in high schools arrives at the same negative evaluation: technical training in schools is based on an outmoded assessment of future needs. Students are trained without any real knowledge of how they might apply their skills in the future. All they have is an increasing recognition that the technological concepts they are learning are outdated or will be before they can use them.

These conclusions are important, not only because they document the failure of attempts to relate high school education directly to work, but also because of the new interest in "career education." If career education is modeled on vocational education—if specific skills or clusters of skills are taught in traditional schools—it will very likely follow the same dismal course. Another consequence of infusing the high school curricula with career-oriented programs is that educational institutions would be instilling a "single career" concept—the notion that an individual should develop a single, lifetime, occupational role identity. Now, as we are developing systematic evidence that increasing numbers of white-collar and blue-collar workers feel "locked-in" and desire mid-career changes,[22] it is ironic that we would still be trying to put young students on an inflexible career track. (This tendency is compounded by the invidious distinction made between "academic," "general," and "vocational" high school diplomas which often brands young people for life by locking them into a career and educational path from which they cannot escape. Worse, perhaps, this distinction between credentials tends to ossify the class structure along the lines of a similar but more pervasive system found in Great Britain.)

By equating education to a youth activity and by confusing the notions of education and schooling, we have placed too many of our resources in traditional schools designed for people under 21 years of age. We have neglected the fact that education is a lifelong experience, and often occurs outside the classroom. And, as many educators feel, the desire for education often increases with age, as does the seriousness with which students approach it. Recognition of these facts would open up several important options for worker training—from making education available to workers at later stages in their lives to encouraging education in places other than the traditional schools.

Workplaces and Schoolplaces It may be useful to look at the concept of career education from a vantage point that views schools as a workplace, influenced by, and influencing, other workplaces. In *Future Shock,* Alvin Toffler argues that the pre-industrial educational means of transmitting knowledge and skills crumbled before the onslaught of the mechanical age, because "industrialism required a new kind of man." He goes on to say:

Mass education was the ingenious machine constructed by industrialism to produce the kind of adults it needed. The problem was inordinately complex. How to pre-adapt children for a new world—a world of repetitive indoor toil, smoke, noise, machines, crowded living conditions, collective discipline, a world in which time was to be regulated not by the cycle of sun and moon, but by the factory whistle and clock.

The solution was an educational system that, in its very structure, simulated this new world. . . . Yet the whole idea of assembling masses of students (raw material) to be processed by teachers (workers) in a centrally located school (factory) was a stroke of industrial genius. The whole administrative hierarchy of education, as it grew up, followed the model of industrial bureaucracy. The very organization of knowledge into permanent disciplines was grounded on industrial assumptions. Children marched from place to place and sat in assigned stations. Bells rang to announce changes in time.

The inner life of the school thus became an anticipatory mirror, a perfect introduction to industrial society. The most criticized features of education today—the regimentation, lack of individualization, the rigid system of seating, grouping, grading, and marking, the authoritarian role of the teacher—are precisely those that made mass public education so effective an instrument of adaptation for its place and time.[23]

This relationship between authoritarianism and rigidity in the schoolroom and the workplace—with the implicit view of man as inherently undisciplined and ignorant—probably has not directly occurred to modern educators. But the similarities between the processes were clear to Frederick Winslow Taylor, who wrote:

No schoolteacher would think of telling children in a general way to study a certain book or subject. It is practically universal to assign each day a definite lesson beginning on one specified page and line and ending on another; and the best progress is made when . . . a definite study hour or period can be assigned in which the lesson must be learned. Most of us remain, through a great part of our lives, in this respect, grown-up children, and do our best only under pressure of a task of comparatively short duration.[24]

Although mass education may have served its purpose well of preparing our youth for the kind of work served up in the past, the fact that today's workers are not "grown-up children," but are revolting against authoritarianism, fragmentation, routine, and other aspects of the inherited workplace, suggests that the schools are anachronistic in *their* "production" methods. The success of the schools in helping to produce Industrial Man indicates they could be successful in helping to produce the Satisfied Worker; yet they are mired in the model of Industrial Man.

If, to produce Industrial Man, the schools had to become an "anticipatory mirror, a perfect introduction to industrial society," then to help produce the Satisfied Worker, the schools need to become another kind of anticipatory mirror, providing another perfect introduction to a changed world of work. It may be the case that a Satisfying Education would be the best precursor of Satisfying Work, and, in that sense, be a major component of "career" education.

The *process* by which education may be made more satisfying is suggested by the criticisms of the contemporary workplace: we would expect the school to become more satisfying as a place of work, just as we expect the same of other workplaces, by removing the equivalent necessity of punching a time-clock, by increasing the autonomy of the "worker," by enlarging tasks and by reducing rigidities. If students were viewed as workers

and teachers as team leaders, school workplaces might be redesigned along the lines of other workplaces illustrated in this
report, with a high degree of participation among all the "workers" and "team leaders" in the choice of procedures to reach
the goals.

Some teachers may have the same authoritarian personalities
that some managers in private industry have—so that greater
autonomy among the "workers" is undesirable to them. But we
cannot ignore the fact that teachers are subject to fixed hours of
instruction, uniformity in subject matter, and lack of discretion
in choosing the content of courses. We would expect teachers to
find *their* work more satisfying if they were to function as team
leaders, with a considerable amount of autonomy, rather than
as supervisors demanding submissiveness and control, and if
they were given what workers are asking for—the assistance,
equipment, and information to do their job. In short, if we
think of the school as a workplace and that like every other
workplace it should be satisfying, then changes have to be introduced that will increase the satisfaction of the workers, students and teachers alike.

If the goals of education were maintaining curiosity, maintaining and building self-confidence, inducing a love of learning, and developing competence, education would be directly
relevant to the major needs expressed by the workers. Some of
these, it may be recalled, are the opportunity to use one's skills
and education to the full, to be reasonably autonomous in doing one's work, to have a sense of accomplishment, and to have
the opportunity to learn while on the job. Earlier remarks on
the importance of self-esteem are also applicable, for the school-
work satisfactions that would evolve through curiosity, resource-
fulness, and mastery would contribute to productivity and self-
esteem on the job as well as in school.

Educational experiments, like those in industry, suggest that
school-work can be advantageously redesigned. Some schools
have stopped the practice of lumping children by age, now

enabling them to progress individually, and to compete not with each other but with themselves over time. Some enable the student's interest rather than a bell to determine the length of a "period" with the result that 75% to 90% of the students achieve at the same level as the top 25% do under traditional conditions.[25] There are probably as many different ways to re-design school-work as there are to redesign other kinds of work to make it more satisfying.

We are suggesting that "career education" will succeed to the extent that the concept develops within an understanding of the nature of work and once again *anticipates* the world of work by developing within its own workplace exemplary re-structurings, and not by attempting to impart specific voca-tional skills.

Before leaving this topic, we should like to note a recent career education experiment which, at first glance, appears to be teaching certain vocational skills, but which is responding, in fact, to a fundamental social need. A newspaper story re-counts that in Des Moines, "Grade school pupils . . . visit lo-cal businesses and see people at work in many kinds of jobs. There will be more role-playing and field trips." [26] The impor-tance of this activity cannot be over-estimated. Simone Weil, in *The Need for Roots,* lamented how modern work has destroyed the easy awareness of their parental occupations that children had in more traditional societies.[27] More recently, Bronfenbren-ner has observed:

Although there is no systematic evidence on this subject, it appears likely that the absence of such exposure (to adults at work) contributes significantly to the growing alienation among children and youth . . .[28]

(It should be noted that our rules regarding nepotism inadver-tently serve as an obstacle to reducing this source of alienation.)

Every worker is a teacher and every workplace is a school, not because of the skills that the one may impart, nor the organization or technology that is apparent in the other, but because they deal with the real world and man's mastery therein.

Alternative Career Education Strategies If specific skills are learned best on the job, in public and proprietary vocational schools, in community colleges, and in professional and graduate schools of universities, what occupational role remains for the high school? Particularly, what happens to traditional vocational education in secondary schools if education becomes a lifelong process?

Again, as with other questions we have raised in this report, there are many answers that can be offered. But an analysis from the perspective of the institution of work suggests that the regular secondary school appears to be an appropriate place to broaden formal education to include an introduction to the world of work, its meaning, its necessity for life, its rewards, its requirements, and its shortcomings.

The secondary school can prepare the young person for the transition from dependency to self-support. Perhaps through the schools some of the current unreal expectations about work that are held by young people can be dispelled, thus avoiding much of the disappointment and frustration they feel when they take their first jobs.

Basically, most young people simply do not know what to expect from work or what work will require them to give. Surely, to give them this information presents a broad challenge to our high schools. Some of the alternative approaches to introducing young people to and preparing them for the world of work might be academic, benefiting from what the schools do best: providing information. In this case the information might concern the manner in which work is organized in our society, how people work alone and together to achieve certain goals. Other activities would be designed to be "action-rich," and would present a contrast to traditional, passive schooling.

Information-Rich Alternatives General education for work should probably be aimed at enhancing the young person's reading comprehension, arithmetical skills, the ability to write and speak clearly, and the capacity for working closely with other people. We seem to have forgotten that these skills are the ones most sought after by employers. Typically, employers find that young workers who have "learned how to learn" can quickly master the specifics of most jobs. The satisfaction of young people with their future jobs would probably be increased by this kind of training—for competence is often a great part of job satisfaction. A good general education, restructured along lines suggested above, is probably the best career education a young person can receive. Still, curricula might be widened to meet the curiosity of young people about the adult world by incorporating such information-rich topics as the following:

COURSES IN INSTITUTIONAL MANAGEMENT AND ADMINISTRATION Given that bureaucracies and large institutions (corporations, universities, government) are, and will continue to be, the dominant source of employment in the United States, it might be useful to offer courses in which students learn the procedures of large work organizations. They might explore how institutions are formed, and why they are formed. They might try to discover how these organizations operate, what they produce, how they relate to other organizations, and what roles people play in them. They could learn some of the basics that are taught in MBA programs—the basic principles of management and administration, such as how to organize a group of people to complete a given task in a given time. They could be introduced to some of the administrative problems that people are likely to face in any organization, and how people might think about such problems rationally to find solutions that are satisfying to both humans and to institutions. Such courses might help to dispel some of the unrealistic expectations young people have about work by candidly exploring the personal advantages and disadvantages (e.g., security vs. independence) of working in large organizations. A central component of such a course should be the basic principles of organizing work in order to provide for factors that lead to job satisfaction.

COURSES IN ENTREPRENEURIAL SKILLS One of the ironies of our system is that for all of our verbal commitment to the American Dream we seldom teach our youth the basic knowledge that anyone would need who wanted to go into business for himself. In fact, this knowledge is usually transmitted from father to son in middle-class families, and is thus difficult for women or the poor to obtain. Except for those young Americans who take part in Junior Achievement, knowledge about self-employment in this country is a quite well-kept secret. Young people might benefit from learning what it means to keep books, to accumulate capital, to borrow and to invest, to buy and to sell, to take risks, to wholesale, to retail, to provide services or to manufacture and sell a good by oneself.

These examples are intended only to be illustrative. But, any course would be effective only to the degree that it is intellectually honest. If we attempt to teach an ideology of work, rather than examining and discussing that ideology, then the courses will be worse than no courses at all.

Action-Rich Alternatives To acknowledge that the high schools are inappropriate places to learn specific, marketable technical skills is not to say that it is necessary to board up all the shops in the nation's schools. To the contrary, much of what is taught in present vocational courses could be modified into valuable, practical courses available to all students. Domestic skills, crafts, and mechanics courses need not be justified in terms of future employment, but as contributing to the educated person's basic knowledge. The young woman who does not understand how a car operates and how it is repaired, and the young man who cannot cook, are at a considerable disadvantage in life. Learning to use tools is a basic necessity that all students would benefit from learning. (Other skills, such as how to prepare one's income tax form, how to go about buying a house, and how to be an effective consumer are practical skills that can be utilized in whatever career one chooses. Also, concepts from such "academic" subjects as mathematics and physics could be integrated with a work-related curriculum.) The important issue about work-oriented courses is that they be directed at a set of skills that the students can use while they are taking the course or ones they will need no matter what jobs they eventually take. As a prime example of this, there is no reason why every high school student should not learn how to type. Not only does it make most jobs easier, the skill also can be used at home or at school. Also, if we all could type, this would be the most important step in reducing both the sex-stereotyping of the secretary role, and eliminating many hours of the least interesting aspect of the secretary's job. In conclusion, occupational courses should not be allowed to become tracking courses and might better be labeled "survival courses for an imperfect service economy."

There are other means by which education can become action-rich within the confines of the school. One such format that is attracting increasing interest among educators consists of so-called "games and simulations." As defined by James Coleman, these are games "in which certain social processes are explicitly mirrored in the structure and functioning of the game." [29]

In simulating work environments the emphasis is not on decisions *per se* but on the processes through which decisions are reached. The players assume simulated roles and play according to a set of rules that provide choices and create behavior which leads to certain outcomes. These games provide a way for students to learn about "real costs" and possible long-range outcomes of various decisions—in career choice, in education, and in work. But if education is to become more than a game played in lieu of life, one goal may be to free students from the confines of school and to provide them with opportunities to mingle, associate, and work with older members of society. Cooperative education programs appear to provide at least partial responses to this need. Nearly 300,000 high school youths are currently involved in cooperative education programs that provide part-time employment while they are enrolled in school.[30] Some jobs involve only one afternoon a week, others are half-time jobs. There are several advantages to such programs—particularly when the student has had the opportunity to try two or three jobs before he finally makes up his mind to take a full-time job:

—Such jobs help to overcome age segregation and allow students the opportunity to observe adults at work and, in so doing, learn what it is like to work all day in various occupations.

—In many cases, the students are able to acquire some actual occupational skills.

—Students who have the opportunity to do blue-collar work will have a chance to overcome stereotypes about manual laborers. That many manual jobs are well paid and offer the chance to solve problems no doubt comes as a surprise to some students.

—Students are given the opportunity to make contacts in the world of work, thus enlarging their options when they come to choose what full-time jobs to take.

—Cooperative education often makes school work more meaningful for students, particularly those from disadvantaged backgrounds.

—Success is rewarded with earned income—an important badge of adulthood.

—Young people may come to know themselves better, to learn what they can and cannot do and, thus, develop realistic aspirations.

While obvious difficulties abound in expanding current cooperative education in high schools—child labor laws, lack of jobs, rigid class scheduling—the benefits would seem to make the effort worthwhile. Congress has authorized some funds for cooperative education in the 1972 Higher Education Act, but it would appear to be worth exploring further possibilities of trade-offs with other vocational education programs in order that all high school students could have the option of a cooperative experience.

Another role for the high schools might be to provide more relevant and effective career counseling. Current occupational counseling, on the whole, does not appear to be as responsive to the world of work and the needs of work-bound students as educational counseling is to the world of higher education and the needs of college-bound students. For example, a recent survey found that high school counselors spend twice as much time on college-related counseling as they do on vocational topics.[31] In part, counselors are responding to the pressures of a society that values college preparation very highly. Also, the orientation of counselors may be influenced by the fact that one-half of all high school graduates now go on to college. This is a misleading fact, however, because fully two-thirds of these students never complete a four-year degree program and soon find themselves looking for a job.[32] A second myth is that most young students will find white-collar jobs. Recent statistics show that over 63% of all young men will take a blue-collar first job.[33] Perhaps our counselors have anticipated a revolution in which all of our young people become college graduates and all take white-collar jobs in the burgeoning service sector of our economy. This revolution has not yet taken place. Therefore, the drop-out and the student who is probably heading for a blue-collar job clearly require a greater share of the time of the counselors. Yet, the 1968 Manpower Report of the President states that 56% of high school graduates received some form of job guidance or counseling compared to only 22% for high-school drop-outs.[34]

In summary, we have argued that to lodge skill training (especially training for a single occupation or a related cluster of occupations) in the high school invites a too-early career tracking and seldom provides students with usable skills. We have further argued that the most advantageous acquisition of specific skills occurs either on the job or in post-secondary institutions such as community colleges where there is a much closer relationship to true demand than in high schools.

Where training cannot be obtained on the job, there remains the problem of access to the educational institutions offering skills training. Young people who seek this kind of training seldom have sufficient funds for tuition or living expenses; thus, there is clearly a need for society to help them to receive the skills they need to earn a living. There are several options for achieving this; among them are the following:

—As a first step, all Federal regulations relating to student loans and scholarships to colleges and universities could be rewritten to make them applicable to community colleges, and public and proprietary vocational schools.

—Tax credits or other incentives could be offered to employers who provide or underwrite training for workers, including on-the-job training.

—If manpower programs are made universal, as we suggest in the next chapter that they should be, some young people could have their occupational education financed in this fashion.

—One could extend the concept of the Worker Self-Renewal proposal to make younger workers eligible. Alternatively, at the age of 18 each person could be entitled to a given amount of support for further education. He could draw on this account at any point in his lifetime (a kind of universal, permanent G.I. Bill). To the extent that he draws on his account, he might repay it through an addition to his social security tax. (The account would not be a grant, but a loan which might or might not be used depending on the individual's own best judgments of his interests.)

Perhaps the most important thing that could come out of this analysis of work and education would be to draw educators out of the schools, boards of education, and offices of education and periodically into the world of work. Without a thorough knowledge of this world, they probably will never be able to design a career education program that is responsive to the needs of young students and workers. Likewise, it would be well to attract employers and supervisors periodically into the world of education where they could acquire a greater sensitivity to the changing values of youth and, thus, a greater knowledge of the kinds of jobs they will have to provide for tomorrow's workers.

6
FEDERAL WORK STRATEGIES

Federal activities are deeply enmeshed in the world of work, both directly and indirectly. Federal programs support the training of people for specific careers—in health professions, teaching, scientific research, and the like; Federal spending encourages the growth of certain industries and occupations; and, to mention only one other instance, national military service removes some young people from the labor market, training them for many occupations, and returns others in mid-career through early retirement. A systematic review of Federal policies and programs affecting work—which we shall not undertake here—would reveal the Government's deep penetration into the factors determining the quantity of jobs, and no small incursion into the factors determining their quality.

Our venture, in this report, into Federal policies and strategies on work is inescapably determined by conclusions reached earlier: that the health of workers is influenced by the quantity and quality of work, that a large number of problems with which HEW contends very likely arise because of insufficient employment opportunities, and that many of the potential improvements that could be made in the quality of work depend in part on an abundance of work.

We also felt it would be remiss, if not irresponsible, merely to call for more jobs without facing up squarely to one of the most difficult economic problems of today—the trade-off between inflation and unemployment. Accordingly, we have tried to show in this chapter how several work policies, if pursued, would have a dampening effect on inflation, which would permit a much greater effort in the private and public sectors to expand employment opportunities without the inflationary dangers that prevail today.

Furthermore, although it is clearly the case that the *sine qua non* of job satisfaction is the possession of a job, the creation of dissatisfying jobs would be an inadequate response to the problems of unemployment. A primary public policy position advanced here, in recognition of the foregoing, is that the quality considerations that play a role in the *redesign* of jobs and in the retraining of workers must go hand in hand with the quantity issues in a comprehensive approach to *creating* jobs. That this important relationship is not self-evident is, in part, a result of the way in which we have thought about work in the past.

We have tended to develop shifting and contradictory responses to the problems of work, in part because we have lacked a full enough understanding of the meaning of work in our lives. Public assistance programs present an example of this confusion: while they were designed as income maintenance programs for those who could not work, in recent years they have become entwined with employment and manpower programs.[1] Because of this shift, we have begun to look to work as the solution to our welfare "mess." Work *is* the key to ending dependency, but as we shall illustrate in this chapter, we may have put that key in the wrong lock. Rhetorically, and often administratively, the nation has demanded that those on welfare take jobs. Forcing these people to work would not end dependency since about ninety-five percent of those receiving welfare benefits are women with children. They are on welfare precisely because they cannot work or do not have a husband to support them. But a great part of this welfare "mess" might be straightened out if we were to provide steady jobs for the millions of fathers of welfare children, whether or not they are currently living in the same household with their children. These under-employed men need jobs in order that they may establish stable households. Work, then, offers a partial, preventive solution to the problem of dependency.

From the perspective of work, it would seem that welfare, manpower, and employment programs might be both more effective and more equitable if they were disaggregated. They should work in tandem, but each should do different things. Employment policies should aim at creating jobs for all of those who want to work. The existence of a job will be sufficient, in most cases, to get people to work; the importance of work to life obviates the need for compulsion.

There will remain some individuals, of course, for whom the availability of work is not enough, and they will need manpower training. Again, motivation, not coercion, should be sufficient to bring people into training programs. Finally, there will remain those who cannot work (primarily for physical reasons) and those who choose to care for their young children instead of taking jobs, and these people will require income maintenance assistance.

Such a work-oriented perspective of Federal programs establishes the primacy of employment policies, makes manpower training an essential but supportive function, and leaves income maintenance programs as a truly residual category, a fallback for family support. We shall now look briefly at some policy alternatives based on this construct.

Pursuing Full Employment

The statistical artifact of a "labor force" conceals the fluidity of the employment market and shifts attention from those who are not "workers"—the millions of people who are not in the "labor force" because they cannot find work. For example, in 1969, there were 92.5 million civilian men and women 16 years of age and older who had some kind of "work experience." But our "labor force" for the same year was reported as only 80.7 million.[2] Although this narrower concept of a "labor force" is useful for many economic indices, it is inadequate as a tool for creating employment policy. Its primary shortcoming is that it excludes from consideration the millions of people who answer "no" to the question "are you seeking work," but who would in fact desire a job if one were available and under reasonably satisfactory conditions. For example, the ranks of the "unemployed" would be swelled were we to include such individuals from the categories listed below:

—The millions of women who do not look for part- or full-time employment because they know it is not available at all, or unavailable under conditions that would enable them to discharge their family responsibilities

—The large numbers of younger and some older persons who are in school or in training programs because they have been unable to find suitable jobs

—Young women, for the most part in low-income families, who remain at home because they find it difficult to secure a suitable job

—Persons on welfare, many of whom are female heads of households, who cannot support their families by holding down the types of jobs available to them

—The many physically, mentally, and socially handicapped persons who cannot work, at least initially, except under sheltered conditions

—Prisoners and other people in institutions who are denied access to meaningful work

—Older persons who no longer seek jobs because they are not hired even though they might be able to work full-time or part-time, or trained to do so

—Large numbers of people who make a living in illicit or illegal work, in part because of their failure to find suitable legitimate employment. (One of the ironies of crime is that it keeps "unemployment" down.)[3]

It is significant that we have fallen short of "full employment" even while using a narrow definition of the worker that excludes the above categories of potential workers.

Inflation and Unemployment With the adoption in the early 1960's of a Keynesian approach to Federal economic policies it appeared that we were embarking on a path that would lead to "full employment." The concept of a balanced full employment budget was embraced and the encumbrance of a balanced budget was shorne. It became part of the conventional wisdom that what heretofore had been thought of as "structural" unemployment could be substantially reduced by the stimulation of aggregate demand (which was accomplished initially by a major tax cut, then by a rapid expansion of both domestic programs and defense expenditures). However, this particular rosebush contained two very sharp thorns. One was the fact that despite the low unemployment rates and concomitant economic growth, there were sizable subgroups of the population who were still bearing the disproportionate brunt of the remaining unemployment. These were largely the "disadvantaged" toward whom the attention of most Federal manpower policies were turned. These policies are discussed later in this chapter.

The other thorn was inflation. As we progressed through the mid-sixties, it became increasingly apparent that lower unemployment rates could be "bought" with the application of economic policy instruments only at the expense of increased inflation. The concept of the Phillips curve, which depicts a presumed inverse relationship between unemployment and inflation, became a standard part of every policymaker's vocabulary. Finally, in the late sixties, the Federal government concluded that the "costs" of inflation were too high (despite the benefits of low unemployment) and monetary and fiscal measures were employed to control inflation—in the process causing the unemployment rate to rise.

As a result of the economic experience of the last ten years there is a growing consensus among economists on the following:

—Even under the most favorable assumptions about a Phillips curve for this country, what empirical evidence there is suggests that the inflation-unemployment trade-off facing us using traditional economic weapons is highly unfavorable. The most optimistic estimates of economists indicate that a 4% rate of unemployment is attainable (and maintainable) only at the expense of an equal or greater rate of inflation

—Inflation is fueled by factors other than its relationship with unemployment. For example, if people *anticipate* inflation (whether or not it would naturally occur for structural reasons) they will demand salary increases that will lead to further inflation. This "inflation mentality" makes the trade-off between inflation and unemployment more adverse

—Our macroeconomic policy instruments as generally applied are fairly imprecise tools—we cannot have any confidence that their application will, in fact, enable us to achieve the lowest feasible rate of unemployment compatible with any given rate of inflation.

In view of these considerations, it is clear that a continuation of our present types of economic policies will not permit us to deal effectively with the employment problems that have been documented in this study. They may not even permit us to reduce drastically the 5 million plus who are presently classified as unemployed, much less provide large quantities of jobs for the 10 to 30 million who are underemployed, on welfare, or who are out of the labor market but would take a job.

But a policy that took into account the social and personal values of work might begin with the need to maintain what might be termed total employment—in which everyone who desires a job is able to find a reasonably satisfying one—as opposed to just "full employment" which is inadequate because it is a function of our current "labor force" participation rate. Such a policy that begins with the need to maintain total employment would *then* determine how to maintain price stability within that context.

Toward a Total Employment Strategy One could not expect the country to adopt a total employment policy overnight because the structural changes that this would require in the economy and society would be difficult to achieve.

However, we could make some marked strides in this direction in the near future. Following is an examination of some of the important elements of such an employment strategy, particularly as they relate to other policies recommended in this report.

A significant movement toward total employment for our economy means two things:

—The existence of considerably more employment opportunities (of a satisfactory nature) than now exist

—A distribution of job opportunities that will be more equitable for youth, the aged, women, and minorities.

Past experience indicates that the pursuit of the former will do much to achieve the latter—but not enough. Therefore, as long as we fall short of total employment, it will be necessary to some extent to focus job creation efforts on those demographic subgroups of the population that traditionally face employment difficulties.

In view of the adverse inflation-unemployment trade-off there are two main steps that the Federal government might take to ensure the existence of a greater number of, and more equitably distributed, employment opportunities:

—The initiation of largescale programs aimed at significantly improving the inflation-unemployment trade-off

—The simultaneous use of expansionary monetary and (selective) fiscal policies to maintain the maximum amount of employment consistent with "tolerable" rates of inflation. Fiscal policies would be selective in the sense that they would be designed to (1) have the least adverse impact on the inflation-unemployment situation and (2) create job opportunities that would result in a more equitable distribution of employment.

The first of the steps is the most difficult to develop. Despite the plethora of recent research on the subject of the inflation-unemployment relationship, not enough is known about it to give clear guidance to public policy. However, it is quite likely that several of the major policies suggested in this report for improving job satisfaction would also have a major impact on the problem of inflation. The basic Worker Self-Renewal program would remove hundreds of thousands of workers from the labor force who would otherwise have been underproductive. It would decrease unnecessary labor oversupply in declining industries and occupations by retraining workers for industries and occupations where they will be more productive and where critical manpower shortages might otherwise have created inflationary bottlenecks. Studies undertaken at the Urban Institute indicate that such a program would have a significant impact on the problem of inflation.[4] Similarly, the redesign of work, accompanied by profit sharing, has a high potential for increasing productivity—particularly through reductions in wasteful turnover and work stoppages. Other suggestions developed in the report could be expected to have lesser, but still important, effects on inflation. The reorganization of secondary education would increase the efficiency with which youth are able to move between school and work. Eliminating race and sex discrimination in the workplace would reduce the dispersion of unemployment rates in the economy, thus helping to reduce the rate of inflation associated with a given level of employment. Fuller portability and vesting of pensions would permit increased worker mobility, which should promote efficiency. And finally, some of the reforms of current manpower programs that are discussed later in this chapter could also have a favorable impact on the Phillips curve. One cannot predict the exact degree of change that would occur in the unemployment-inflation relationship as a result of any one of these actions, but taken together they appear to present a formidable arsenal in the war on inflation.

Pursuing such anti-inflationary policies would permit more expansionary use of traditional monetary and fiscal policies and, therefore, a higher level of employment than would otherwise be possible. Furthermore, maintaining full employment by stimulating aggregate demand will create an atmosphere that is more conducive to making many of the personal and organizational adjustments that are needed for the restructuring of work and upgrading of lower-skilled workers. But in order to obtain the greatest benefits possible from the job creation and redistribution of employment opportunities that arise from expansionary monetary and fiscal policies, it may be necessary to utilize the latter in a more selective fashion than we have previously. On the taxation side, this would argue in favor of such policies as:

—Employer tax-incentives for hiring, training, and upgrading workers from traditionally low-employment groups

—Greater tax breaks for low-income families and individuals (such as deductions for employment-necessitated child care, "forgiveness" of social security taxes, and lower marginal tax rates on earnings for those on welfare) to both encourage greater work effort and put more money (almost all of which would be used for consumption purposes) into low-income areas so it will create jobs where they are needed.

On the expenditure side this would argue for:

—A generous funding of the efforts suggested in this report that would have a favorable impact on the inflation-unemployment relationship

—A greater targeting of expenditures in general on purchases of goods and services that create relatively more jobs for the disadvantaged (e.g., regional development of Appalachia)

—A program of public service employment for those for whom this is the only alternative to dependency on the state. To the extent possible, this should involve filling existing vacancies— thus minimizing the adverse inflationary impact.

It should be noted that while in the short run these various anti-inflationary measures for job creation might require expansion in the Federal budget, in the longer run the increased employment should result in significant reductions in costs for welfare, unemployment compensation, manpower programs, crime protection and control, and social services. There will be less need for continued growth in these essentially compensatory programs if we have fuller employment.

Beyond the Problem of Inflation The policies we have discussed should have the effect of dampening the effect on inflation to a degree that would permit greater government stimulation of demand. In this way, most new jobs would be created in the private sector. But the use of expansionary fiscal policy to create jobs raises the important question of what kinds of jobs will be created. Because economic issues tend to monopolize discussions of job creation, this issue tends to take a back seat to the question of inflation. But, as a direct result of every expenditure it makes, the government creates jobs, and, therefore, we must ask what jobs we want done in the society, who we want to do them, and under what working conditions.

To begin, there are many jobs—obvious to the naked eye—that patently need doing, either for the survival or the improvement of our civilization: our cities need to be restored or rebuilt; our transportation systems are in disarray; our air, water, and land are fouled with pollution from coast to coast. In carrying out these activities, the government can choose to do those things itself or it can buy such public goods predominantly from *private* contractors. Because of budget constraints, the government cannot do all these things, even if all are beneficial for society. It must choose among these public goods. In so doing it can target its purchases in such a way that it can determine the kinds of *jobs* it is buying, because the population groups affected by expenditures varies greatly. This does not argue that we should buy things we do not need simply because they create the right kinds of jobs. Rather, in choosing among the tasks that need to be done we should attempt to maximize the quantity and quality of jobs we are buying with public dollars. For example, expenditures on space, research, higher education, and rural highways may have little significance for the traditionally unemployed, while purchases of urban development and pollution control should produce more jobs for these groups. The mix of skill levels required for different projects also varies greatly. Health care, space, and research stimulate those levels of jobs for which there is already considerable demand, but few blue-collar jobs are created. On the other hand, environmental protection programs in the area of water supply and sewage services are estimated to offer a job mix of 61% unskilled or semi-skilled blue-collar jobs, 26% skilled operators, and only 9.4% professional jobs.[5]

Where such expenditures are made also affects their impact. A maximum amount of jobs per public dollar would probably result from expenditures made by State and local governments (in large part funded by Federal revenue sharing or formula grants). On the average, a billion dollar investment at the Federal level creates 89,900 jobs while a similar investment creates 110,900 jobs if it is made at the State or local level.[6] Indeed, over the past decade the greatest rate of job growth in the *private* sector is attributable to State and local government purchases of goods and services: private sector employment that is directly attributable to such purchases increased by 58%, while total employment as a whole rose by only 19%.[7]

In this framework, "public-service" employment (usually called "leaf-raking") would be a misnomer. Many meaningful tasks serving public needs could be accomplished by the private sector. What must be recognized is that the private sector *can* provide satisfying work on public goods. An example of this might be made by a comparison of the garbage men of New York with the garbage men of San Francisco. In New York, where garbage men work for the city, and receive decent wages, they often go on strike, the service they deliver is generally regarded as poor, and the status of their job is low. In San Francisco, where the garbage men have formed private co-operatives and have high incomes, they never go on strike, the service they deliver is generally regarded as both cheap and excellent, and the status of their job is surprisingly high. It is not because they arc involved in a private enterprise that the garbage man's lot in San Francisco is better than his peer's in New York, but the private sector employment allows for two things: greater participation in the management of the operation and participation in profits. Although one cannot draw strong conclusions from one example, the greater possibility of designing rewarding work in the private sector probably should not be discounted when choosing between direct government provision of services and buying such services from the private sector.

Another problem with the jobs we create through public expenditures is that they often do not reach the rural poor and those in the ghettos who need the employment the most. The response to this problem is complicated. First, government and private employers would probably have to address a whole range of options to deal with other sources of employment difficulties, including education, housing, transportation, and plant location, that might include:

—Adoption of educational policies at the local level to increase the employability of members of disadvantaged groups

—Expansion of on-the-job training

—Acceleration of the training, placement, and promotion of the disadvantaged

—Assumption of responsibility by employers for insuring that transportation systems link their establishments with lower-income neighborhoods. Alternatively, policies that influence the location and relocation of plants and offices, including industrial promotion and highway construction, could be designed to aid marginal workers.

These suggestions assume that fairly traditional measures can be utilized to overcome the employment difficulties of marginal workers. There are also less conventional alternatives. For example, it has been proposed that the Federal Government encourage large corporations to franchise personal services companies in the ghettos. Community groups or individuals could obtain such a franchise and the large corporation would handle the administrative and bonding problems, provide training and the capital needed to start the enterprise. These franchise companies could train teams of ghetto residents to provide such services as car and appliance repair and home cleaning and repair. In some cities, enterprising ghetto residents have already organized themselves into such teams to provide services for both ghetto and non-ghetto residents.

What probably prevents the natural spread of this idea is the shortage of business "know-how" and capital. Such a job creation program would answer the needs for more personal services (for example, it is nearly impossible for ghetto residents to get a plumber), for work under less structured conditions, for opportunities for community control of business, and for opportunities for underemployed ghetto residents.

This suggestion is not offered as a panacea. Rather, it is an imaginative alternative for providing meaningful work for the underemployed; there are undoubtedly other ideas that should be explored.

Self-Employment Another job creation strategy might be to encourage certain types of self-employment. We have seen that self-employment is the most satisfactory of all kinds of employment, and that the closing of most entrepreneurial options has exacerbated the feeling of workers that they are locked-in to their current jobs.

But there are many obstacles to self-employment today—one being that large institutions benefit from economies of scale and thus drive out small "inefficient" concerns. If we decide that job satisfaction and greater employment opportunities add to social efficiency, we might rewrite our tax laws to give the self-employed and small business proprietor a better chance to compete with larger institutions. At the Federal, State, and local level, this might require the exemption of certain categories of the self-employed and the smallest businesses (e.g., under ten employees) from certain licensing, insurance regulations, and expensive and time-consuming reporting to government agencies. Also, we might make more risk capital available through the Economic Development Administration and the Small Business Administration and through incentives to private investors. In the previous chapter of the report, for example, we suggest an educational method for encouraging self-employment. Many other ideas, no doubt, can be developed to support self-employment and small businesses.

Job Information Finally, there are those who claim that our unemployment problem would be eased considerably if we had an information system that provided workers and employers with increased knowledge about the supply and demand of labor and jobs. For workers at all levels, fate plays the greatest part in how jobs are obtained. People fall into jobs. They get jobs because they know somebody who knows somebody. Yet, few of us even know enough people to have more than a couple of options when we are seeking employment. At the lowest end of the occupational scale, one may have only one or two options among similar jobs. Most often, lower-level workers see no choice: a job is available and they take it without knowledge of any alternatives. This suggests that many people are in unsatisfactory jobs because of a dearth of information about their options. It also suggests that there may be—but this is not certain—a larger supply of unfilled jobs than we had supposed.

It is difficult to design a way of dealing with this information problem. As a start, the Labor Department has begun to install computerized "job banks." The success of their effort will depend on the willingness of employers to report job openings, something they are often reluctant to do, preferring instead "personal recommendations."

Whatever job creation options the government might pursue, it is important that the jobs that are created are meaningful.

Now we turn to the problem of workers who seem unable to attain or hold jobs even when they are available.

Manpower Training

The concentration of unemployment among minorities, youth, older persons, and those who live in rural areas was essentially unaltered by the economic expansion of the 1960's. The existence of these groups was considered a "structural" problem of the workforce—the abilities of these unemployed persons did not meet the demands of the labor market. The Government attempted to alleviate this "structural unemployment" with manpower development policies to supplement macroeconomic policy. The central issue was poverty amid affluence. Although cash grants to the poor would have been a more direct attack on poverty, the Economic Opportunity Act of 1964 reflected our national preference for work over non-work; accordingly, the law advocated training and education to improve the opportunity of poor people for employment.

Some Reasons for the Failure of Present Manpower Training Programs To be eligible for the bulk of our public manpower training programs, one must be "disadvantaged"—a poor person who does not have suitable employment, and who is either a high school drop-out, under 22 or over 45, handicapped, or subject to special obstacles to employment, such as racial discrimination. Other manpower training programs pinpoint specific groups facing barriers to employment: veterans, Indians, ex-prisoners, displaced workers, older persons, migrant workers, and so forth.

Most of these programs do not create permanent jobs, but attempt to "upgrade" the unemployed so they better fit some estimated demand for labor. Yet, evaluations of the MDTA, for example, indicate that such programs are not fully effective in producing trained individuals who, indeed, "fit" the characteristics of the demand for labor.[8] Similarly, under the Work

Incentive Program, of the 3 million welfare recipients who were eligible in 1971, only 300,000 received training, and placement rates for those who had gone through training never bettered 20%.

Such manpower policies and programs may be faulted on several other grounds.[9] First, assistance is fragmented into far too many categories. Some people who could be helped and who want to be helped are not because their "category" falls between administrative cracks. Others are confused by a bewildering array of programs with unclear and overlapping eligibility. Probably the most important factor in the success of a training program is the motivation of the enrollee, a factor too subtle for categorical eligibility standards. This suggests the need for a system based on motivation—one that would be a totally voluntary program. No one would be forced to enroll, but special access could still be assured the disadvantaged by assigning them some priority within a voluntary scheme. In addition, fragmentation makes efforts too diffuse to achieve the critical mass needed for impact, effectiveness, or public acceptance.

The second deficiency in our present manpower strategy is that it has become too entwined with income maintenance policies. Income programs were aimed at those who are poor because they are incapable of working. The categories of assistance have developed to give benefits to those who are unemployable for reasons beyond their control, and to exclude the "undeserving" who are thought to have some control over their employment status. In deference to the work ethic, and in part out of suspicion that some public assistance recipients might be able to work, the income programs have incorporated measures expressing a preference for work over welfare—in the treatment of outside income, in the rehabilitative social services accompanying assistance, and in work/training requirements. In the effort to get the poor to work, the welfare system has become a combination income maintenance and rehabilitation/man-power program.

At the same time, manpower programs have become, to a great extent, a part of the government's anti-poverty strategy. Eligibility for manpower programs is drawn from categories quite similar to those for income programs: the aged, the disabled, poor persons. Some manpower programs (WIN, special state employment services, Emergency Employment Act) are specifically designed to get people off welfare and into jobs.

The majority of these programs for the disadvantaged would undoubtedly be more effective if we distinguished between the purposes of the income maintenance and the manpower strategies. Income policy should strive for maintenance of some minimum standard of living. Its concern should be for anyone who is below that standard, for whatever reason he may be in need. But the thrust of the argument here is that a decent and satisfying job with adequate pay would be *the* work incentive, and none other would be required. Instead of building a welfare strategy with so-called work incentives, we need to have a work strategy which does not penalize people who want to work. If work itself were refurbished and made the incentive, neither coercion nor pressure on existing welfare recipients—who are in no position to resist—would be needed. Some people assume that if the income for maintaining a minimum standard of living were sufficiently high (whatever that may be), a significant portion of the population would withdraw from work. That may be true—but what evidence there is suggests that most people will prefer employment and self-sufficiency to unemployment and dependency. Work withdrawal on a significant scale may be more a theoretical than a *real* possibility and this mere possibility should not be permitted to deter us from the work-based strategy suggested here.

For many recipients, an income supplement will not be sufficient—they will need and want help in order to obtain work.

However, there is neither need nor rationale for separate man-power training for the very poor; rather, there is a need for manpower training for all, separate from the income mainte-nance system, in which welfare recipients can take part. One reason for this is that programs designed specifically for the poor seldom generate the broad public support needed for con-tinued funding at a level high enough to have impact on the problem. Thus, programs for the poor quickly become poor programs. Also, the existence of a plethora of programs—for Indians, the aged, veterans, etc.—leads to unconstructive com-petition for funds.

Another argument against a link between manpower training and welfare programs is that their combination prevents us from designing each program optimally. For example, if it is decided that welfare mothers who do not work should forfeit their benefits, it becomes necessary not only to provide man-power training for them but also day care for their children. Since existing day care facilities are inadequate to meet the influx of thousands of welfare children, the government must then create a new, costly, federally sponsored and supervised in-dustry. Thus, the decision to make welfare mothers work leads not only to the government impinging on the freedom of choice of mothers who would want to raise their children at home, but also to an obligation to provide a service that may have a low cost/benefit ratio. Furthermore, it hinders the rational design of a responsive system of *voluntary* day care for the children of working mothers.

It also is most important that manpower programs emphasize on-the-job training, rather than institutional training, for the former has proven more successful in placing enrollees in per-manent jobs.[10] In addition, this approach would further the government's job creation strategy of stimulating and subsi-dizing private sector employment.

But even if these adjustments were made, there would still be left unattended the need to fit work to the workers, rather than the other way around. The lower down the scale of employability one descends, the greater the necessity to provide something akin to a "sheltered workshop" in order for these people to benefit from work. This is one reason why the National Alliance of Businessmen's "Jobs" program was far from a success. The hard-core unemployed failed to cope with the discipline of work as interpreted by mainstream culture, and when the economy turned sour, these marginal workers were the first to be laid off.

With respect to the problem of discipline, it is well known that many poor people have little or no work experience and, consequently, have high rates of absenteeism, tardiness, and other problems on the job. Many of the methods we suggest in Chapter 4 for making work schedules and work rules more flexible for workers in general, can be adapted to meet the needs of these "hard-core" unemployed. But a major limitation on a policy of expanding private or public jobs is that we may have a *dual* labor market—a theory that is not verified, but one that is nevertheless a useful tool for characterizing the employment problems of the very poor.

Dual Labor Market Most policy analyses of poverty and employment have tended to follow the classical economic approach of viewing labor as relatively homogeneous except for a hierarchy based on skill levels. Under this theory, the stimulation of the economy through traditional macroeconomic policy should create full employment. But the anomalies between this view and observed behavior in the labor market has led to the development of the dual labor market theory. Apparently, there may not be one, but rather two labor queues, and macro-policy often fails to generate jobs for those in the second queue. Michael Piore describes the dual labor market in the following terms:

One sector of [the labor] market . . . the primary market, offers jobs which possess several of the following traits: high wages, good working conditions, employment stability and job security, equity and due process in the administration of work rules, and chances for advancement. The secondary sector has jobs that . . . tend to involve low wages, poor working conditions, considerable variability in employment, harsh and arbitrary discipline, and little opportunity to advance.

The factors which generate the dual market structure and confine the poor to the secondary sector are complex. . . . the most important characteristic distinguishing primary from secondary jobs appears to be the behavioral requirements they impose upon the work force, particularly that of employment stability. Insofar as secondary workers are barred from primary employment by a real qualification [not race, sex, or ethnicity], it is generally their inability to show up for work regularly and on time. Secondary employers are far more tolerant of lateness and absenteeism, and many secondary jobs are of such short duration that these do not matter. Work skills, which receive considerable emphasis in most discussions of poverty and employment, do not appear a major barrier to primary employment (although, because regularity and punctuality are important to successful learning in school and on the job, such behavioral traits tend to be highly correlated with skills).[11]

Piore then goes on to describe the factors that generate the secondary labor market, draw the poor to it, and tend over time to lock in even the poor who initially had appropriate traits for the primary labor market. There are indications that Federal manpower programs are insensitive to the problems of the secondary labor market. Indeed, there is some evidence that the MDTA has made use of it as a source of jobs. One evaluation of the MDTA claims that it has chosen to train for jobs where openings occur because of high turnover, whether or not they are characterized by high demand.[12] Thus, instead of facilitating mobility, the manpower program may have recirculated the working poor among the secondary jobs that were, in part, responsible for their poverty. (An advantage of the Worker Self-Renewal programs that we described is that they would be particularly sensitive to the difference between the primary and secondary markets and would train workers specifically for jobs in the former.)

It would be a mistake to consider the secondary labor market as intrinsically bad. It fits the needs of the young who tend to be excluded from the primary labor market until they are in their twenties, and matches the preferred life style of those who don't want to be tied down to a job. However, it does not meet the needs of those who wish to establish a stable, economically secure family, as we illustrate in the next section.

Consequently, the following problem emerges with respect to expanding employment: If the expansion comes in the primary job market it may not appreciably benefit the unskilled, under-employed in the secondary labor market, nor those potential workers on welfare who generally possess secondary labor market characteristics. There is some mobility between the primary and secondary labor market and an opening up of the primary labor market would tend to increase this mobility. However, based upon the analysis of Piore and others, it appears much more likely that such expansion would result either in drawing more working-class or middle-class women (who have the required behavioral traits—or "adaptive skills") into the primary labor force or in redesigning primary jobs to have secondary characteristics.[13]

On the other hand, expansion of the secondary labor market does not solve the poverty problem for families and in addition tends not to reduce primary unemployment. Economically, but even more psychologically, many poor families need the rewards of primary employment.

Dual-labor-market economists suggest changes in manpower training and equal-opportunity law enforcement to aid the poor in finding primary employment. But their suggestions can only bear fruit if the total amount of primary employment expands.

In this report we discuss several options for retraining and for creating primary jobs. We feel that imaginative policies designed to tap the demonstrated desire of poor people to work will overcome many of the obstacles to employing them in the primary labor market. The fact that these people hold secondary jobs, if they hold any job at all, suggests that employment for them could be increased without significantly increasing inflation. One of the main causes of inflation is an excess demand for the highly skilled. By providing people in secondary jobs (or the unemployed) with the requisite skills, we can reduce this type of inflation by meeting the demand for skilled labor, thereby holding down its cost. Thus, there are potential benefits to employers and to society from developing meaningful manpower policies. The Urban Institute's study estimates that changes in our total concept of our manpower "system" (including improvements in the quality of jobs) would provide an annual increase in the GNP of $30 billion.[14]

As promising as such a conceptual change may seem, we must acknowledge its limitations. Some workers are either incapable or too accustomed to failure to learn a new skill. The question for them will be simply the availability of a job. In America, we like to think that all workers should be "mobile." The sad truth is that for some we can expect nothing more than low-level employment. The challenge here is not just for manpower training, but for the creation of jobs that are steady and pay a living wage—in short, some form of sheltered employment.

In summary, an effective manpower program would be one that is broad—encompassing all present categorical programs and more—and sufficiently flexible to be able to respond to diverse reasons for unemployment. Unencumbered by welfare considerations and unconstrained by categorical red tape, the manpower program should be able to train those who are employable but lack certain skills, create jobs for those who have adequate training but for whom there is no current demand, and provide such alternatives as sheltered workshops for those who are handicapped in ways that leave them unable to compete in the job market.

Such a program would do much to alleviate our welfare "mess" through providing decent jobs for central providers—who are not the prime recipients of welfare benefits—and through separating manpower requirements for welfare mothers from income maintenance programs. When welfare is examined through the lens of work, we can see the role that job creation and manpower policies can play in limiting dependency, and the legitimate burden of income maintenance that remains.

Work and Welfare

In original conception and intent, welfare is an income maintenance program for those who cannot take care of themselves. The main programs provide categorical aid to the blind, the aged, the disabled, and to families with dependent children (a program originally designed to make it possible for widows and mothers without employable husbands to stay at home and raise their children.)

Increasingly, however, the original purposes and definitions of welfare have lost their force, especially with respect to the Aid to Families with Dependent Children. What was originally defined as a population dependent on the larger community for maintenance and support tends now to be defined in the public's mind as a population of malingerers who ought to be forced to accept work. The result is that persons who cannot take jobs or, by social agreement, should not take jobs, are now the target of programs designed to make them take jobs.

This change in public perception and policy has two main roots. One is the frustration born of the now-certain knowledge that the need for a Federal public assistance program will always be with us and will not, as was originally hoped, wither away as a result of the growth of a comprehensive contributory social insurance system.[15] The other is the change from widows and orphans to unmarried mothers and illegitimate children as models or prototypes of the AFDC family.[16] ("The AFDC example always thought about," remembers the first Executive Secretary of the Social Security Board, "was the poor lady in West Virginia whose husband was killed in a mining accident, and the problem of how she could feed those kids.")[17] Where the original model of the miner's widow evoked compassion, the new model of the unwed mother evokes deep and widespread resentment.

Underneath the resentment and the frustration, and giving rise to them, are a host of unverified assumptions about the character and composition of the welfare population: most poor people don't want to work; most people on welfare are black; welfare mothers have babies to increase their welfare benefits; people on welfare live well and easy; most people on welfare want to be on welfare; etc.

Every one of these assumptions is demonstrably false as a generalization, and is true only in the occasional particular. The facts are that most poor people are not on welfare and the majority of poor people not only want to work but do work, year round and full time; black families, though over-represented, make up less than half of the AFDC caseload; the average monthly payment per recipient on AFDC is $49.60; most mothers on AFDC do want to work—it is not difficult to add to the factual side of this misunderstood issue.[18]

What is so terribly damaging to the prospect of developing constructive programs for dealing with the problems of welfare is that these false stereotypes of poor people, black people, and AFDC families are widely held by the general public. The negative attitudes of most Americans about welfare thus constrain national leaders in their development of policy. Indeed, the existence of these feelings leads to a situation in which the public's "price" for welfare reform is the inclusion of mandatory work requirements for those on welfare, including mothers.

The variety of recent attempts to reform the welfare system are characterized by the inclusion of mandatory work provisions. These reflect the public's belief that there are many people on welfare who don't belong there, who could and should be working, and that we can deal with "the welfare mess" by forcing these people off the rolls. Realistically, then, we cannot expect a welfare reform program that does not have a work requirement for mothers until there is general public agreement that the great majority of people on welfare belong there (in the sense that they have no other place to go). The only able-bodied adults on welfare are those on the AFDC rolls, but since less than 5 percent of the families receiving AFDC include an able-bodied man, the only category of recipients with any potential for joining the work force are women with dependent children, the very persons AFDC was designed to assist in staying home.

From the analysis we present in this section, the present public attitudes may very well lead to a worse welfare problem in the future. A welfare program with a compulsory work requirement for mothers will not help the mothers, the children, or the society at large, and, as we will discuss later, it will not enhance the all-important role of the central provider in establishing family stability. We believe that the alternative presented here, that of viewing mothers as working and of making jobs available for central providers, would better achieve the major objectives of the general public—a decreasing welfare caseload in the long run.

Should Welfare Mothers Be Required to Take a Job? The question of whether the mother in a fatherless family (76 percent of AFDC families)[19] should take a job or not is a complex one. It is not even clear that anyone other than the mother has the legal or moral right to make that decision, or that anyone other than the mother can make the decision that is best for her and her children. Some mothers prefer outside jobs to keeping house and raising children; others prefer to stay home. To force all AFDC mothers to do one or the other is to do violence to what we know about human development and family relationships: mothers who work because they prefer to work, and mothers who stay home because they prefer to stay home, probably make better and happier mothers (and children) than those who do one or the other because of circumstances or coercion.[20] It follows that the public interest and the interests of the mother and her children will be best served if the mother herself makes the choice. This choice, of course, must be essentially a free one: a decision either way must not carry with it any special penalties, rewards, or forfeitures.

The easiest part of the problem has to do with those women now on AFDC—perhaps a majority—who, other things being equal, would prefer to work and support their families. But other things are not equal. They do not take jobs because there aren't suitable child care facilities, or because the costs associated with having a job and paying for child care often leave them with less than they would be receiving on welfare. These women do not need to be coerced into the labor force; they need the freedom to join it: adequate child care facilities and a decent job at a living wage.[21]

The more difficult part of the problem lies with those AFDC mothers who choose to remain home and raise their children themselves. More accurately, the problem lies not with them but rather with our system of public values regarding women and women's roles and our definition of work. When we say to the AFDC mother, for example, "You must go to work or take work-training in order to be eligible for public assistance," we are, in effect, telling her that, from society's point of view, she is not now working, that keeping house and raising children are not socially useful, at least not as useful as "a job." But we are able to make this judgment of the AFDC mother who stays home and raises her children only because we make this same judgment of all housewives.

Thus, the public devaluation of keeping house and raising children is, for the AFDC mother, only a special case of the more general problem faced by women throughout our society. Indeed, it is one of the principal sources of the deep discontent experienced by women in all social classes. The failure of society to acknowledge housekeeping and child rearing as socially useful work on a par with paid employment makes it increasingly difficult for the married woman who is "just a housewife" to see herself as a valued contributor in the eyes of her family, her neighbors, and the larger society. The pressures generated by such social values tend to push women into the labor force in their search for recognition as full and valued participants in society. The result is that some women who would perhaps prefer to remain at home are, in effect, pushed into the labor force against their will.

It is with the AFDC mother who would prefer to stay home that the social undervaluing of housekeeping and child rearing appears in its clearest, most perfect form. In this case, it is precisely the social undervaluing of housekeeping and child rearing that provides the rationale for telling her that she must take a job to be eligible for welfare, and also for the notion that she is "getting something for doing nothing."

The clear fact is that keeping house and raising children is work—work that is, on the average, as difficult to do well and as useful to the larger society as almost any paid job involving the production of goods or services. The difficulty is not that most people don't believe this or accept it (we pay lip service to it all the time) but that, whatever our private and informal belief systems, we have not, as a society, acknowledged this fact in our public system of values and rewards. Such an acknowledgment might begin with simply counting housewives in the labor force, assigning a money value to their work and including it in the calculation of the gross national product, and including housewives in social security or other pension systems. The question arises, "if the housewife is to be considered 'employed,' who is her employer?" One answer might be, her husband's employer, for it is the wife's labor and her support that enables her husband to do whatever he does for the man or the firm he works for. In this case, the husband and the wife would be viewed as a production unit and money for the housewife's pension plan might take the form of a payroll tax paid by the employer or shared by him and his employees. In the case of widows or other husbandless women with dependent children who do not work outside the home, they, too, would be "covered" workers, self-employed, and pay their own retirement premiums out of their own resources or, if on welfare, out of their welfare checks. Alternatively, one might consider them simply public service workers and pay the premiums out of the general fund.

In either event, the choice confronting the AFDC mother would no longer be between taking a job or receiving no assistance (which is really no choice at all) but rather the choice between working at home, in her own house with her own children, or working outside the home. In the long run, such a change in the choice offered to welfare mothers would not only cost less, but it would also permit the welfare family to keep its self-respect and at the same time enlarge an important area of choice in our society.

How Work Is a Key to Ending Dependency But the more significant link between work and welfare is not with welfare recipients, most of whom are on the welfare roles precisely because they can't work, but rather with those men who are not themselves on welfare but whose wives and children are. The statistical magnitude of the problem is easy to state. In January 1971, there were 2,523,900 families on the AFDC rolls. The father was absent in 1,924,800 of the families (76 percent), mainly through divorce, separation, desertion, or never having been married to the mother.[22] Thus, there is a clear and striking relationship between family instability and poverty. But if family instability causes poverty, what causes family instability? Among the lower classes, at least, one of the main causes seems to be poverty, thus completing the circle and presenting an especially difficult problem because it feeds on itself.

If poverty is a cause of marital or family instability, it should not surprise us that marriages in lower-class families end in separation and divorce far more often than in higher-income families. In addition to breaking up for many of the same reasons that higher-income couples do, low-income husbands and wives also break up because they do not have enough money to maintain family life.

In general, rates of marital instability are roughly twice as high among laborers and service workers as among professionals, with the other occupations falling in between. In Jesse Bernard's study of the relative effects of income, education, and occupation, income was the most powerful correlate of marital instability.[23] Crucial to an understanding of dependency is the research finding that at the end of ten years of marriage, a woman married to a man with earnings in the poverty range is twice as likely to have lost her husband through divorce or desertion as is the woman whose husband earns the median income or more.[24]

Does this mean that, by itself, an income maintenance policy in dole form would solve the problem of destructively high rates of divorce and desertion among poor people? Probably not, although poor people would surely be less poor if they had more money and be better off for it. To see what direction national policy should take with respect to family instability among the poor, we must look more closely at the connection between low income and marital break-up.

What specifically, is the connection between a man with a wife and two children earning, say, $3,000–$4,000 a year and his leaving the family? By itself, a poverty income does not explain the break-up of the marriage. Something else must be going on and all the evidence points to the fact that this something else is that the man sees himself, in his own eyes and in the eyes of all those around him, as a failure—a failure as breadwinner, and therefore a failure as husband, father, and man. The inability to support one's family constitutes a daily, unremitting reminder of failure that is too much for most men in that position to endure and sooner or later they leave. And how much more biting this failure if the man is earning so little that, if he leaves, his wife and children then will be eligible for welfare and actually be better off—not worse.[25]

It is important for our understanding of how AFDC families are generated to keep in mind that although many woman-headed families are the direct product of the process outlined above, other woman-headed families have appeared not because these events actually occurred, but in anticipation of them or in dread of them. Thus, even before marriage, lower-class girls' involvement in sexual activity that leads to pregnancy and illegitimate births, or to forced marriages, often seems to arise from the girls' perceptions that their present and future prospects for a better life (dependent as they are on their mates' occupational prospects) are not good and they have little to lose by beginning a family early even if it is in a not fully respectable way. (This is not to say, however, that girls who become pregnant before marriage are necessarily choosing to have a child. Indeed, the very high rates of abortion for premarital pregnancies where abortion is freely available indicate that the pregnancies are overwhelmingly unwanted.)[26]

Frank Furstenberg, drawing on the work of several sociological studies, attributes the high rate of illegitimacy among poor people generally and blacks in particular to this same occupational uncertainty of the men.[27] Lee Rainwater found expectant mothers rejecting marriage if their sexual partners were unemployed or had poor occupational prospects.[28]

We have already seen how low income leads to the self-definition of failure of the husband and father during marriage. And, if he is slow to see his failure, the chances are that his wife will point it out. Since neither partner can properly carry out the job of wife/mother or husband/father on the available resources, the inducement for self- and other-blame is always present. The tension generated by chronic money shortages is raised to even higher levels if the husband also experiences intermittent or prolonged unemployment. There is always the question in everyone's mind that his being unemployed may be "his own fault." He is "surplus man" around the house, because the sharp division of labor in the lower-class family gives him a minimally active role in housekeeping and child-rearing, and because the wife feels he should be out working or looking for work. And since unemployment in low-income households is often a reality and always a prospect—or even if he works steadily, he may not be bringing home enough to live on—the man is constantly vulnerable to the definition, his own or others' or both, that something is wrong with him, that he does not want to work, or if he is working, that he is simply not worth enough to be paid a living wage.

Finally, after divorce or desertion, the man's poor job situation tends to retard second marriages and to lengthen the amount of time men and women spend in divorced status. Among middle-class women, divorces tend to be followed by remarriage relatively quickly, but equally lonely lower-class separated and divorced women are not so fortunate: they are more likely to take boyfriends. These relationships are often institutionalized in such a way that the boyfriend is included within the family in a quasi-father role. Many women on AFDC give serious consideration to the possibility of marrying their boyfriends—indeed, they are often pressed toward marriage by the boyfriend. But even when the boyfriend is earning more than the woman receives on AFDC, she must think in a very tough-minded way about her family's likely future within a new marriage compared to being on welfare. She knows that welfare, though inadequate, is a steady source of income. Her prospective husband's income, she has good reason to fear, is not likely to be as steady; or in the event that he seems to be a steady worker with a steady job, the chances are that they couldn't live on what he makes. She can marry her boyfriend and take her chances, knowing that it will be touch-and-go at best, or she can maintain the less-than-satis-factory boyfriend relationship as long as it will last, and count on her secure source of welfare income.

Policy Implications In summary, family and marital stability may be functions of many things, but economic sufficiency and the part played by the man in providing it is surely one of them. Piecing together the findings from 46 studies relating work experience and family life, Frank Furstenberg concludes that "economic uncertainty brought on by unemployment and marginal employment is a principal reason why family rela-tions deteriorate." [29]

The implications of this conclusion for public policy are clear: If our society provided stable employment at above-poverty level wages for all men, and if all women could there-fore look forward to marrying men who could serve them in the provider role and for whom they could serve in the home-maker role, then it is likely that fewer girls would become pregnant before marriage, that lower-class couples would marry at a somewhat later age, that relationships in lower-class mar-riages would be less tense, that fewer lower-class marriages would break up, and for those that did, remarriage would take place more quickly. All these tendencies would be strengthened if women, too, could readily find stable part- and full-time em-ployment. (It should be noted that the work demands of women's liberation are essentially a middle-class phenomenon; among the lower-income classes, particularly among blacks, the crucial problems is work for the male.)[30]

Thus, the key to reducing familial dependency on the gov-ernment lies in the opportunity for the central provider to work full-time at a living wage. The provision of this oppor-tunity should be the first goal of public policy. Although a combination of income maintenance and work policies may be needed as a beginning step, it is unfortunate that so much of the reformist energies of the past decade or so have gone into the issue of guaranteed income and so little into the issue of guaranteed, rewarding work. It is difficult to avoid the impression that guaranteed income has been appealing both because it is simpler—one thing the Federal Government knows how to do easily and well is write checks—and perhaps because a guaranteed income program is less likely than a guaranteed job program to require or result in deep structural changes in the organization of work in our society. Another contributing factor may be that those who have been most vocal in their concern with problems of social welfare in recent times have tended to be identified with educational and welfare institutions rather than institutions more directly oriented to work and the labor market.

In any event, it is important to recognize the probability that an income maintenance program alone is not likely to do more—however crucial this "more" is—than keep families from living in utter degradation. Continued failure to provide decent job opportunities for everyone is to commit our society to a large, intractable, and costly dependent population. And the costs are not merely the cost of public assistance payments, but the incalculable, indirect costs of lost productivity, crime, and public discontent and private misery.

The solution to the "welfare mess"—if there is one—is to be found in meaningful and dignified work, in our society's explicit revelation of need for each person's contribution.

7
CONCLUSION

Albert Camus wrote that "Without work all life goes rotten. But when work is soulless, life stifles and dies." Our analysis of work in America leads to much the same conclusion: Because work is central to the lives of so many Americans, either the absence of work or employment in meaningless work is creating an increasingly intolerable situation. The human costs of this state of affairs are manifested in worker alienation, alcoholism, drug addiction, and other symptoms of poor mental health. Moreover, much of our tax money is expended in an effort to compensate for problems with at least a part of their genesis in the world of work. A great part of the staggering national bill in the areas of crime and delinquency, mental and physical health, manpower and welfare are generated in our national policies and attitudes toward work. Likewise, industry is paying for its continued attachment to Tayloristic practices through low worker productivity and high rates of sabotage, absenteeism, and turnover. Unions are paying through the faltering loyalty of a young membership that is increasingly concerned about the apparent disinterest of its leadership in problems of job satisfaction. Most important, there are the high costs of lost opportunities to encourage citizen participation: the discontent of women, minorities, blue-collar workers, youth, and older adults would be considerably less were these Americans to have an active voice in the decisions in the workplace that most directly affect their lives.

Our analysis of health, education, welfare, and manpower programs from the unique perspective of work indicates that to do nothing about these problems in the short run is to increase costs to society in the long run. Much of the capital needed to redesign jobs, increase worker mobility, and create new jobs can be directed to these activities through trade-offs with existing expenditures. More capital can be obtained by lowering the waste of unemployment and through increasing worker productivity. But the essential first step toward these goals is the commitment on the part of policy makers in business, labor, and government to the improvement of the quality of working life in America.

APPENDIX—CASE STUDIES IN THE HUMANIZATION OF WORK *

	General Foods	AT&T	AT&T	Bell System	Polaroid Corp.
1. Establishment(s) or Employee Groups	Pet Food Plant Topeka, Kans. All plant employees.	Long Lines Plant, N. Y. Private Line Telephone District. Framemen.	Shareholder Correspondents, Treasury Department.	17 groups of workers in diverse occupations, including toll operators, installers, clerks, equipment engineers.	Production-line employees.
2. Year Initiated	1971	1966	1965	1967	1959
3. No. Employees Affected	70	35–40	95–120	about 1,200	2,000+
4. Problem	In designing this new plant management sought to solve problems of frequent shut downs, costly recycling and low morale that plagued an existing plant making the same product.	There was low productivity, high errors, schedule slippage and no worker's pride.	High turnover, absenteeism, low morale, low productivity.	Are the methods and results of the AT&T Shareholder Correspondents Study transferable to other employee groups?	Top management wanted to increase the meaningfulness of work.
5. Technique Used	Workers were organized into relatively autonomous work groups with each group responsible for a pro-	The framemen's work was expanded to include taking full responsibility for the job and negotiating with	Workers were given less supervision and more job freedom. The authors of letters to complainants were	Same as AT&T Shareholder Correspondents Study.	Factory operators were rotated between their factory jobs and more

	duction process. Pay is based on the total number of jobs an employee can do.	the "customer."	allowed to sign without review by supervisors.		desirable non-factory jobs.
6. *Human Results*	Job attitudes a few months after the plant opened indicated "positive assessments" by both team members and leaders. Increased democracy in the plant may have led to more civic activity.	Grievances were practically eliminated (from rate of one per week). Morale was higher in the year's experiment.	There was more pride in group achievement. Higher job satisfaction was measured.	After a year's experience, where measured, attitudes improved and grievances dropped.	For some there was challenge and reward while learning, then frustration until they were permanently transferred
7. *Economic Results*	The plant is operated by 70 workers, rather than the 110 originally estimated by industrial engineers. Also, there were "improved yields, minimized waste and avoidance of shut downs."	There was no significant change in absenteeism or tardiness. However, at the end there was a slight increase in productivity with fewer workers and less overtime.	After a year's trial, absenteeism decreased from 2% to 1.4%. Turnover practically eliminated.	Turnover decreased by 9.3% in the experimental group and increased 13.1% in the control group. Overtime hours decreased about 50%.	Turnover and absenteeism decreased. Recruitment was easier for factory jobs, since they were no longer dead-end.
8. *Reference(s)*	Walton, Richard E.—*Workplace Alienation and the Need for Major Innovation*, May 1972 (unpublished)	Ford, R. N., *Motivation Through The Work Itself*, AMA, 1969, pp. 211–256	Ford, R. N., *op. cit.* at pp. 20–44 Foulks, F. K., *Creating More Meaningful Work*, AMA, 1969, pp. 97–120	Ford, R. N., *op. cit.* at pp. 45–79	Foulks, F. K., *op. cit.* at pp. 35–55

* This appendix was prepared by Ward McCreedy, Deborah Bond, Shirley King, and Pat Forkel under the direction of Vincent Macaluso, the Division of Planning, Office of Program Development, Employment Standards Administration, U.S. Department of Labor.

	Texas Instruments, Inc.	Hunsfos Pulp & Paper Mill Kristiansand, Norway	Nobø Fabrikker A/S Trandheim, Norway	H. P. Hood & Sons Boston, Mass.	Rade Koncar Zagreb, Yugoslavia
1. *Establishment(s) or Employee Groups*	Small group of women—electronic instrument assemblers.	Chemical pulp department of papermill.	New unit making electrical panels for metal manufacturing plant.	Unspecified number of company plants and occupations.	Plant manufacturing heavy electrical equipment. All employees.
2. *Year Initiated*	1967	1964	1965	Over 20 years ago.	1945
3. *No. Employees Affected*	600	32	10 to 40	Not specified.	1946—890; 1966—7,946
4. *Problem*	Top management wanted better utilization of human resources.	Segregation of jobs, lack of overlapping skills and permanent shifts increasingly hindered work as the process became more complex.	Management wished to improve simple repetitive jobs.	There was no specific problem. The goal was to improve operations and to involve employees more in the affairs of the company.	National need for rapid industrialization and a desire to transfer management to the worker-producer.
5. *Technique Used*	The group was asked to set its own production goal and given more information concerning costs and terms of the government contract on which it was working.	The group of 32 workers was given greater responsibility for the operation of the department as a whole and was encouraged to increase its control of the process.	Production groups and subgroups were established and put on group bonus rates. A "contact person" (with department head) was substituted for the supervisor and was chosen by election.	On numerous occasions workers teamed with supervisors to simplify work, often using films of actual operations. Workers with two or more years of seniority are secure against layoff.	Under worker's self-management, all workers are members of working units, and have the right and obligation to manage their units, make decisions, establish economic policy, and to

					submit suggestions, criticisms, questions, etc. "to authoritative management," who is obligated to consider them.
6. Human Results	A survey revealed that employees were deriving more satisfaction from their work and had fewer complaints about so-called maintenance items.	Workers showed greater job interest through their suggestions.	The program manager reported, "the employees do not resist the approach, an attitude which may have been fostered by a cash award system for suggestions."	. . . general satisfaction among the workers . . . and absenteeism . . . much lower than for the factory as a whole.	Not explicitly stated.
7. Economic Results	During the experiment, assembly time per unit decreased from 138 to 32 hours. Absenteeism, turnover, leaving time, complaints and trips to health center decreased.	In the four-year experiment, the average quality bonus increased about 24%.	In the one-year experiment, production rates increased 22% and hourly earnings increased 11%.	Not explicitly stated.	From a small company in 1945, Rade Koncar has taken a leading role in equipment for power plants, including nuclear, and transformer plants.
8. Reference(s)	Foulks, F. K., op. cit. at pp. 56–96	P. H. Engelstad, Socio-Technical Approach to Problems of Process Control, Papermaking Systems And Their Control, 1970	Ødegaard, L. A., Summary of Third Field Experiment, Industrial Democracy Project, Phase B (unpub.)	Foulks, F. K., op. cit. at pp. 169–176	Mladen, K.; Self-Management in the Enterprise, Medunarodna Stampa Interpress, 1967

	Sisak Ironworks Yugoslavia	I. C. I.	P. P. G. Industries	Monsanto	Monsanto Chemical
1. Establishment(s) or Employee Groups	Iron and Steel Industry in Sisak, Caprag	Imperial Chemical Industries—Gloucester, Great Britain Factory floor workers.	P. P. G. Industries Lexington, N. C. Twist frame operators.	Electronics Division West Caldwell, N.J. Foremen.	Textile Division Pensacola, Fla. Chemical operators.
2. Year Initiated	1961	1968	1969	Not specified.	1968
3. No. Employees Affected	About 6,000	19,500	675	Not specified.	50
4. Problem	Low productivity of labor.	Low morale. "Five walkouts in a week."	Loss of efficiency in twist frame machines because frame cleaning was dirty work; repetitive and routine.	High employee turnover among new hires.	Rising production costs beset the automated control room for chemical reaction and conversion.
5. Technique Used	Self-management bodies were established in each department in which the workers decided on production norms and pay rates (including incentives).	Weekly staff assignments provide job rotation. Small groups (8) input "own ideas" into work process.	The frame cleaner job was eliminated. Since cleaning takes 15% of the time on each job, the machine operators took over the cleaning function.	The foremen were given responsibility for interviewing, indoctrinating, and giving skills training to new hires.	Four employee "task forces" (one from each shift) restructured certain jobs and eliminated some dirty jobs through automation. Operators now manage their own restructured jobs.

6. Human Results	Not specified.	"... it's their (the workers) factory, not just a place where they come to work," a supervisor reported.	Personnel and production managers report that "morale is high."	Not specified.	Employee suggestions increased 300%.
7. Economic Results	In eight years, product quality improved. Production was expanded and modernized.	Since the experiment there has been a 20% reduction in labor, 20% increase in production, 25% increase in pay, and a 30% cut in supervision.	Productivity increased by 12% over the previous two years.	Turnover, which had been high among unskilled jobs, averaged 6% annually in the five years of the program.	Waste loss dropped to zero, operators monitor 50% more instruments and half of the old supervisors not needed.
8. Reference(s)	The Economic Resources of the Production Departments and Distribution According to the Results of Labor in the Sisak Ironworks; Beograd, 1970	Smith, Dan, *In Place of Strife at ICI*, HR 13, Info Service, Steel House, London, Sept. 1970, pp. 420–426	Rush, Harold M. F., *Job Design for Motivation*, Report from the Conference Board, 1971, pp. 67–70	Rush, Harold M. F., *op. cit.* at pp. 75–76	Rush, Harold M. F., *op. cit.* at pp. 70–73

	Weyerhauser	Araphoe	Syntex	American Velvet Co.	Monsanto
1. Establishment(s) or Employee Groups	Weyerhauser Co. Tacoma, Wash. Paper production employees.	Araphoe Chemical Boulder, Colo. Chemists.	Syntex Corporation Mexico City, Mexico; Research Center Palo Alto, Calif. Salesmen.	All employees of manufacturer of velvet. Stonington, Conn.	Agriculture Division Muscatine, Iowa Machine operators.
2. Year Initiated	1968	1968	1966	Not specified.	1967
3. No. Employees Affected	300 (pilot project)	125	Not specified.	400	150
4. Problem	Low productivity.	Low productivity and morale.	The innovativeness of scientists was not being utilized.	None specified.	There was a production "bottleneck" in the bagging section.
5. Technique Used	An "I Am" plan (short for "I Am Manager of My Job") was implemented, based on the assumption that all people want to be responsible, to succeed, and can best manage their own jobs.	Each chemist was made directly responsible for an entire project.	Team work groups were formed "where employee set own standards and quotas."	Workers plan and organize own work and have profit sharing plan.	Seminars were held with employees who analyzed their own jobs and made changes. Production goals were set by baggers.
6. Human Results	The project manager said, "they became a fraternity . . . and	Not specified.	A vice president reports, "less skepticism, more volunteering,	"Consultation, participation, and involvement are a way of life	Not specified.

were enthusiastic about the challenge of their new jobs."			more introspection an instantaneous feedback, managers more concerned with career paths—career planning of employees, rank-and-file employees appear more committed and involved."	at the top of the company and at the production level as well."
7. Economic Results "Increased productivity" according to an executive.	Productivity increased and deadlines on customer orders were met more promptly.	Volume sales in the two experimental groups increased by 116% and 20% over the control groups.	Not specified.	Production increased 75% in the four months after the change.
8. Reference(s) Rush, Harold M. F., op. cit. at pp. 55–60	Rush, Harold M. F., op. cit. at pp. 33–39	Rush, Harold M. F., Behavioral Science, Concepts and Management Application, 1970, pp. 130–138	Foulks, F. K., op. cit. at pp. 176–184	Rush, Harold M. F., Job Design for Motivation, Report from the Conference Board, 1971, pp. 73–74

	Oldsmobile	Norsk	Texas Instruments	Corning Glass Works Medfield, Mass.	Donnelly Mirrors, Inc. Holland, Mich.
1. *Establishment(s) or Employee Groups*	Oldsmobile Division, GM Lansing, Mich. Engineering and assembly employees.	Norsk Hydro Oslo, Norway Production workers.	Texas Instruments Inc. Dallas, Tex. Maintenance personnel.	Instrument assembly workers.	Auto mirror mfg. All employees.
2. *Year Initiated*	1970	1966	1967	1965	Long term project
3. *No. Employees Affected*	Two plants	About 50	120	6	460
4. *Problem*	High absenteeism and turnover.	Competition was becoming tougher and profits were declining.	100% quarterly turnover and failure to get buildings clean.	Not specified.	To "come to grips with the problems of productivity."
5. *Technique Used*	A volunteer hourly employee task force held meetings with foremen and other employees, conducted surveys, and made broad recommendations to improve employee relations.	Autonomous work groups were established without first hands (supervisors). A group bonus plan was installed based on productivity.	Workers were organized into 19 member cleaning teams. Each member voice in planning, problem-solving, goal-setting, and scheduling.	Assembly line techniques were abandoned. Workers were allowed to assemble entire electrical hot plates with the freedom to schedule their work as a group so as to meet weekly objectives.	Workers determine their annual salaries. They receive productivity bonuses and must find ways to assure that the bonuses are paid through higher production, elimination of needless jobs, etc.

6. Human Results	Not specified.	"I feel like a human being. You know what you have to do and you push to do it," says an employee.	Not specified.	The percentage of workers expressing overall job satisfaction increased from 58 to 100.	"The results included more positive employee relations."
7. Economic Results	Wages, costs, and profits all have increased during the past few years, even as the company has lowered its prices.	In the six months after the change, rejects dropped from 23% to 1% and absenteeism from 8% to 1%.	Quarterly turnover dropped from 100% to 9.8%. Personnel requirements dropped from 120 to 71. Cost savings averaged $103,000 annually between 1967–1969. Building cleanliness ratings increased from 65% to 85%.	Production costs per ton decreased 30% over the first six months of the project, but other factors were also involved. Absenteeism was 4% in the experimental factory vs. 7% for the control factory.	Absenteeism decreased 6% in engineering and 6.5% in assembly —while rising 11% in the rest of Oldsmobile. There were "improved product quality . . . and reduced costs."
8. Reference(s)	U.S. News and World Report, op. cit. at p. 51	U.S. News and World Report, July 17, 1972, p. 50	Rush, Harold M. F., Job Design for Motivation, Report from the Conference Board, 1971, pp. 39–49	Bregard, A., Gulowsen J., et al. Norsk Hydro, Experiment in the Fertilizer Factories, Work Research Institute, Jan. 1968	GM Publication, Oldsmobile's Action on Absenteeism and Turnover, Nov. 1971

	Monsanto-Textiles Co. Pensacola, Fla.	Alcan Aluminum Corp. Oswego, N.Y.	Micro-Wax Dept.—Shell Stanlow Refinery, Ellesmere Port; Cheshire, England	Philips Electrical Industries—Holland	Ferado Company United Kingdom
1. Establishment(s) or Employee Groups	Production workers of nylon tire yarn.	Rolling mill operators.	Chemical operators.	Assembly workers.	Production workers making brake linings.
2. Year Initiated	1971	1965	1963	1960	Not specified.
3. No. Employees Affected	6,000	Not specified.	Not specified.	240–300	Not specified.
4. Problem	Not specified.	High rates of absenteeism and tardiness.	Low productivity, low morale, and possibility of "shutdown."	Not specified.	Not specified.
5. Technique Used	Four-day classroom sessions were held to involve production workers in problem-solving. Also, employees set production goals and rotated jobs.	Time clocks were removed and production jobs designed to give workers unusual freedom and decision-making responsibilities. Salaries were guaranteed during absences or layoffs.	Operators formed group teams that provided both more flexibility within shift teams and rotation in jobs. Time clocks were also removed.	Independent work groups were formed and made responsible for job allocations, material and quality control, and providing delegates for management talks.	Groups of six men were trained to use all machines involved in the process and allowed to move from one machine to the other. Each group sees the batch of marketable products they have made.

6. Human Results	"For the employee the program means 'humanized' working conditions," the plant manager reported.	"Monotony is relieved," says the plant manager.	"It is well known that absence and sickness may be symptomatic of alienation . . . from the work situation. Thus . . . [these] statistics are partly an indication of morale," said that plant manager.	The members of semi-autonomous groups derived more satisfaction from their work compared with workers in the old situation.	Job satisfaction in the plant has been found to increase.
7. Economic Results	"The cost of the program more than pays for itself in higher productivity through fewer idle machines and lower repair costs—a possible gain of 100,000 pounds of yarn a year," says the plant manager.	Absenteeism decreased to about 2.5% compared to an industry average of about 10%. Productivity increased.	"Output" in three sections increased by 35%, 40%, and 100% over 1965. Absence and sickness decreased from 4.3% in 1963 to 3.3% in 1969.	By 1967, waste and repairs decreased by 4% and there was an unspecified savings of lower managerial personnel.	There is less turnover, and original delivery times have been cut by seven-eighths.
8. Reference(s)	U.S. News and World Report, op. cit. at p. 52	"The Honor System," Wall Street Journal, May 22, 1970 "Alcan Hails in Dumping Time Clock," The Plain Dealer, Sept. 29, 1969	Burden, Derek, A Participative Approach to Management, Shell U.K., April 15, 1970	Davis & Trist—Work In America, Approaches to Improving Quality of Working Life, June 1972, p. 18	Wilson, N. A. B., On the Quality of Working Life, A Personal Report to the NATO Committee on Challenges of Modern Society, p. 40

	Netherlands PTT	Kaiser Aluminum Corporation Ravenswood, W.Va.	Bankers Trust Company New York	Operations Division, Bureau of Traffic— Ohio Dept. of Highways
1. Establishment(s) or Employee Groups	Clerical workers— data collection.	Maintenance workers in reduction plant.	Production typists in stock transfer operations.	Six field construction crews.
2. Year Initiated	Not specified.	1971	1969	Not specified.
3. No. Employees Affected	100	60	200	Not specified.
4. Problem	Jobs were routine. Workers and supervisors were both "notably uninterested" in their work.	Productivity was low. There were walkouts and slowdowns.	Production was low and quality poor. Absenteeism and turnover were high and employee attitudes were poor . . . Jobs were routine, repetitive and devoid of intrinsic interest . . . Too much overseeing.	Low productivity and poor quality of performance.
5. Technique Used	Jobs were enlarged to comprise a whole collaborative process (e.g., listing, punching, control punching, corrections, etc.) in-	Time clocks were removed and supervision virtually eliminated. Workers now decide what maintenance jobs are to be done and in	Typists were given the opportunity (1) to change their own computer output tapes, (2) to handle typing for a specific	Three experimental groups were established, each with a different degree of self-determination of work schedules. Crews

	stead of a single stage of this process.	what priority and keep their own time cards.	group of customers, (3) to check their own work, and (4) to schedule their own work. Training was given in these areas.	were unaware that they were participating in an experiment.
6. *Human Results*	88% of the workers in the experimental group said the work had become more interesting.	"Morale has improved along with pride in workmanship," says the maintenance chief.	A quantitative survey disclosed improved attitudes and greater satisfaction.	Data showed that as participation increased, so did morale.
7. *Economic Results*	There was a 15% increase in output per man-hour.	Tardiness is now "non-existent." Maintenance costs are down 5.5%. Maintenance work is done with more "quality."	Absenteeism and tardiness were reduced while production and quality increased. Job enrichment programs were extended.	There was no significant change in productivity.
8. *Reference(s)*	Wilson, N. A. B., *op. cit.* at p. 36	Thompson, Donald B., "Enrichment in Action Convinces Skeptics," *Industry Week*, Feb. 14, 1971	Detteback, William W., Assistant Vice Pres. Bankers Trust, and Kraft, Philip, Partner, Roy W. Walters Associates, "Organization Change Through Job Enrichment," *Training and Development Journal*, August 1971	Powell, Reed M., and Schlacter, John L., "Participative Management: A Panacea?," *Academy of Management Journal*, June 1971, pp. 165–173

NOTES *

Chapter 1

1. Historical references from Harold Wilensky, "Work as a Social Problem," 1966.

2. Thorstein Veblen, *The Theory of the Leisure Class*, 1934.

3. Harry Levinson, "Various Approaches to Understanding Man at Work," 1971.

4. Harry Kahn and J. R. P. French, in *Social Issues*, July 1962.

5. Erich Fromm, *The Revolution of Hope*, 1971.

6. Robert Coles, "On the Meaning of Work," 1971.

7. Ben Seligman, "On Work, Alienation and Leisure," 1965.

8. Elliot Jacques, *Equitable Payment*, 1961.

9. T. S. McPartland and J. H. Cummings, "Self-Conception, Social Class and Mental Health," 1958.

10. Kahn and French, *op. cit.*

11. Wilensky, *op. cit.*

12. Paul Dickson, "Striking Out on Your Own," 1971.

13. Eli Ginzberg, *Grass on the Slag Heaps*, 1942; and E. W. Bakke, *The Unemployed Worker*, 1940.

14. Bakke, *Ibid.*

15. Charles Winick, "Atonie: The Psychology of the Unemployed and Marginal Worker," 1964.

16. E. Frankel, "Studies in Biographical Psychology," 1936.

17. Winick, *op. cit.*

18. *Ibid.*

19. Eli Ginzberg, "Work: The Eye of the Hurricane," 1971.

20. Winick, *op. cit.*

21. James N. Morgan, Survey Research Center.

22. Robert Morse and Nancy Weiss, "The Function and Meaning of Work and the Job," 1955.

23. Leonard Goodwin, "A Study of Work Orientations of Welfare Recipients," 1971.

24. Joseph E. Champagne and Donald King, "Job Satisfaction Factors Among Underprivileged Workers," 1967.

25. Harold Watts, "New Jersey Experiment: Notes for Discussion," 1972.

* Notes are presented in short form. Full citations are to be found in the bibliography.

26. Richard Walton, "Workplace Alienation and the Need for Major Innovation," 1972.

27. Abraham Maslow, *Motivation and Personality,* 1954.

28. Frederick Herzberg, *Work and the Nature of Man,* 1966.

29. For a review of the literature, see Robert Kahn, "The Meaning of Work: Interpretation and Proposals for Measurement," 1972.

30. Based on an analysis of Bureau of Labor Statistics for the number of "operatives" and other job categories likely to have "assemblyline" features.

31. Kahn, *op. cit.*

32. George Strauss, "Is There a Blue Collar Revolt Against Work?," 1972.

33. Kahn, *op. cit.*

34. Harold Sheppard and Neal Herrick, *Where Have All the Robots Gone?,* 1972.

35. Robert Kahn, "The Work Module," 1972.

36. Wilensky, *op. cit.*

37. Peter Rossi, "The Prestige Standing of Occupations," 1972.

38. Elton Mayo's work is an example of this school's thought.

39. Louis Davis and Eric Trist, "Improving the Quality of Working Life," 1972.

40. All figures in this section from Michael Maccoby and Katherine Terzi, "Work and the American Character," 1972.

41. Robert Blauner, *Alienation and Freedom,* 1964.

42. *Ibid.*

43. See Chapter 2 for a discussion of this phenomenon.

44. Willis Harman, "Key Choices of the Next Two Decades," 1972.

45. Judson Gooding, "The Fraying White Collar," 1970.

46. *Ibid.*

47. Sidney Harman, "Responsibilities of Businessmen," 1972.

48. *Ibid.*

49. U.S. Bureau of the Census, *Statistical Abstract of the United States: 1971.*

50. Patricia Cayo Sexton and Brendan Sexton, *Blue Collars and Hard Hats,* 1972.

51. *Ibid.*

52. *Time,* June 2, 1971.

53. Walton, *op. cit.,* See discussion in Chapter 4.

Chapter 2

1. Letter to the *Washington Post* in 1972.

2. Studs Terkel, "A Steelworker Speaks," *Dissent,* Winter 1972.

3. *Occupational Mental Health,* Vol. 1, No. 2, Winter 1971.

4. Martin Meissner "The Long Arm of the Job: A Study of Work and Leisure," 1971.

5. Stanley Seashore and Thad J. Barnowe, "Demographic and Job Factors Associated With the 'Blue-Collar Blues'," 1972.

6. Sheppard and Herrick, *op. cit.*

7. Wilensky, *op. cit.*

8. Robert Dahl, *After the Revolution?,* Yale University Press, New Haven, 1970.

9. Robert Quinn, "Locking-in as a Moderator of the Relationship Between Job Satisfaction and Mental Health," 1972.

10. Robert Schrank and Susan Stein, "Yearning, Learning and Status," in Levitan, ed., *The Blue Collar Workers,* 1971.

11. *Ibid.*

12. This can be supported by Sheppard and Herrick's (*op. cit.*) study that showed young workers *in the same jobs* as older workers *with equal pay* to be less satisfied.

13. Schrank and Stein, *op. cit.*

14. Melvin DeFleur, "Occupational Roles as Portrayed on Television," 1964.

15. U.S. Bureau of the Census, *Characteristics of the Population by Ethnic Origin,* 1970.

16. Basil Whiting, "The Suddenly Remembered American," 1971.

17. *Wall Street Journal,* December 3, 1971, p. 4.

18. Shrank and Stein, *op. cit.*

19. Simone Weil, *The Need for Roots,* 1952.

20. N. A. B. Wilson, *The Quality of Working Life,* 1971.

21. Judson Gooding, *op. cit.*

22. *Ibid.*

23. *Ibid.*

24. Damon Stetson, "For Many Concerns: An Inadvertent 4-Day Week," *New York Times,* May 14, 1972.

25. American Management Association, *Manager Unions,* 1972.

26. Elliot Jacques, *Work, Creativity and Social Justice,* 1970; and Harry Levinson, "On Being a Middle-Aged Manager," 1969.

27. L. M. Cone, Jr., "Society's Latest Disease—M.O.," 1969.

28. Emmanuel Kay, "Middle Managers," 1972.

29. Dale Hiestand, "Obligations of Employers and the Society to Minority Workers," 1972.

30. *Economist,* April 30, 1972.

31. Daniel Yankelovich, *The Changing Values on Campus,* 1972.

32. Joyce Starr, "Adaptation to the Working World," 1972.

33. *Ibid.*

34. *Project Talent: Progress in Education, a Sample Survey,* American Institutes for Research, 1971.

35. Sheppard and Herrick, *op. cit.*

36. John Haynes, "The New Workers: A Report," 1970.

37. Harman, *op. cit.*

38. Judson Gooding, "The Accelerated Generation Moves Into Management," 1971.

39. *Ibid.*

40. Sebastian deGrazia, *Of Time, Work and Leisure,* 1962.

41. See Chapter 5 for a further discussion of this point.

42. Quoted in Paul Campanis, "You Are What You Work At," 1972.

43. Hiestand, *op. cit.*

44. William H. Grier and Price M. Cobbs, *Black Rage,* 1965.

45. Hiestand, *op. cit.*

46. Max Ways, "Equality: A Steep and Endless Stair," 1972.

47. "Myths and Reality," U.S. Department of Labor, April 1971.

48. Aileen Jacobson, "Marriage Rethought: The Very Private Impact of the Women's Movement," 1972.

49. Judy Klemesrud, "Secretary Image: A Tempest in a Typewriter," 1972.

50. Angus Campbell, *The Quality of Life,* Institute of Social Research, University of Michigan.

51. Virgil Schein, "Implications and Obstacles to Full Participation of the Woman Worker," 1972.

52. "Myths and Reality," *op. cit.*

53. Isabel Sawhill, "Perspectives on Women and Work in America," 1972.

54. Norton Dodge, *Women in the Soviet Economy,* 1966.

55. Sawhill, *op. cit.*

56. *Time,* March 20, 1972.

57. Sawhill, *op. cit.*

58. *Voices of the New Feminism,* 1968.

59. U.S. Department of Labor, *1969 Handbook on Women Workers.*

60. Caroline Bell, "Unemployed Women: Do They Matter?," 1972.

61. Susan B. Orden, "Working Wives and Marriage Happiness, 1969.

62. Joan Jordan, "The Economics of Women's Liberation," 1969.

63. Juanita Kreps, *Sex in the Marketplace,* 1971.

64. J. H. Plumb, *The Death of the Past,* 1971.

65. Philip Slater, *The Pursuit of Loneliness,* 1970.

66. *Business Week,* "Thirty-and-Outers Opt for Late Retirement," October 9, 1971.

67. *Business Week,* "Getting an Early Start on Those Golden Years," April 27, 1968.

68. Riley et al., *Aging and Society,* Russell Sage Foundation, 1968.

69. A. J. Jaffee, "The Retirement Dilemma," *Journal of Industrial Gerontology,* Summer 1972.

70. U.S. Department of Health, Education and Welfare, Social Security Administration, *Social Security Bulletin,* April 1971; and U.S. Department of Labor, Bureau of Labor Statistics, *Monthly Report: Employment and Earnings,* 1971.

71. *Ibid.*

72. U.S. Senate, Committee on Labor and Public Welfare, Subcommittee on Labor: *Hearings,* Private Welfare and Private Pension Plan Study, Part I, July 27–29, 1971, and Part II, October 12–13, 1971, U.S. Government Printing Office, Washington, D.C., 1971.

73. U.S. Department of Labor, Bureau of Labor Statistics: "Private Pension Plans 1960–69, An Overview," 1970; and Edward J. O'Boyle, "Job Tenure: How it Relates to Race and Age," 1969.

Chapter 3

1. Erdman Palmore, "Predicting Longevity: A Follow-Up Controlling for Age," 1969.

2. Sula Benet, "Why They Live to be 100, or Even Older, in Abkhasia," 1972.

3. Charles J. Karcher and Leonard L. Linden, "Family Rejection of the Aged and Nursing Home Utilization," 1972.

4. Marian Mariotti, "Worker Conditions and Manner of Aging" in *Work and Aging,* International Center of Social Gerontology, Paris, 1971.

5. Bruce Margolis and William Kroes, "Work and the Health of Man," 1972.

6. John R. P. French, Jr., and Robert D. Caplan, "Organizational Stress and Individual Strain," 1972.

7. Harry Levinson, "Emotional Toxicity of the Work Environment," 1969.

8. French and Caplan, *op. cit.*

9. C. D. Jenkins, "Psychologic and Social Precursors of Coronary Disease," 1971; and S. Sales and J. House, "Job Dissatisfaction as a Possible Risk Factor in Coronary Heart Disease," 1971.

10. S. Cobb and S. V. Kasl, "Blood Pressure Changes in Men Undergoing Job Loss: A Preliminary Report," 1970.

11. J. R. P. French, J. Tupper, and E. Mueller, *Work Load of University Professors,* 1965.

12. M. Friedman, R. H. Rosenman, and V. Carroll, "Changes in the Serum Cholesterol and Blood Clotting Time of Men Subject to Cyclic Variation of Occupational Stress," 1957.

13. S. M. Sales, "Organizational Roles as a Risk Factor in Coronary Heart Disease," 1969.

14. A. Pepitone, "Self, Social Environment, and Stress," 1967.

15. H. J. Montoye, et al., "Serum Uric Acid Concentration Among Business Executives With Observations on Other Coronary Heart Disease Risk Factors," 1967.

16. H. H. W. Miles, et al., "Psychosomatic Study of 46 Young Men With Coronary Artery Disease," 1954; and H. I. Russek, "Stress, Tobacco, and Coronary Heart Diseases," 1965.

17. Cary P. McCord, "Life and Death by the Minute," 1948.

18. J. S. House, "The Relationship of Intrinsic and Extrinsic Work Motivations to Occupational Stress and Coronary Heart Disease Risk," 1972.

19. H. I. Russek, "Emotional Stress and Coronary Heart Disease in American Physicians, Dentists, and Lawyers," 1962.

20. R. Caplan, "Organizational Stress and Individual Strain: A Social-Psychological Study of Risk Factors in Coronary Heart Disease Among Administrators, Engineers, and Scientists," 1971; and Thomasina Smith, "Sociocultural Incongruity and Change: A Review of Empirical Findings," 1967.

21. Stanislav Kasl and Sidney Cobb, "Physical and Mental Health Correlates of Status Incongruence," 1971.

22. C. D. Jenkins, R. H. Rosenman, and M. Friedman, "Development of an Objective Psychological Test for Determination of Coronary-Prone Behavior Pattern," 1967; and S. Sales and J. House, "Job Dissatisfaction as a Possible Risk Factor in Coronary Heart Disease," 1971.

23. Caplan, *op. cit.*

24. Melvin Kohn and Carmi Schooler, "Occupational Experience and Psychological Functioning: An Asessment of Reciprocal Effects," N.I.M.H., 1972.

25. Caplan, *op. cit.*

26. *Ibid.*

27. S. Seashore, *Group Cohesiveness in the Industrial Work Group,* 1954.

28. Y. S. Matsumoto, "Social Stress and Coronary Heart Disease in Japan; A Hypothesis," 1970.

29. M. Susser, "Causes of Peptic Ulcer: A Selective Epidemiologic Review," 1967; and J. V. Brady, "Ulcers in the 'Executive' Monkeys," *Scientific American,* 1958.

30. S. H. King and S. Cobb, "Psychosocial Factors in the Epidemiology of Rheumatoid Arthritis," 1958.

31. S. Cobb, *The Frequency of the Rheumatic Diseases,* 1971.

32. Cobb and Kasl, *op. cit.,* 1971.

33. C. M. Sulley and K. J. Munden, "Behavior of the Mentally Healthy," 1962.

34. Studies undertaken at the Survey Research Center, University of Michigan, over the last twenty years.

35. A. Zaleznik, J. Ondrack, and A. Silver, "Social Class, Occupation, and Mental Illness," 1970.

36. Arthur Kornhauser, *Mental Health of the Industrial Worker,* 1965.

37. Charles R. DeCarlo, "Technological Change and Mental Health," in A. McLean, ed., *Mental Health and Work Organization,* 1970.

38. E. Chinoy, *Automobile Workers and the American Dream,* 1955.

39. Stanislav Kasl, "Work in America: Work and Mental Health," 1972.

40. C. L. Hulin and M. R. Blood, "Job Enlargement, Individual Differences and Worker Responses," 1968; and W. P. Sexton, "Industrial Work: Who Calls It Psychologically Devastating?," 1968.

41. Kornhauser, *op. cit.*

42. Alan McLean, *Mental Health and Work Organizations,* 1970.

43. New York Narcotics Addiction Control Commission, "Differential Drug Use Within the New York State Labor Force," July 1971.

44. Special Action Office for Drug Abuse Prevention, Executive Office of the President, 1972.

45. P. M. Roman and H. M. Trice, "The Development of Deviant Drinking Behavior," March 1970.

46. Frederick P. Li, "Suicide Among Chemists," *Archives of Environmental Health,* 1970.

47. The *Washington Evening Star and Daily News,* July 20, 1972.

48. *Ibid.*

49. Erich Fromm, "The Erich Fromm Theory of Aggression," 1972.

50. Studs Terkel, *op. cit.*

51. *Washington Post: Potomac Magazine,* June 25, 1972.

52. Milton F. Shore and Joseph L. Massimo, "Job-Focused Treatment for Antisocial Youth," *Children,* July/August, 1964.

53. Milton Shore and Joseph L. Massimo, "Five Years Later: A Follow-Up Study of Comprehensive Vocationally Oriented Psychotherapy," 1969.

54. Lewis Bartlett, "Productive Participation," 1971.

55. Margolis and Kroes, *op. cit.*

Chapter 4

1. For a thorough review of the documentation for the following factors see Robert Kahn "The Meaning of Work: Interpretation and Proposals for Measurement," 1972.

2. Richard E. Walton, "Workplace Alienation and the Need for Major Innovation," 1972.

3. *Ibid.*

4. Louis Davis and Eric Trist, "Approaches to Improving the Quality of Working Life," 1972.

5. William W. Dettleback and Philip Kraft, "Organization Change Through Job Enrichment," 1971.

6. Carl Jacobs, "Job Redesign," 1972.

7. Harold M. F. Rush, "Job Design for Motivation," 1971.

8. Bert Metzger, "Socio-Economic Participation: Key to a Better World of Work in the Future," 1972.

9. Davis and Trist, *op. cit.*

10. *Ibid.*

11. French and Caplan, *op. cit.*

12. Jacobs, *op. cit.*

13. Metzger, *op. cit.*

14. *Ibid.*

15. *Ibid.*

16. *Ibid.*

17. *Ibid.*

18. Personal interview with our Task Force.

19. Sheppard and Herrick, *op. cit.*

20. Albert Epstein, "In the Beginning Was the Work," 1972.

21. Irving Bluestone, "Democratizing the Work Place," 1972.

22. Davis and Trist, *op. cit.*

23. I. M. Moriyama, D. E. Krueger, and J. Stamler, *Cardiovascular Disease in the United States*, 1971.

24. "Die Gleitzeit" A Report by the German Industry Institute for Social Politics, 1971.

25. Alan McLean and Charles R. DeCarlo, "Work, New Styles, New Environment, New Attitudes," *Innovation*, No. 30, 1972.

26. Robert Kahn, "The Work Module," 1972.

Chapter 5

1. Sheppard and Herrick, *op. cit.*

2. "Occupational Manpower and Training Needs," *Bulletin 1701*, U.S. Department of Labor, 1971.

3. Herbert Striner, *Continuing Education as a National Capital Investment*, 1972.

4. "Occupational Manpower and Training Needs," *op. cit.*

5. *Ibid.*

6. Charles Holt et al., *Manpower Programs to Reduce Inflation and Unemployment*, 1971.

7. Arthur Okun, "The Gap Between Actual and Potential Output," 1963.

8. Harold Clark and Harold Sloan, *Classrooms in the Factories*, Institute of Research, Farleigh-Dickinson University, 1958.

9. *Manpower Report of the President*, 1971.

10. Sar Levitan, Garth Mangum, and Ray Marshall, *Human Resources and the Labor Market: Labor and Manpower in the American Economy*, 1972.

11. Ivar Berg, *Education and Jobs: The Great Training Robbery*, 1970.

12. Hugh Folk, "The Surplus of College Graduates," *New Generation*, Spring 1971.

13. C. M. Arensberg and S. T. Kimball, "The Small Farm Family in Rural Ireland," 1971.

14. Jerald G. Bachman, Swayzer Green, Ilona D. Wirtanen, "Dropping Out —Problem or Symptom?," 1971.

15. *Ibid.*

16. Gerald Somers, *The Effectiveness of Vocational and Technical Programs*, 1971.

17. *Ibid.*

18. Harold T. Smith and Henry C. Thole, "Secondary and Post-Secondary Occupational Education in Kalamazoo, Michigan," in Levitan and Siegel, eds., *Dimensions of Manpower Policy*, 1966.

19. Somers, *op. cit.*

20. Jacob Kaufman et al., *The Role of the Secondary Schools in the Preparation of Youth for Employment,* 1967.

21. "Vocational Education," Supplement to *Journal of Human Resources,* 1968.

22. Sheppard and Herrick, *op. cit.*

23. Alvin Toffler, *Future Shock,* 1970.

24. Frederick Taylor, *Principles of Scientific Management,* 1911.

25. J. H. Block et al., *Mastery Learning,* 1971.

26. Des Moines (Iowa) *Tribune,* July 14, 1972.

27. Simone Weil, *The Need for Roots,* 1971.

28. Urie Bronfenbrenner, "The Roots of Alienation."

29. S. Boocock and E. O Schild, eds., *Simulation Games in Learning,* 1968.

30. *Manpower Report of the President,* 1972.

31. Robert E. Campbell, *Vocational Guidance in Secondary Education: Results of a National Survey,* 1968.

32. F. Newman et al., *Report on Higher Education,* 1971.

33. Seymour Wolfbein, *Work in American Society,* 1971.

34. *Manpower Report of the President,* 1968.

Chapter 6

1. L. Hausman, "From Welfare Rolls to Pay Rolls? The Welfare System as a Manpower and Rehabilitation System," in Weber et al., *Public-Private Manpower Policies,* 1969.

2. *Manpower Report of the President,* 1970.

3. Eli Ginzberg, "Who Is a Worker," 1972.

4. Holt et al., *op. cit.*

5. *Manpower Report of the President,* 1971.

6. *Ibid.*

7. *Manpower Report of the President,* 1972.

8. G. Mangum, *MDTA: Foundation of Federal Manpower Policy,* 1968.

9. *Manpower Report of the President,* 1972.

10. Mangum, *op. cit.*

11. Michael J. Piore, "Jobs and Training," 1970.

12. Testimony of Bennet Harrison before the Senate Subcommittee on Employment Manpower and Poverty, 26 April 1972.

13. Piore, *op. cit.*

14. Holt et al., *op. cit.*

15. Gilbert Steiner, *Social Insecurity: The Politics of Welfare*, 1966.

16. Steiner, *ibid.*

17. Steiner, *op. cit.*

18. "Findings of the 1971 AFDC STUDY: PART I," 1971.

19. *Ibid.*

20. Leonard Goodwin, "Summary of Findings and Discussion," 1971, and Betty Burnside, "The Employment Potential of AFDC Mothers in Six States," 1971.

21. *Ibid.*

22. "Findings of the 1971 AFDC STUDY: PART II," 1972.

23. Jesse Bernard, "Women and the Public Interest," 1971.

24. Frank Furstenberg, "Work Experience and Family Life," 1972.

25. Liebow, *op. cit.*

26. Lee Rainwater, "Work, Well-Being and Family Life," 1972.

27. Furstenberg, *op. cit.*

28. Lee Rainwater, "Poverty, Living Standards and Family Well-Being," 1972.

29. Furstenberg, *op. cit.*

30. James O'Toole, *Watts and Woodstock,* Holt, Rinehart and Winston, New York, 1973.

TASK FORCE MEMBERS

James O'Toole, Chairman of the Task Force, received his doctorate in 1970 in social anthropology from Oxford University, where he was a Rhodes Scholar. He was formerly the Coordinator of Field Investigations for the President's Commission on Campus Unrest. He is the author of *Watts and Woodstock,* a study of minority group identity and culture in the United States and South Africa.

Elizabeth Hansot is a Program Officer at the National Endowment for the Humanities. She received her doctorate from Columbia University, where she also taught political science. Before joining the Endowment, she worked with the Education Sub-Committee of the Senate Committee on Labor and Public Welfare.

William R. Herman is Special Assistant for Policy Analysis, in the office of the Assistant Secretary for Planning and Evaluation, Department of Health, Education, and Welfare. He formerly directed the Department's health planning and analyses. His education includes graduate work in philosophy, literature, and economics.

Neal Herrick is the director of the Office of Program Development, Employment Standards Administration, U.S. Department of Labor. He was head of the Labor-HEW Task Force that drafted the Occupational Safety and Health Bill first submitted to the Congress in 1968, and is the co-author of the recently published, *Where Have All the Robots Gone?*

Elliot Liebow is Chief, Center for Studies of Metropolitan Problems, Division of Special Mental Programs, National Institute for Mental Health. He received his doctorate in anthropology from Catholic University. He is the author of *Tally's Corner,* a study of unemployed streetcorner men.

Bruce Lusignan, doctor of electrical engineering, is an associate professor in the School of Engineering at Stanford University. For the past seven years he has led teams of graduate students in studies of the economic and social effects of technological advances. Currently he is spending his sabbatical with the Office of Telecommunications Policy of the Department of Health, Education, and Welfare.

Harold Richman is Professor of Social Welfare Policy and Dean of the School of Social Services Administration at the University of Chicago. He was formerly a White House Fellow with the Secretary of Labor and has served as a vice-chairman of the Secretary of HEW's Task Force on Medicaid and Related Programs. He received his M.A. and Ph.D. from the University of Chicago.

Harold Sheppard has been on the Washington staff of the W. E. Upjohn Institute for Employment Research since 1963. Prior to that he was Assistant Administrator of the Area Redevelopment Administration in the Department of Commerce. He received his doctorate from the University of Wisconsin in 1949. Among the books he has authored or co-authored are: *When Labor Votes: A Study of Auto Workers, The Job Hunt, Poverty and Wealth in America, Economic Failure, Alienation and Extremism?* and *Where Have All the Robots Gone?*

Ben Stephansky is the director of the Washington office of the W. E. Upjohn Institute for Employment Research. He has been United States Ambassador to Bolivia and the Deputy Assistant Secretary of State for Latin American Affairs. He has also served as the executive director of the United States-Puerto Rico Commission on the Status of Puerto Rico. He received his doctorate in economics from the University of Wisconsin.

James Wright is a former steelworker from Gary, Indiana who is now a community organizer with the National Center for Urban Ethnic Affairs in Washington, D.C. He is currently engaged in a study on drug use among blue-collar workers for the President's Special Action Office for Drug Abuse.

AUTHORS OF COMMISSIONED PAPERS AND CONSULTANTS TO THE TASK FORCE

Ivar Berg, Columbia University

Irving Bluestone, United Auto Workers

David S. Bushnell, Human Resources Research Organization

Paul Campanis, Boston University

Reginald Carter, Michigan State University

Gary M. Cook, Department of Commerce

Louis E. Davis, University of California, Los Angeles

Robert Dubin, University of California, Irvine

Albert S. Epstein, International Association of Machinists and Aerospace Workers

Otto Feinstein, Wayne State University

Frank Furstenberg, Jr., University of Pennsylvania

Eli Ginzberg, Columbia University

Stefan Halper, Special Action Office for Drug Abuse Prevention

Sidney Harman, Jervis Corporation

Willis Harman, Stanford Research Institute

Dale L. Hiestand, Columbia University

Charles Holt, Urban Institute

James S. House, Duke University

Carl D. Jacobs, Xerox Corporation

Robert Kahn, University of Michigan

Stanislav V. Kasl, Yale University

Emanuel Kay, Gellerman Kay Corporation

Steve Kidder, Johns Hopkins University

Melvin Kohn, National Institute of Mental Health

Michael Koleda, National Planning Association

Kenneth Kramer, American Red Cross

Elliot A. Krause, Northeastern University

William H. Kroes, National Institute for Occupational Safety and Health

Barbara Lutzker, Library of Congress

Michael Maccoby, Institute for Policy Studies, Washington, D.C.

David C. MacMichael, Stanford Research Institute

Bruce L. Margolis, National Institute for Occupational Safety and Health

Alan McLean, International Business Machines

Bert Metzger, Profit Sharing Research Foundation

Heinz Pagels, Rockefeller University

John Palmer, Department of Health, Education, and Welfare

Robert Perloff, University of Pittsburgh

Michael Piore, Massachusetts Institute of Technology

Lee Rainwater, Joint Center for Urban Studies, Harvard University and the Massachusetts Institute of Technology

Beatrice G. Reubens, Columbia University

Mae Rosenberg, Stanford Research Institute

Joel Rosenblatt, Office of Management and the Budget

Peter H. Rossi, Johns Hopkins University

Isabel Sawhill, Goucher College

Milton F. Shore, National Institute for Mental Health

Richard Shore, Department of Labor

Joyce Starr, Northwestern University

George Strauss, University of California, Berkeley

Herbert E. Striner, American University

Katherine A. Terzi, Institute for Policy Studies

Thomas C. Thomas, Stanford Research Institute

Eric L. Trist, University of Pennsylvania

Tom Veblen, Cargill Incorporated

Regis Walther, George Washington University

Richard E. Walton, Harvard University

Rolland H. Wright, Wayne State University

Jerry Wurf, American Federation of State, County and Municipal Employees

Research Associates

Martin Beiser, Coordinator
Susan Downs
Pamela Johnson
Zeta Jordan
Laurence Liu
Howard Sklar
Robert Smith

COMMISSIONED PAPERS, BY AUTHOR

Ivar Berg, "The Protestant Ethic: A Troubled Demiurge."

Irving Bluestone, "Democratizing the Work Place."

David S. Bushnell, "Continuing Education: Problems and Prospect."

Paul Campanis, "You Are What You Work At."

Reginald Carter, "Busy Hands Are Happy Hands."

Louis E. Davis and Eric L. Trist, "Approaches to Improving the Quality of Working Life."

Robert Dubin, "Some Notes on the Quality of Working Life."

Albert S. Epstein, "In the Beginning Was the Work."

Otto Feinstein and Rolland H. Wright, "The Ethnic Revival: Work and Community Satisfaction and the Work Ethic."

Frank F. Furstenberg, Jr., "Work Experience and Family Life."

Eli Ginzberg, "Who Is a Worker?"

Stefan Halper and Heinz Pagels, "Mass Media and the American Work Culture."

Sidney Harman, "Responsibilities of Businessmen."

Dale L. Hiestand, "Obligations of Employers and the Society to Minority Workers."

James S. House, "The Effects of Occupational Stress on Physical Health."

Carl D. Jacobs, "Job Redesign."

Robert L. Kahn, "The Work Module: A Proposal for the Humanization of Work."

Stanislav V. Kasl, "Work in America: Work and Mental Health."

Emanuel Kay, "Middle Management."

Kenneth Kramer, "Productivity and Unions."

Elliot A. Krause, "The Politics of Work Experience."

Michael Maccoby and Katherine A. Terzi, "Work and the American Character."

David C. MacMichael, "Occupational Bias in Formal Education and Its Effect on Preparing Children for Work."

Bruce L. Margolis and William H. Kroes, "Work and the Health of Man."

Bert L. Metzger, "Socio-Economic Participation: Key to a Better World of Work in the Future."

Robert Perloff and Michael Koleda, "The Work Ethic."

Michael Piore, "Notes on Welfare Reform and the Design of Income Maintenance Systems."

Lee Rainwater, "Work, Well-Being and Family Life."

Beatrice Reubens, "Vocational Education For *All* in High School?"

Mae Rosenberg, "Curriculum Issues and Career Education."

Peter H. Rossi, "The Prestige Standing of Occupations: Characteristics and Consequences."

Isabel Sawhill, "Perspectives on Women and Work in America."

Milton F. Shore, "Youth and Jobs: Educational, Vocational and Mental Health Aspects."

Joyce Starr, "Adaptation to the Working World."

George Strauss, "Is There a Blue-Collar Revolt Against Work?"

Thomas C. Thomas, "Work and Welfare."

Tom Veblen, "Some Thoughts on Work Organization."

Regis Walther, "The Socialization of Youth for Work."

Richard E. Walton, "Work Place Alienation and the Need for Major Innovation."

BIBLIOGRAPHY

Chapter 1

"America: A Special Section," *The Atlantic,* October 1971.

"America's Growing Anti-Business Mood," *Business Week,* June 17, 1972.

Arendt, H. *The Human Condition,* Chicago University Press, Chicago, 1958.

Argyris, Chris. *Human Behavior in Organizations,* Harper and Row, New York, 1954.

Bakke, E. W. *Citizens Without Work,* Yale University Press, New Haven, 1940.

————. *The Unemployed Worker,* Yale University Press, New Haven, 1940.

Bell, Daniel. "The Corporation and Society in the 1970's," *Public Interest,* Summer, 1971.

————. "Work and Its Discontents," in *The End of Ideology: On the Exhaustion of Political Ideas in the Fifties,* Free Press, 1960.

Bennis, W. G. *Changing Organizations,* McGraw-Hill, New York, 1966.

Blau, Peter M. and Duncan, O. D. *The American Occupational Structure,* Wiley, New York, 1965.

Blauner, Robert. *Alienation and Freedom; The Factory Worker and His Industry.* University of Chicago Press, Chicago, 1964.

————. "Work Satisfaction and Industrial Trends in Modern Society," in W. Galenson and S. Lipset, eds., *Labor and Trade Unionism,* Wiley, New York, 1960.

Blood, M. R. and Hulin, C. L. "Alienation, Environmental Characteristics and Worker Responses," *Journal of Applied Psychology,* Vol. 51, 1967.

Blum, A. A. "The Office Employee," in A. A. Blum et al., eds., *White Collar Workers,* Random House, New York, 1971.

Blum, Zahava and Rossi, Peter N. "Social Class Research and Images of the Poor: A Bibliograph Research," in Daniel P. Moynihan, ed., *On Understanding Poverty,* Basic Books, New York, 1968.

Bortner, R. W. and Hultsch, D. F. "A Multivariate Analysis of Correlates of Life Satisfaction in Adulthood," *Journal of Gerontology,* Vol. 25, 1970.

Bose, Keith W. "Searching for Meaning in Work: The Loss of Purpose," *Washington Post,* February 6, 1972.

Boulding, Kenneth E. "The Qualified Uproarious Success," in J. G. Kirk, ed., *America Now,* Atheneum, New York, 1968.

Brayfield, A. H., Wells, R. V., and Strate, M. W. "Interrelationships Among Measures of Job Satisfaction and General Satisfaction," *Journal of Applied Psychology,* Vol. 41, 1957.

Burck, Gilbert. "There'll Be Less Leisure Than You Think," *Fortune,* March 1970.

Carter, Reginald. "The Myth of Increasing Non-work vs. Work Activities," *Social Problems*, Vol. 18, 1970.

Chew, Peter T. "Why Do We Need to Work?," *The National Observer*, July 5, 1971.

Chinoy, Ely. "Manning the Machines—The Assembly Line Worker," in P. C. Berger, ed., *The Human Shape of Work*, Macmillan, New York, 1964.

Coles, Robert. "On the Meaning of Work," *The Atlantic*, October 1971.

DeGrazia, Sebastian. *Of Time, Work and Leisure*, Twentieth Century Fund, New York, 1962.

DeWitt, George. "Man at Work," *Personnel Journal*, Vol. 49, No. 10, October 1970.

Dickson, Paul. "Striking Out on Your Own," *Washington Monthly*, August 1971.

Drucker, Peter F. *The Practice of Management*, Harper and Row, New York, 1954.

Dubin, Robert. "Industrial Workers' Worlds: A Study of the Central Life Interests of Industrial Workers," *Social Problems*, January 1956.

———. "Work and Non-work: Institutional Perspectives," unpublished paper, University of California, Riverside. *The Failure Record Through 1970*, Dun and Bradstreet, Inc. Fenn, Dan H. "Responding to the Employee Voice," *Harvard Business Review*, May/June 1972.

Frankel, E. "Studies in Biographical Psychology," *Character and Personality*, Vol. 5, 1936.

Freud, Sigmund. *Civilization and Its Discontents*, W. W. Norton, New York, 1961.

Friedmann, Georges. *Industrial Society*, The Free Press, New York, 1955.

Fromm, Erich. *The Heart of Man*, Harper and Row, New York, 1964.

———. *The Revolution of Hope*, Bantam Books, New York, 1971.

Galbraith, John Kenneth. *The New Industrial State*, revised edition, Houghton Mifflin, Boston, 1972.

Gallup, George. "Productivity Seen on Downswing," *Washington Post*, April 10, 1972.

Garson, Barbara. "Luddites in Lordstown," *Harper's*, June 1972.

Ginzberg, Eli. *Grass on the Slag Heaps*, Harper, New York, 1942.

———. *The Unemployed*, Harper, New York, 1943.

———. "Work: The Eye of the Hurricane," *Humanitas*, Vol. VII, No. 2, Fall 1971.

Goldthorpe, J. H., Lochwood, D., Bachofer, F., and Platt, J. *The Affluent Worker: Industrial Attitudes and Behavior*, Vol. I, Cambridge University Press, New York, 1968.

Goodenough, Ward. *Cooperation and Change,* The Russell Sage Foundation, New York, 1963.

Gordon, T. J. *Ideas in Conflict,* St. Martin's Press, New York, 1966.

Gouldner, A. W. *Patterns of Industrial Bureaucracy,* The Free Press, New York, 1954.

Harmon, Willis. "Key Choices of the Next Two Decades," address before the "White House Conference on the Industrial World Ahead," February 1972.

Herrick, Neal. "Who's Unhappy At Work and Why," *Manpower,* Vol. 4, No. 1, January 1972.

Herzberg, Frederick. *Work and the Nature of Man,* World Publishing, Cleveland, 1966.

————, Mausner B., and Snyderman, B. *The Motivation to Work,* Wiley, New York, 1959.

———— et al. *Job Attitudes: Review of Research and Opinion,* Psychological Service of Pittsburgh, Pittsburgh, 1957.

Inkeles, Alex and Rossi, Peter H. "National Comparisons of Occupational Prestige," *American Journal of Sociology,* Vol. LXI, January 1956.

Kahn, Robert L. "The Meaning of Work: Interpretation and Proposals for Measurement," in A. A. Campbell and P. E. Converse, eds., *The Human Meaning of Social Change,* Basic Books, 1972.

Komarovsky, M. *The Unemployed Man and His Family,* The Dryden Press, New York, 1940.

Krause, Elliot. *The Sociology of Occupations,* Little, Brown, Boston, 1971.

Lessard, Suzannah. "America the Featherbedded," *The Washington Monthly,* March 1971.

————. "America's Time Traps: The Youth Cult, The Work Prisons, The Emptiness of Age," *The Washington Monthly,* February 1971.

————. "What Do People Do All Day?," *The Washington Monthly,* March 1972.

Lieberman, Jethro K. *The Tyranny of the Experts: How Professionals Are Closing the Open Society,* Random House, New York, 1967.

Liebow, Elliot. *Tally's Corner,* Little, Brown, Boston, 1967.

Levinson, Harry. "Various Approaches to Understanding Man at Work," *Archives of Environmental Health,* Vol. 22, May 1971.

Maccoby, M. "Emotional Attitudes and Political Choice," *Politics and Society,* Winter 1972.

Marx, Karl. *Economic and Philosophical Manuscripts of 1844* (Martin Milligan, trans.), Lawrence and Wishert, London, 1959.

Maslow, Abraham. *Motivation and Personality,* Harper and Row, New York, 1954.

McLean, Alan. "Work as a Four Letter Word," *Journal of Occupational Medicine,* Vol. 12, No. 10, October 1970.

McPartland, T. S. and Cummings, J. H. "Self-conception, Social Class and Mental Health," in *Human Organization,* Vol. 17, 1958.

Meissner, Martin. *Technology and the Worker,* Chandler Publishing, San Francisco, 1969.

Merton, Robert K. "Social Structure and Anomie," in *Social Theory and Social Structure,* The Free Press, Glencoe, Illinois, 1957.

Miller, Delbert C., and Form, William H. *Industrial Sociology: The Sociology of Work Organizations,* Harper and Row, New York, 1951.

Mishan, E. J. "On Making the Future Safe For Mankind," *Public Interest,* Summer 1971.

Morse, Nancy C. and Weiss, Robert S. "The Function and Meaning of Work and the Job," *American Sociological Review,* Vol. 20, April 1955.

Nosow, Sigmund and Form, William H., eds. *Man, Work and Society,* Basic Books, New York, 1962.

Orzack, L. H. "Work as a Central Life Interest of Professionals," *Social Problems,* Vol. 7, 1959.

Price, Charlton R. *New Directions in the World of Work: A Conference Report,* W. E. Upjohn Institute for Employment Research, Washington, D.C., 1972.

"Promoting Human Productivity," *Wall Street Journal,* April 21, 1972.

Reiss, A. J. and Katt, P. K. *Occupations and Social Status,* The Free Press, Glencoe, Illinois.

Reuther, Walter P. "The Human Goals of Manpower Policy," in Irving Siegel, ed., *Manpower Tomorrow: Prospects and Priorities,* Augustus M. Kelley Publishers, New York, 1967.

Ritti, R. *Engineers in Industrial Organizations,* Columbia University Press, New York.

Roche, William and MacKinnon, Neil L. "Motivating People with Meaningful Work," *Harvard Business Review,* May/June 1970.

Roethlisberger, F. J. and Dickson, W. J. *Management and the Worker,* Harvard University Press, Cambridge, Massachusetts, 1939.

Rosen, Bernard C. and Crockett, Harry J., eds. *Achievement in American Society,* Schenkman Publishing, Cambridge, Massachusetts.

Rosen, R. A. Hudson. "The Hard Core and the Puritan Ethic," *Manpower,* Vol. 2, No. 1, January 1970.

Seligman, Ben. "On Work, Alienation, and Leisure," *The American Journal of Economics and Sociology,* Vol. 23, No. 4, 1965.

Sexton, Patricia Cayo and Sexton, Brendan. *Blue Collars and Hard Hats: The Working Class and the Future of American Politics,* Random House, New York, 1972.

Sheppard, Harold L. and Herrick, Neal. *Where Have All the Robots Gone?*, The Free Press, New York, 1972.

Sherwin, Douglas S. "Strategy for Winning Employee Commitment," *Harvard Business Review*, May/June 1972.

Statistical Abstract of the U.S.: 1971, Bureau of the Census, U.S. Department of Commerce, Washington, D.C., 1971.

Stein, Maurice. *The Eclipse of Community*, Princeton University Press, Princeton, New Jersey, 1960.

Striner, Herbert E. "1984 and Beyond: The World of Work," staff paper, W. E. Upjohn Institute for Employment Research, Washington, D.C., 1967. *Survey of Working Conditions*, Survey Research Center, University of Michigan, 1970.

Taylor, F. W. *The Principles of Scientific Management*, Harper, New York, 1911.

Tiffany, D. W., Cowan, J. R., and Tiffany, P. M. *The Unemployed: A Social-Psychological Portrait*, Prentice-Hall, Englewood Cliffs, New Jersey, 1970.

Tilgher, A. *Work: What It Has Meant To Men Through the Ages*, Harcourt, Brace, and World, New York, 1930.

Time (Law Section), June 2, 1971.

Toffler, Alvin. *Future Shock*, Bantam Books, New York, 1970.

Touraine, Alain. *The Post-Industrial Society*, Random House, New York, 1971.

Trist, Eric. "A Socio-Technical Critique of Scientific Management," paper contributed to the Edinburgh Conference on the Impact of Science and Technology, Edinburgh University, May 24–26, 1970.

"U.S. 1960 Census of the Population, Detailed Characteristics, Summary Final Report," U.S. Department of Commerce, U.S. Government Printing Office, Washington, D.C., 1963.

Veblen, Thorstein. *The Theory of the Leisure Class*, Modern Library, 1934.

Vroom, Victor H. *Work and Motivation*, Wiley, New York, 1964.

Walker, E. R. and Guest, R. H. *The Man on the Assembly Line*, Harvard University Press, Cambridge, Massachusetts.

Weber, Max. *The Protestant Ethic and the Spirit of Capitalism*, Scribner, New York, 1958.

Weil, Simone. *The Need for Roots*, Harper Colophon, New York, 1952.

Whyte, William H., Jr. *The Practice of Management*, Simon and Schuster, New York, 1956.

Wilcock, R. C. and Franke, W. H. *Unwanted Workers*, The Free Press, Glencoe, Illinois, 1963.

Wilensky, Harold. "Work as a Social Problem," in Howard S. Becker, ed., *Social Problems: A Modern Approach*, Wiley, New York, 1966.

Winick, Charles. "Atonie: The Psychology of the Unemployed and the Marginal Worker," in George Fish, ed., *The Frontiers of Management Psychology,* Harper and Row, New York, 1964.

Wolfbein, Seymour. *Work in American Society,* Scott, Foresman, Glenview, Illinois, 1971.

"Work—Some Ramifications," *The Rehabilitation Record,* January/February 1972.

Yankelovich, Daniel. "The New Naturalism," *Saturday Review,* April 1, 1972.

Zagoria, Sam. "Searching For Meaning in Work: Rebellion and Reform," *The Washington Post,* February 6, 1972.

Chapter 2

Aiken, M., Ferman, L. A., and Sheppard, H. L. *Economic Failure, Alienation, and Extremism,* University of Michigan Press, Ann Arbor, 1968.

Anderson, Nels. *Dimensions of Work: The Sociology of a Work Culture,* D. McKay, New York, 1964.

Anundsen, Kristin. "The Rise of Womanagement," *Innovation,* No. 24, September 1971.

Barfield, R. and Morgan, J. N. *Early Retirement: The Decision and the Experience,* Institute for Social Research, The University of Michigan, Ann Arbor, 1969.

Becker, Gary S. *The Economics of Discrimination,* The University of Chicago Press, Chicago, 1957.

Bell, Caroline. "Unemployed Women: Do They Matter?," *Wall Street Journal,* March 15, 1972.

Berger, Bennett. *Working-Class Suburb: A Study of Auto Workers in Suburbia,* University of California Press, Berkeley, 1969.

Bergmann, Barbara. "The Effect on White Incomes of Discrimination in Employment," *Journal of Political Economy,* March/April 1971.

Bernard, Jessie. *Women and the Public Interest,* Aldine, New York, 1971.

Bird, Caroline. "Welcome, Class of '72, to the Female Job Ghetto," *New York,* Vol. 5, May 1972.

Blauner, Robert. *Alienation and Freedom,* University of Chicago Press, Chicago, 1964.

———. "Work Satisfaction and Industrial Trends in Modern Society," in Walter Galenson and S. M. Lipset, eds., *Labor and Trade Unionism: An Interdisciplinary Reader,* Wiley, New York, 1960.

"The Blue Collar Blues," *Newsweek,* May 17, 1971.

Bowen, William G. and Finegan, T. A. *The Economics of Labor Force Participation,* Princeton University Press, Princeton, 1969.

Boyer, Elizabeth. "Equal Opportunity for Women in Our Time," *Women Lawyers Journal*, Vol. 56, 1970.

"The Busy Boss: How Tense Is He? Latest Findings . . . ," *U.S. News and World Report*, March 13, 1972.

Cain, Glenn. *Married Women in the Labor Force*, University of Chicago Press, Chicago, 1966.

Carlson, Elliot. "Focusing on 'Blue Collar Blues,' " *Wall Street Journal*, April 6, 1972.

"Central Influences on American Life," *The Wall Street Journal*, April 4, 1972.

"Characteristics of the Population by Ethnic Origin," U.S. Department of Commerce, U.S. Government Printing Office, Washington, D.C., 1970.

"Children of Women in the Labor Force, March, 1970," U.S. Department of Labor, U.S. Government Printing Office, Washington, D.C., 1971.

Cobb, William L. "Black-White Differences in the Importance of Aspects of Work," unpublished paper, University of Michigan, 1971.

Cohen, Malcolm S. "Sex Differences in Compensation," *Journal of Human Resources*, Fall 1971.

Coleman, James S. et al. "Black and White Careers During the First Decade of Labor Force Experience," *Social Science Research*, Vol. I, No. 3, September 1972.

Cone, L. M. "Society's Latest Disease—M.O.," *Marketing Review*, Vol. 24, 1969.

Cooper, George. "Working Wives and the Tax Law," *Rutgers Law Review*, Vol. 25, Fall 1970.

DeFleur, Melvin. "Occupational Roles as Portrayed on Television," *Public Opinion Quarterly*, Vol. 28, No. 57, 1964.

Derryck, Dennis. "Young Blacks vs. the Work World," *New Generation*.

Dewey, Lucretia M. "Women in Labor Unions," *Monthly Labor Review*, Vol. 94, February 1971.

Dodge, Norton. *Women in the Soviet Economy: Their Role in Economic, Scientific, and Technical Development*, Johns Hopkins, Baltimore, 1966.

Donahue, W., Orbach, H. L., and Pollack, O. "Retirement: The Emerging Social Pattern," in C. Tibbitts, ed., *Handbook of Social Gerontology*, The University of Chicago Press, Chicago, 1960.

Draper, Jean E., Lundrgre, Earl F., and Strother, George B. *Work Attitudes and Retirement Adjustment*, University of Wisconsin, Madison, 1967.

Drapkin, Michael K. "False Security—Union Men, Workers Worry About Safety of Their Pension Funds," *Wall Street Journal*, March 7, 1972.

Drucker, Peter. "The Surprising Seventies," *Harper's*, July 1971.

Eidson, Bettye. *Institutional Racism: Minority Group Manpower Policies of Major Urban Employers,* unpublished dissertation, Johns Hopkins, 1971.

Ellis, Charles D. "Danger Ahead for Pension Funds," *Harvard Business Review,* May/June 1971.

"The Employment Problems of Older Workers," U.S. Department of Labor, Government Printing Office, Washington, D.C., 1971.

Faunce, W. D. "Automation and the Automobile Worker," *Social Problems,* No. 6, 1958.

Ferriss, Abbott L. *Indicators of Trends in the States of American Women,* Russell Sage Foundation, New York, 1971.

Friedan, Betty. *The Feminine Mystique,* Norton, New York, 1963.

Friedmann, Eugene A. and Havighurst, Robert J. *The Meaning of Work and Retirement,* University of Chicago Press, Chicago, 1954.

Fuchs, Victor. "Differences in Hourly Earnings Between Men and Women," *Monthly Labor Review,* May 1971.

Fuentes, Sonia Pressman. "The Law Against Sex Discrimination in Employment and Its Relationship to Statistics," *The American Statistician,* Vol. 26, No. 2, April 1972.

"Getting an Early Start on Those Golden Years," *Business Week,* April 27, 1968.

Gilman, Charlotte P. *Women and Economics,* Harper and Row, New York, 1966.

Ginzberg, Eli and Yohalem, Alice M., eds. *Women's Challenge to Management,* Praeger, New York, in press.

Gitlow, Abraham L. "Women in the American Economy: Today and Tomorrow," *Labor Law Journal,* Vol. 23, April 1972.

Gooding, Judson. "The Accelerated Generation Moves Into Management," *Fortune,* March 1971.

———. "Blue Collar Blues on the Assembly Line," *Fortune,* July 1970.

———. "The Fraying White Collar," *Fortune,* December 1970.

———. "It Pays to Wake Up the Blue Collar Worker," *Fortune,* September 1970.

Gray, Betty MacMorran. "The Economics of Sex Bias," *Nation,* Vol. 212, June 14, 1971.

Grier, William H. and Cobbs, Price M. *Black Rage,* Bantam Books, 1969.

Gwertzman, Bernard. "Be Nice to Secretaries, Diplomats are Advised," *New York Times,* March 6, 1972.

Hackamack, Lawrence C. and Solid, Alan B. "The Woman Executive: There is Still Ample Room for Progress," *Business Horizons,* Vol. 15, April 1972.

1969 Handbook on Women Workers, U.S. Department of Labor, U.S. Government Printing Office, Washington, D.C.

Harris, L. "Pleasant Retirement Expected," *Washington Post,* November 28, 1965.

Harwood, Edwin. "Youth Unemployment: A Tale of Two Ghettos," *Public Interest,* Vol. 1, 1969.

Haynes, John. "The New Workers: A Report," *New Generation,* Vol. 52, No. 4, Fall 1972.

Hedges, J. N. "Women Workers and Manpower Demands in the 1970's," *Monthly Labor Review,* June 1970.

Henderson, Holly M. "When Retirement Becomes a Way of Life," *The Conference Board Record,* March 1972.

Hodgson, J. D. "The Changing Character of America's Workforce," *Personnel Administration,* Vol. 34, No. 4, 1971.

Hollowell, Donald L. "Women and Equal Employment," *Woman Lawyers Journal,* Vol. 56, 1970.

Hyatt, Jim. "Out in the Cold—Increasing Layoffs Rob Many of Their Pensions as Well as Their Jobs," *Wall Street Journal,* November 4, 1970.

Jacobson, Aileen. "Marriage Rethought: The Very Private Impact of the Women's Movement," *Washington Post: Potomac Magazine,* June 4, 1972.

Janeway, Elizabeth. *Man's World, Woman's Place: A Study in Social Mythology,* Morrow, New York, 1971.

Jeger, Lana. "Equal Pay: Making it Work," *New Statesman,* Vol. 76, 1968.

Jordan, Joan. "The Economics of Women's Liberation," *New Generation,* Fall 1969.

————. "Comment: Working Woman and the Equal Rights Amendment," *Transaction,* Vol. 8, Nos. 1 and 2, November/December 1970.

Kassalow, E. M. "White Collar Unionism in the United States," in Adolf Sturmthal, ed., *White Collar Trade Unions,* University of Illinois, Chicago, 1967.

Keniston, Kenneth. *The Uncommitted,* Dell Publishing, New York, 1960.

Kennedy, Joseph P. "Sex Discrimination: State Protective Law Since Title VII," *Notre Dame Lawyer,* Vol. 47, No. 3, February 1972.

Kidder, Alice H. "Job Search Among Negroes," *Labor Law Journal,* August 1968.

Killian, Ray A. *The Working Woman: A Male Manager's View,* American Managers Association, New York, 1971.

Klemesrud, Judy. "Secretary Image: A Tempest in a Typewriter," *New York Times,* March 7, 1972.

Kohn, Melvin I. "Bureaucratic Man: A Portrait and an Interpretation," *American Sociological Review,* Vol. 36, June 1971.

Koontz, Elizabeth Duncan. "Childbirth and Childrearing Leave: Job Related Benefits," *New York Law Forum,* Vol. XVII, No. 2, 1971.

Kreps, Juanita. *Sex in the Marketplace: American Women at Work,* Johns Hopkins, Baltimore, 1971.

Landau, Eliot A. and Dunahoo, Kermit L. "Women's Legal Employment Rights and Their Application," *The Hastings Law Journal,* Vol. 23, No. 1, November 1971.

Landes, William M. "The Economics of Fair Employment Laws," *Journal of Political Economy,* July/August 1968.

Langner, Elinor. "The Women of the Telephone Company," *New York Review of Books,* March 26, 1970.

Lasson, Kenneth. *The Workers,* Bantam Books, New York, 1972.

Levenstein, Asron. *Why People Work: Changing Incentives in a Troubled World,* Crowell-Collier Press, New York, 1962.

Levinson, Harry. "On Being a Middle-Aged Manager," *Harvard Business Review,* July/August 1969.

Levitan, Sar A., ed. *Blue Collar Workers: A Symposium on Middle America,* McGraw-Hill, New York, 1971.

Lewis, Edwin. *Developing Women's Potential,* Iowa State University Press, Ames, 1968.

Long, Clarence D. *The Labor Force Under Changing Income and Employment,* Princeton University Press, Princeton, 1958.

Lurie, Melvin and Rayack, Elton. "Racial Differences in Migration and Job Search: A Case Study," *Southern Economic Journal,* 1966.

Lyons, Richard D. "Unions for Doctors Are Growing Trend," *New York Times,* June 18, 1972.

"Managers Militant . . . Revolt or a Bill of Rights?," *Industry Week,* March 22, 1971.

"Manager Unions," American Management Association, New York, June 1972.

Marcson, S., ed. *Automation, Alienation and Anomie,* Harper and Row, New York, 1970.

Markoff, Helene S. "Federal Women's Program," *Public Administration Review,* Vol. XXXII, No. 2, March/April 1972.

Marshall, Patricia. "Women at Work," *Manpower,* Vol. 4, June 1972.

McCarthy, Colman. "Superworkers in the Rat Race—What Makes Them Run," *Los Angeles Times,* March 26, 1972.

McNally, G. B. "Patterns of Female Labor Force Activity," *Industrial Relations,* Vol. 7, May 1968.

Meissner, Martin. "The Long Arm of the Job: A Study of Work and Leisure," *Industrial Relations,* Vol. 10, October 1971.

Miller, S. M. "The Blue Collars," *The New Society,* March 16, 1972.

Mills, C. Wright. *White Collar,* Oxford University Press, New York, 1971.

Mincer, Jacob. "Labor Force Participation of Married Women: A Study of Labor Supply," in *Aspects of Labor Economics,* Princeton University Press, Princeton, 1962.

Morgan, Robin, ed. *Sisterhood Is Powerful,* Random House, New York, 1970.

Morse, Dean. *The Peripheral Worker,* Columbia University Press, New York, 1969.

Neff, Walter S. *Work and Human Behavior,* Atherton Press, New York, 1968.

Nobile, Philip., ed. *The Con III Controversy: The Critics Look at the Greening of America,* Pocket Books, New York, 1971.

Novak, Michael. "White Ethnic," *Harper's,* October 1971.

Nye, F. Ivan and Hoffman, Lois W. *The Employed Mother in America,* Rand McNally, Chicago, 1963.

O'Boyle, Edward J. "Job Tenure: How It Relates to Race and Age," *Monthly Labor Review,* September 1969.

Oppenheimer, Valerie K. *The Female Labor Force in the U.S.,* University of California, Berkeley, 1970.

Orden, Susan R. "Working Wives and Marriage Happiness," *American Journal of Sociology,* Vol. 74, No. 4, January 1969.

Plumb, J. H. *The Death of the Past,* Houghton Mifflin, Sentry Editions, Boston, 1971.

Pope, Harrison. *Voices From the Drug Culture,* Beacon Press, Boston, 1971.

The President's Commission on the Status of Women, *Report of the Committee on Private Employment,* U.S. Government Printing Office, Washington, D.C., 1963.

"Private Pension Plans, 1960–69, An Overview," *Monthly Labor Review,* July 1970.

Quinn, Robert P. "Locking-in As a Moderator of the Relationship Between Job Satisfaction and Mental Health," Survey Research Center, University of Michigan, 1972.

Reis, Albert J., Duncan, Otis D., Hatt, P., and Novch, N. *Occupations and Social Status,* The Free Press of Glencoe, New York, 1962.

Reische, Diana. *Women and Society,* The H. W. Wilson Co., New York, 1972.

The Report of the President's Commission on Campus Unrest, U.S. Government Printing Office, Washington, D.C., 1970.

"The Revolt of the Middle Managers," *Dun's Review,* Vol. 94, No. 3, September 1969.

Ribicoff, Abraham. "The Alienation of the American Worker," *Saturday Review,* April 22, 1972.

Robertson, Nan. "A Wallace Backer Stirred by Busing," *New York Times,* May 14, 1972.

Rossi, Alice. "Job Discrimination and What Women Can Do About It," *Atlantic Monthly,* Vol. 225, March 1970.

Roszak, Theodore. *The Making of a Counter Culture,* Anchor Books, New York, 1969.

Salpukas, Agis. "Workers Increasingly Rebel Against Boredom on Assembly Line," *New York Times,* April 2, 1972.

———. "Young Workers Disrupt Key G.M. Plant," *New York Times,* January 23, 1972.

Sanborn, Henry. "Pay Differences Between Men and Women," *Industrial and Labor Relations Review,* July 1964.

Sawhill, Isabel V. "The Economics of Discrimination Against Women: Some New Findings," *Journal of Human Resources,* forthcoming.

———. *The Relative Earnings of Women in the U.S.,* unpublished dissertation, New York University, 1968.

Sayles, Leonard R. "Wildcat Strikes," *Harvard Business Review,* Vol. 32, No. 6, October 1964.

———, and Strauss, George. *The Local Union,* Harcourt, New York, 1967.

Scott, Donald I. *The Psychology of Work,* Duckworth, London, 1970.

Schein, Virgil. "Implications and Obstacles To Full Participation of the Woman Worker," *Best's Review,* Vol. 72, April 1972.

Schonberger, R. J. "Inflexible Working Conditions Keep Women 'Unliberated,' " *Personnel Journal,* Vol. 50, No. 11, November 1971.

———. "Ten Million Housewives Want to Work," *Labor Law Review,* Vol. 21, June 1970.

Schrank, Robert. "It Makes No Difference Now," *New Generation,* October 1970.

———. "The Young Workers—Their Influence on the Workplace," National Committee on the Unemployment of Youth, Board Meeting, Spring 1971.

Schwartz, Eleanor B. "The Sex Barrier in Business," *Atlanta Economic Review,* Vol. 21, June 1971.

Seashore, Stanley E. and Barnowe, J. Thad. "Demographic and Job Factors Associated With the 'Blue Collar Blues,' " mimeographed, 1972.

Shepard, Jon M. "Functional Specialization, Alienation, and Job Satisfaction," *Industrial and Labor Relations Review,* Vol. 23, January 1970.

———. Functional Specialization and Work Attitudes," *Industrial Relations,* Vol. 8, No. 2, May 1969.

Sheppard, Harold L. "Discontented Blue Collar Workers—A Case Study," *Monthly Labor Review,* April 1971.

———. *Toward an Industrial Gerontology,* Johns Hopkins, Baltimore, 1970.

Simchak, Morag MacLeod. "Equal Pay in the United States," *International Labour Review*, Vol. 103, June 1971.

Simon, William and Gagnon, John H. "The White Working Class and Its Youth: An Overview," paper prepared for the National Institute of Health, contract #70-511.

Slater, Philip. *The Pursuit of Loneliness*, Beacon Press, Boston, 1970.

Sliven, Dennis P. "What Companies Are Doing About Women's Job Equality," *Personnel*, Vol. 48, July/August 1971.

Smuts, Robert W. *Women and Work in America*, Columbia, New York, 1959.

Strauss, George. "Some Notes on Power Equalization," in Harold J. Leavitt, ed., *The Social Science of Organizations*, Prentice-Hall, Englewood Cliffs, New Jersey, 1963.

Suter, Larry E. and Miller, Herman P. "Components of Income Differences Between Men and Career Women," paper presented at the September 1971 American Statistical Association Meetings.

Tausky, Curt. "Meaning of Work Among Blue Collar Men," paper presented to the annual meeting of the American Sociological Association in San Francisco, 1968.

Telly, Charles S., French, Wendell, and Scott, William G. "The Relationship of Inequity to Turnover Among Hourly Workers," *Administrative Science Quarterly*, Vol. 16, No. 2, June 1971.

" 'Thirty-and-Outers' Opt for Late Retirement," *Business Week*, October 9, 1971.

"Time Lost From Work Among the Currently Employed Population," U.S. Department of Health, Education, and Welfare, U.S. Government Printing Office, Washington, D.C., 1968.

Trice, H. M. and Belasco, J. A. "The Aging Collegian: Drinking Pathologies Among Executive and Professional Alumni," in G. L. Maddox, ed., *The Domesticated Drug—Drinking Among Collegians*, College and University Press, New Haven, 1970.

"The Troubled American: A Special Report on the White Majority," *Newsweek*, October 6, 1969.

Turner, Arthur and Lawrence, Paul. *Industrial Jobs and the Worker*, Harvard Graduate School of Business Administration, Boston, 1965.

Walton, R. E. "Alienation in Work Organizing," a project in the Graduate School of Business Administration, Harvard University.

Ways, Max. "Equality: A Steep and Endless Stair," *Fortune*, March 1972.

Weisskoff, Francine Blau. " 'Women's Place' in the Labor Market," *American Economic Review*, May 1972.

Whiting, Basil. *The Suddenly Remembered American*, draft, Ford Foundation, 1971.

Whyte, William H., Jr. *Organization Man*, Anchor Books, Garden City, New York, 1957.

Wilson, N.A.B. "The Quality of Working Life: A Personal Report to the NATO Committee on Challenges of Modern Society," 1971.

"The World of the Blue Collar Worker, (Special Issue)," *Dissent*, Winter 1972.

"Work Attitudes of Disadvantaged Black Men," U.S. Department of Labor, U.S. Government Printing Office, Washington, D.C., 1972.

Yankelovich, Daniel. *The Changing Values on Campus: Political and Personal Attitudes on Campus*, Washington Square Press, New York, 1972.

Zellner, Harriet. "Discrimination Against Women, Occupational Segregation, and the Relative Wage," *American Economic Review*, May 1972.

Chapter 3

Alderfer, C. P. "Job Enlargement and the Organizational Context," *Personnel Psychology*, Vol. 22, 1969.

Antonovsky, A. "Social Class and the Major Cardiovascular Diseases," *Journal of Chronic Diseases*, Vol. 21, 1968.

Argyris, C. "Individual Actualization in Complex Organizations," *Mental Hygiene*, Vol. 44, 1960.

Auster, Simon L. "Psychological Problems in the Context of Work and Industry," address before conference on Nursing Practices and Occupational Mental Health, February 1966.

Back, K. W. and Gergen, K. J. "Personal Orientation and Morale of the Aged," in I. H. Simpson and J. C. McKinney, eds., *Social Aspects of Aging*, Duke University Press, Durham, North Carolina, 1966.

Bartlett, Lewis. "Productive Participation," *Occupational Mental Health*, Vol. I, No. 2, Winter 1972.

Benet, Sula. "Why They Live to Be 100, or Even Older, in Abkhasia," *New York Times Magazine*, December 26, 1972.

Bisgeier, George. "How Many New Employees Are Drug Abusers?," *Industrial Medicine*, Vol. 39, No. 8, August 1970.

Bradburn, N. *The Structure of Psychological Well-Being*, Aldine Press, Chicago, 1969.

Brady, J. V. "Ulcers in the Executive Monkeys," *Scientific American*, Vol. 99, 1958.

Breed, W. "Occupational Mobility and Suicide," *American Sociological Review*, Vol. 28, 1963.

Brenner, M. H. "Patterns of Psychiatric Hospitalization Among Different Socioeconomic Groups in Response to Economic Stress," *Journal of Nervous and Mental Diseases*, Vol. 148, 1968.

————. "Economic Change and Mental Hospitalization: New York State, 1910–1960," *Social Psychiatry*, Vol. 2, 1967.

Brown, G. W. "The Experiences of Discharged Chronic Schizophrenic Patients in Various Types of Living Groups," *Milbank Memorial Fund Quarterly*, Vol. 37, 1959.

Caplan, R. *Organizational Stress and Individual Strain: A Social-Psychological Study of Risk Factors in Coronary Heart Disease Among Administrators, Engineers, and Scientists*, unpublished Ph.D. thesis, University of Michigan, 1971.

————, and French, J. R. P., Jr. "Final Report to NASA," unpublished manuscript, University of Michigan, 1968.

Cassel, J. and Tyroler, H. A. "Epidemiological Studies of Culture Change," *Archives of Environmental Health*, Vol. 3, 1961.

Chinoy, Ely. *Automobile Workers and the American Dream*, Doubleday, Garden City, 1955.

"Clinical Health Age: 30–40," *Business Week*, March 3, 1956.

Cobb, S. *The Frequency of the Rheumatic Diseases*, Harvard University Press, Cambridge, Massachusetts, 1971.

————. "A Report on the Health of Air Traffic Controllers Based on Aeromedical Examination Data," unpublished report to the Federal Aviation Agency, University of Michigan, 1972.

———— et al. "Social Class Gradient of Serum Uric Acid Levels in Males," *The Journal of the American Medical Association*, Vol. 189, August 10, 1963.

————, Brooks, G. W., Kasl, S. V., and Connelly, W. E. "The Health of People Changing Jobs: A Description of a Longitudinal Study," *American Journal of Public Health*, Vol. 56, 1966.

————, and Dunn, James P. "Frequency of Peptic Ulcer Among Executives, Craftsmen, and Foremen," *Journal of Occupational Medicine*, Vol. 4, No. 7, July 1962.

————, and Hall, W. "Newly Identified Cluster of Diseases: Rheumatoid Arthritis, Peptic Ulcer and Tuberculosis," *Journal of the American Medical Association*, Vol. 18, 1965.

————, and Kasl, Stanislav. "Blood Pressure Changes in Men Undergoing Job Loss: A Preliminary Report," *Psychosomatic Medicine*, January/February 1970.

————, "Some Medical Aspects of Unemployment," Institute for Social Research, University of Michigan, 1971.

————, and Lincoln, T. A. "The Prevalence of Mild Rheumatoid Arthritis in Industry," *Journal of Occupational Medicine*, Vol. 5, No. 1, January 1963.

Coffee, Donn and McLean, Alan. "Mental Health in Industry: Whose Responsibility?," *Journal of Occupational Medicine*, Vol. 9, No. 5, May 1967.

Dawis, R. V., England, G. W., and Lofquist, L. H. *Minnesota Studies in Vocational Rehabilitation*, Vol. XV, *A Theory of Work Adjustment*, Industrial Relations Center, University of Minnesota, Minneapolis, 1964.

Dayton, N. A. *New Facts on Mental Disorder*, C. C. Thomas, Springfield, Illinois, 1940.

Dohrenwend, B. P., and Dohrenwend, B. S. *Social Status and Psychological Disorder: A Causal Inquiry*, Wiley, New York, 1969.

"The Effects of Occupational Status on Physical and Mental Health," *Journal of Social Issues*, Vol. XVIII, No. 3, July 1962.

Erikson, E. H. "The Problems of Ego Identity," *Journal of American Psychoanalysis Association*, Vol. 4, 1956.

————. "The Healthy Personality," in *Identity and the Life Cycle, Psychological Issues, Monograph 1*. International Universities Press, New York, 1959.

Felton, J. S. and Cole, R. "The High Cost of Heart Disease," *Circulation*, Vol. 27, 1963.

Freeman, H. E. and Simmons, O. G. "Mental Patients in the Community: Family Settings and Performance Levels," *American Sociological Review*, Vol. 23, 1958.

French, John R. P., Jr. "The Social Environment and Mental Health," *Journal of Social Issues*, Vol. 19, No. 4, 1963.

————, and Caplan, Robert. "Psychosocial Factors in Coronary Heart Disease," *Industrial Medicine*, Vol. 39, No. 9, September 1970.

————, "Organizational Stress and Individual Strain," to appear in A. Marrow, ed., *The Failure of Success*, forthcoming.

————, and Kahn, Robert L. "A Programmatic Approach to Studying the Industrial Environmental and Mental Health," *Social Issues*, Vol. XVIII, No. 3, July 1962.

————, Rodgers, W., and Cobb, S. "Adjustment as Person-Environment Fit," in D. Hamburg and G. Coelho, eds., *Coping*, in press, 1972.

————, Tupper, J., and Mueller, E. *Work Load of University Professors*, Cooperative Research Project No. 2171, U.S. Office of Education, University of Michigan, Ann Arbor, 1965.

Fried, M. "Social Differences in Mental Health," in J. Kosa, A. Antonovsky, and I. K. Zola, eds., *Poverty and Health: A Sociological Analysis*, Harvard University Press, Cambridge, Massachusetts, 1969.

Friedman, M., Rosenman, R. H., and Carroll, V. "Changes in the Serum Cholesterol and Blood Clotting Time of Men Subject to Cyclic Variation of Occupational Stress," *Circulation*, Vol. 17, 1957.

Fromm, Erich. "The Erich Fromm Theory of Aggression," *New York Times Magazine*, February 27, 1972.

Garfield, Frederick M. "The Drug Problem and Industry," *Industrial Medicine*, Vol. 39, No. 8, August 1970.

Gomersall, Earl R. and Myers, M. Scott. "Breakthrough in On the Job Training," *Harvard Business Review,* Vol. 44, No. 4, July/August 1966.

Gross, E. "Work, Organization, and Stress," in S. Levine and N. A. Scotch, eds., *Social Stress,* Aldine, Chicago, 1970.

Gurin, Gerald, Vernoff, Joseph, and Field, Sheila. *Americans View Their Mental Health,* Basic Books, New York, 1960.

Harrington, J. A. and Cross, K. W. "Cases of Attempted Suicide Admitted to a General Hospital," *British Medical Journal,* Vol. 2, 1959.

Henry, A. F. and Short, J. F., Jr. *Suicide and Homicide,* The Free Press, Glencoe, Illinois, 1954.

Hinkle, L. E., Jr. "Physical Health, Mental Health, and the Social Environment: Some Characteristics of Healthy and Unhealthy People," in R. H. Ojemann, ed., *Recent Contributions of Biological and Psychosocial Investigations to Preventive Psychiatry,* State University of Iowa, Iowa City, 1959.

Hinrichs, J. R. "Psychology of Man at Work," in P. H. Mussen and M. R. Rosenzweig, eds., *Annual Review of Psychology,* Annual Reviews, Palo Alto, California, Vol. 21, 1970.

Holmes, T. H. and Rahe, R. H. "The Social Readjustment Rating Scale," *Journal of Psychosomatic Research,* Vol. 11, 1967.

House, J. S. *The Relationship of Intrinsic and Extrinsic Work Motivations to Occupational Stress and Coronary Heart Disease Risk,* unpublished Ph.D. thesis, University of Michigan, 1972.

Jackson, E. F. "Status Consistency and Symptoms of Stress," *American Sociological Review,* Vol. 27, 1962.

Jacques, Elliot. *Work, Creativity, and Social Justice,* International Universities Press, New York, 1970.

Jenkins, C. D. "Psychologic and Social Precursors of Coronary Disease," *New England Journal of Medicine,* Vol. 284, 1971.

———, Rosenman, R. H., and Friedman, M. "Development of an Objective Psychological Test for the Determination of the Coronary-prone Behavior Pattern," *Journal of Chronic Diseases,* Vol. 20, 1967.

Kahn, R. L. and French, J. R. P., Jr. "Status and Conflict: Two Themes in the Study of Stress," in J. McGrath, ed., *Social and Psychological Factors in Stress,* Holt, Rinehart, and Winston, New York, 1970.

———. "A Summary and Some Tentative Conclusions," *Social Issues,* Vol. XVIII, No. 3, July 1962.

———, and Quinn, R. P. "Role Stress: A Framework for Analysis," in A. McLean, ed., *Mental Health and Work Organizations,* Rand McNally, Chicago, 1970.

———, Wolfe, D. M., Quinn, R. P., Snoek, J. D., and Rosenthal, R. H. *Organizational Stress: Studies in Role Conflict and Ambiguity,* Wiley, New York, 1964.

Karcher, Charles J. and Linden, Leonard L. *Family Rejection of the Aged and Nursing Home Utilization,* mimeograph, Department of Sociology, University of Georgia, 1972.

Kasl, S. V. and Cobb, S. "Effects of Parental Status Incongruence and Discrepancy on Physical and Mental Health of Adult Offspring," *Journal of Personnel and Social Psychology Monogram,* Vol. 7, 1967.

———. "The Intrafamilial Transmission of Rheumatoid Arthritis: VI, Association of Rheumatoid Arthritis With Several Types of Status Inconsistency," *Journal of Chronic Diseases,* Vol. 22, 1969.

———. "Some Physical and Mental Health Effects of Job Loss," *Pakistan Medical Forum,* Vol. 6, 1971.

———. "Physical and Mental Health Correlates of Status Incongruence," *Social Psychiatry,* Vol. 6, No. 1, 1971.

———, and Brooks. "Changes in Serum Uric Acid and Cholesterol Levels in Men Undergoing Job Loss," *Journal of the American Medical Association,* Vol. 206, 1968.

———, and Gore, S. "Changes in Reported Illness and Illness Behavior Related to Termination of Employment: A Preliminary Report," in press, 1972.

———, and French, J. R. P., Jr. "The Effects of Occupational Status on Physical and Mental Health," *Journal of Social Issues,* Vol. 18, 1962.

King, S. H. and Cobb, S. "Psychosocial Factors in the Epidemiology of Rheumatoid Arthritis," *Journal of Chronic Diseases,* Vol. 7, 1958.

Kitagawa, Evelyn M. and Hauser, P. M. "Education Differentials in Mortality by Cause of Death: United States, 1960," *Demography,* Vol. 5, 1968.

Kleiner, R. J. and Parker, S. "Goal Striving, Social Status, and Mental Disorder," *American Sociological Review,* Vol. 28, 1963.

Kornhauser, Arthur. *Mental Health of the Industrial Worker,* Wiley, New York, 1965.

———. "Mental Health of Factory Workers," *Human Organization,* Vol. 21, Spring 1962.

Kraut, A. *A Study of Role Conflicts and Their Relationship to Job Satisfaction, Tension, and Performance,* unpublished Ph.D. thesis, University of Michigan, 1965.

Kuhn, David, Slocum, John W., and Chase, Richard. "Does Job Performance Affect Employee Satisfaction?," *Personnel Journal,* Vol. 30, No. 6, June 1971.

Langner, T. S. and Michael, S. T. *Life Stress and Mental Health,* The Free Press of Glencoe, New York, 1963.

Lazarus, R. S. *Psychological Stress and the Coping Process,* McGraw-Hill, New York, 1966.

Lerner, M. "Social Differences in Physical Health," in J. Kosa, A. Antonovsky, and I. K. Zola, eds., *Poverty and Health: A Sociological Analysis*, Harvard University Press, Cambridge, Massachusetts, 1969.

Lester, D. "Suicide and Unemployment," *Archives of Environmental Health*, Vol. 20, 1970.

Levine, S. and Scotch, N. *Social Stress*, Aldine, Chicago, 1971.

Levinson, Harry. *Executive Stress*, Harper and Row, New York, 1964.

————. "Emotional Toxicity of the Work Environment," *Archives of Environmental Health*, Vol. 19, August 1969.

Lewin, K., Lippitt, R., and White, R. "Patterns of Aggressive Behavior in Experimentally Created 'Social Climates,'" *Journal of Social Psychology*, Vol. 10, 1939.

Li, Frederick P. "Suicide Among Chemists," *Archives of Environmental Health*, Vol. 20, March 1970.

Linden, Leonard L. and Reinhart, George. "Suicide By Industry and Occupation: A Structural-Change Approach," presentation before Southern Sociological Society, May 1971.

Mann, F. C. and Williams, L. K. "Some Effects of the Changing Work Environment in the Office," *Journal of Social Issues*, Vol. 18, 1962.

Marcson, S., ed. *Automation, Alienation, and Anomie*, Harper and Row, New York, 1970.

Marks, J., Stouffacher, J., and Lyle, C. "Predicting Outcome in Schizophrenia," *Journal of Abnormal Social Psychology*, Vol. 66, 1963.

Marks, Renee. "Factors Involving Social and Demographic Characteristics: A Review of Empirical Findings," *Milbank Memorial Fund Quarterly*, Vol. 45, Part 2, 1967.

Matsumoto, Y. S. "Social Stress and Coronary Heart Disease in Japan: A Hypothesis," *Milbank Memorial Fund Quarterly*, Vol. 48, 1970.

McCord, Carey P. "Life and Death by the Minute," *Industrial Medicine*, Vol. 17, No. 10, October 1948.

McGrath, J. E., ed. *Social and Psychological Factors in Stress*, Holt, Rinehart and Winston, New York, 1970.

McLean, Alan, ed. *To Work is Human: Mental Health and the Business Community*, Macmillan, New York, 1967.

————., *Mental Health and Work Organizations*, Rand McNally, 1970.

————, and Taylor, G. C. *Mental Health in Industry*, McGraw-Hill, New York, 1958.

McQuade, Walter. "What Stress Can Do To You," *Fortune*, January 1972.

Mechanic, D. *Mental Health and Social Policy*, Prentice-Hall, Englewood Cliffs, New Jersey, 1969.

Meltzer, H. "Mental Health Implications of Aging in Industry," *Journal of Genetic Psychology*, Vol. 107, 1965.

"Mental Health and Work," *Mental Health Digest*, Vol. 4, No. 3, March 1972.

Milbank Memorial Fund Quarterly, Entire Issue: "Social Stress and Cardiovascular Disease," Vol. 24, Part 2, 1967.

Miles, H. H. W., Waldfogel, S., Barrabee, E., and Cobb, S. "Psychosomatic Study of 46 Young Men with Coronary Artery Disease," *Psychosomatic Medicine*, Vol. 16, 1954.

Miller, D. R. "The Study of Social Relationships: Situation, Identity, and Social Interaction," in S. Koch, ed., *Psychology: A Study of A Science*, McGraw-Hill, New York, Vol. 5, 1963.

Montoye, H. J., Faulkner, J. A., Dodge, H. J., Mikkelson, W. M., Willis, R. W. III, and Block, W. D. "Serum Uric Acid Concentration Among Business Executives With Observations On Other Coronary Heart Disease Risk Factors," *Annals of Internal Medicine*, Vol. 66, 1967.

Moriyama, I. M., Krueger, D. E., and Stamler, J. *Cardiovascular Diseases in the United States*, Harvard University Press, Cambridge, Massachusetts, 1971.

Mott, Paul E., et al. *Shift Work: The Social, Psychological and Physical Consequences*, University of Michigan Press, Ann Arbor, 1965.

Mueller, Ernst et al. "Psychological Correlates of Serum Urate Levels," *Psychological Bulletin*, Vol. 73, No. 4, 1970.

Myers, J. K. and Bean, L. L. *A Decade Later: A Follow-up of Social Class and Mental Illness*, Wiley, New York, 1968.

Neel, R. "Nervous Stress in the Industrial Situation, *Personnel Psychology*, Vol. 8, 1955.

Neugarten, B. L. "Adult Personality: Toward a Psychology of the Life Cycle," in B. L. Neugarter, ed., *Middle Age and Aging*, University of Chicago Press, Chicago, 1968.

Palmore, Erdman. "Predicting Longevity: A Follow-up Controlling For Age," *Gerontology*, Winter 1969.

———. "Physical, Mental, and Social Factors in Predicting Longevity," *Gerontology*, Vol. 9, 1969.

———, and Jeffers, F., eds. *Prediction of Life Span*, D. C. Heath, Lexington, Mass., 1971.

Parsons, T. "Definitions of Health and Illness in the Light of American Values and Social Structure," in E. G. Jaco, ed., *Patients, Physicians, and Illness*, The Free Press, Glencoe, Illinois, 1958.

Paykel, E. S., Prusoff, B. A., and Uhlenhuth, E. H. "Scaling Life Events," *Archives of General Psychiatry*, Vol. 25, 1971.

Pearson, H. E. S. and Joseph, J. "Stress and Occlusive Coronary-Artery Disease," *The Lancet*, Vol. I, 1963.

Pepitone, A. "Self, Social Environment, and Stress," in M. H. Appley and D. Trumbull, eds., *Psychological Stress*, Appleton-Century-Crofts, New York, 1967.

Rahe, R. H. "Life Crisis and Health Change," in P.R.A. May and J. R. Wittenborn, eds., *Psychotropic Drug Response: Advances in Prediction*, C. C. Thomas, Springfield, Illinois, 1969.

Roman, P. M. "The Etiology of Psychiatric Disorders in Work Organizations," *Archives of Environmental Health*, Vol. 19, 1969.

———, and Trice, Harrison M. "The Development of Deviant Drinking Behavior," *Archives of Environmental Health*, Vol. 20, March 1970.

Russek, H. I. "Emotional Stress and Coronary Heart Disease in American Physicians, Dentists, and Lawyers," *American Journal of Medical Science*, Vol. 243, 1962.

———. "Stress, Tobacco, and Coronary Heart Disease in North American Professional Groups," *Journal of the American Medical Association*, Vol. 192, 1965.

Sales, S. M. *Differences Among Individuals in Affective, Behavioral, Biochemical, and Physiological Responses to Variations in Work Load*, unpublished Ph.D. thesis, University of Michigan, 1969.

———. "Organizational Roles as a Risk Factor in Coronary Heart Disease," *Administrative Science Quarterly*, Vol. 14, No. 3, 1969.

———, and House, J. "Job Dissatisfaction as a Possible Risk Factor in Coronary Heart Disease," *Journal of Chronic Diseases*, Vol. 23, 1971.

Scott, W. A. "Research Definitions of Mental Health and Mental Illness," *Psychology Bulletin*, Vol. 55, 1958.

Seashore, S. *Group Cohesiveness in the Industrial Work Group*, Institute for Social Research, Ann Arbor, Michigan, 1954.

Seeman, M. "On the Personal Consequences of Alienation in Work," *American Sociological Review*, Vol. 32, 1967.

"Selected Bibliography on Occupational Mental Health," U.S. Department of Health, Education, and Welfare, U.S. Government Printing Office, Washington, D.C.

Sells, S. B., ed. *The Definition and Measurement of Mental Health*, Public Health Service, U.S. Department of Health, Educations, and Welfare, Washington, D.C., 1968.

Selye, H. *The Stress of Life*, McGraw-Hill, New York, 1956.

Sexton, W. P. "Industrial Work: Who Calls it Psychologically Devastating?," *Management of Personnel Quarterly*, Vol. 6, 1968.

Shore, Milton and Massimo, Joseph. "The Chronic Delinquent During Adolescence: A New Opportunity for Intervention," in G. Caplan and S. Lebovici, eds., *Adolescence, Psychosocial Perspectives*, Basic Books, New York, 1969.

―――. "A Comprehensive Vocationally Oriented Psychotherapeutic Program for Delinquent Boys," *The American Journal of Orthopsychiatry,* Vol. 33, No. 4, July 1963.

―――. "Five Years Later: A Follow-up Study of Comprehensive Vocationally Oriented Psychotherapy," *American Journal of Orthopsychiatry,* Vol. 39, No. 5, October 1969.

Simmons, Ozzie G. *Work and Mental Illness: Eight Case Studies,* Wiley, New York, 1965.

Slote, Alfred. *Termination: The Closing of the Baker Plant,* Bobbs-Merrill, Indianapolis, 1969.

Smith, M. B. "Mental Health Reconsidered: A Special Case of the Problem of Values in Psychology," *American Psychologist,* Vol. 16, 1961.

Smith, Thomasina. "Sociocultural Incongruity and Change: A Review of Empirical Findings," *Milbank Memorial Fund Quarterly,* Vol. 45, No. 2, Part 2, 1967.

Strauss, G. "The Set-up Man: A Case Study of Organizational Change," *Human Organization,* Vol. 13, 1954.

Streib, G. "Morale of the Retired," *Social Problems,* Vol. 3, 1956.

Suchman, E. A. "Factors Involving Social and Demographic Characteristics: Appraisal and Implications for Theoretical Development," *Milbank Memorial Fund Quarterly,* Vol. 45, No. 2, Part 2, 1967.

Susser, M. "Causes of Peptic Ulcer: A Selective Epidemiologic Review," *Journal of Chronic Diseases,* Vol. 20, 1967.

Sulley, C. M. and Munden, K. J. "Behavior of the Mentally Healthy," *Bulletin of the Menninger Clinic,* Vol. 26, 1962.

Swados, Harvey. *On the Line,* Little, Brown, Boston, 1957.

Terreberry, Shirley. *The Organization of Environments,* unpublished Ph.D. thesis, University of Michigan, 1968.

Thompson, W. E., and Streib, G. F. "Situational Determinants: Health and Economic Deprivation in Retirement," *Journal of Social Issues,* Vol. 14, 1958.

―――, and Kosa, J. "The Effect of Retirement on Personal Adjustment: A Panel Analysis," *Journal of Gerontology,* Vol. 15, 1960.

Veroff, J. and Feld, S. *Marriage and Work in America: A Study of Motives and Roles,* Von Nostrand-Reinhold, New York, 1970.

Vertin, P. G. *Bedryfsgeneeskundige As Pecten van het ulcus pepticum* (Occupational Health Aspects of Peptic Ulcer), thesis, Groningen, Netherlands, 1954.

Vroom, V. "Industrial Social Psychology," in G. Lindzey and E. Aronson, eds., *Handbook of Social Psychology,* Vol. V (second edition), Addison-Wesley, Reading, Massachusetts, 1968.

Weiss, E., Dlin, B., Rollin, H. R., Fischer, H. K., and Bepler, C. R. "Emotional Factors in Coronary Occlusion," *Archives of Internal Medicine*, Vol. 99, 1957.

Zaleznik, A., Ondrack, J., and Silver, A. "Social Class, Occupation, and Mental Illness," in A. McLean ed., *Mental Health and Work Organizations*, Rand McNally, Chicago, 1970.

Zander, A. and Quinn, R. "The Social Environment and Mental Health: A Review of Past Research at the Institute for Social Research," *Journal of Social Issues*, Vol. 18, No. 3, 1962.

Chapter 4

Argyris, Chris. "The Individual and the Organization: An Empirical Test," *Administrative Science Quarterly*, Vol. 4, No. 2, 1959.

――――. *Integrating the Organization and the Individual*, Wiley, New York, 1964.

――――. *Personality and Organization*, Harper and Row, New York, 1957.

Athanasiou, R. "Job Attitudes and Occupational Performance: A Review of Some Important Literature," in J. P. Robinson, R. Athanasiou, and K. B. Head, eds., *Measures of Occupational Attitudes and Occupational Characteristics*, Survey Research Center, University of Michigan, Ann Arbor, Michigan, 1969.

Brooks, George. "History of Union Efforts to Reduce Working Hours," *Monthly Labor Review*, Vol. 79, 1956.

Burden, D. W. E. "Participative Approach to Management: Microwax Department," Shell U. K. Ltd., unpublished report, 1972.

Chevalier, G. G. "Socio-Technical Experiment in Casting Department," Aluminum Co. of Canada, Ltd., unpublished report, 1972.

Clark, Peter A. *Organizational Design*, Tavistock Publications, London, 1972.

Conant, E. H. and Kilbridge, M. D. "An Interdisciplinary Analysis of Job Enlargement: Technology, Costs and Behavioral Implications," *Industrial and Labor Relations Review*, Vol. XVIII, October 1965.

Constandse, William J. "A Neglected Personnel Problem," *Personnel Journal*, February 1972.

D'Aprix, Roger. "Coping With Company Power," *Industry Week*, May 31, 1971.

Davis, Louis E. "Job Satisfaction Research: The Post-Industrial View," Institute of Industrial Relations, University of California, Los Angeles, 1971.

――――, and Trist, Eric. "Improving the Quality of Work Life: Experience of the Socio-Technical Approach," Management and Behavioral Science Center, University of Pennsylvania, 1972.

————. "The Coming Crisis for Production Management: Technology and Organization," *International Journal of Production Research*, Vol. 9, No. 1, 1971.

————. "Toward a Theory of Job Design," *Journal of Industrial Engineering*, Vol. 8, 1957.

————, and Canter, R. R. "Job Design Research," *Journal of Industrial Engineering*, Vol. VII, 1956.

————, and Taylor, J. C. *The Design of Jobs*, Penguin Books, Baltimore, 1972.

————, and Valfer, E. S. "Supervisor Job Design," Proceedings of the Second International Congress on Ergonomics, *Ergonomics*, Vol. VIII, 1965, and "Intervening Responses to Changes in Supervisor Job Designs," *Occupational Psychology*, Vol. XXXIX, 1965.

————, and Werling, R. "Job Design Factors," *Occupational Psychology*, Vol. XXXIV, 1960.

Dettleback, William and Kraft, Philip. "Organization Change Through Job Enrichment," *Training and Development Journal*, August 1971.

Deutsch, M. "An Experiment Study of the Effects of Cooperation and Competition Upon Group Process," *Human Relations*, Vol. 2, 1949.

Emery, F. E. and Thorsrud, E. *Industrial Democracy*, Tavistock, London, 1969.

Fein, Mitchell. *Motivation for Work*, American Institute of Industrial Engineers, Inc., New York, 1971.

Ford, Robert N. "The Third Revolution in Work," *Bell Telephone Magazine*, March/April 1971.

Gilliam, Marco. "They Really Want To Do a Good Job if We'll Let 'em . . . ," *Bell Telephone Magazine*, January/February 1971.

Herrick, Neal. "Activities to Enrich Work in Other Developed Countries," paper delivered before the American Association for the Advancement of Science, Philadelphia, December 27, 1971.

————. "The Other Side of the Coin," paper delivered before seminar sponsored by the Profit Sharing Research Foundation, Evanston, Illinois, November 17, 1971.

Herzberg, Frederick. "One More Time: How Do You Motivate Employees?," *Harvard Business Review*, January/February 1968.

Hulin, Charles L. "Individual Differences and Job Enrichment—The Case Against General Treatment," in John Maher, ed., *New Perspectives in Job Enrichment*, Von Nostrand-Reinhold, New York, 1971.

"Is Labor Movement Losing Ground?," *U.S. News and World Report*, February 21, 1972.

Jehring, J. J. "Profit Sharing and Economic Change—Some New Ways to Look at Profit Sharing as a Motivator for Increasing Productivity," speech given at Wingspread in Racine, Wisconsin, on November 17, 1971.

"Job Enrichment Bibliography," Roy W. Walters and Associates, Inc., Glen Rock, New Jersey, April 1972.

"Job Enrichment Results," Roy W. Walters and Associates, Inc., April 1972.

Johnson, Haynes and Kotz, Nick. "The Unions," series in *Washington Post*, April 9–15, 1972.

Jones, S. C. and Vroom, V. H. "Division of Labor and Performance Under Cooperative and Competitive Conditions," *Journal of Abnormal and Social Psychology*, Vol. 68, March 1964.

Lawler, E. E., III. "Job Design and Employee Motivation," *Personnel Psychology*, Vol. 22, No. 4, 1969.

Likert, Rensis. *The Human Organization*, McGraw-Hill, New York, 1967.

————. *New Patterns of Management*, McGraw-Hill, New York, 1961.

Marrow, Alfred J., Bowers, David G., and Seashore, Stanley E. *Management by Participation, Creating a Climate for Personal and Organizational Development*, Harper and Row, New York, 1967.

Metzger, Bert. "Socio-Economic Participation: Key to a Better World of Work in the Future," Profit-Sharing Research Foundation, Evanston, Illinois.

————, and Colletti, Jerome A. *Does Profit Sharing Pay?*, Profit Sharing Research Foundation, Evanston, Illinois, 1971.

Morse, Nancy C., and Reimer, E. "The Experimental Change of a Major Organizational Variable," *Journal of Abnormal and Social Psychology*, Vol. 52, 1956.

Pateman, Carole. *Participation and Democratic Theory*, Cambridge University Press, New York, 1970.

Paul, W. J. and Robertson, K. B. *Job Enrichment and Employee Motivation*, Gower Press, London, 1970.

Percy, Senator Charles H. and Javits, Senator Jacob K. "How Good is the News about Productivity?," *Fortune*, May 1972.

Rosow, Jerome M. "Closing the Gap Between Manufacturing Goals and Actual Productivity," *Apparel Manufacturer*, March 1971.

Rush, Harold M. F. "Job Design for Motivation," The Conference Board, New York, 1971.

Sherif, M. and Sherif, Carolyn W. *Groups in Harmony and Tension: An Integration of Studies on Intergroup Relations*, Harper, New York, 1953.

Steiger, William A. "Can We Legislate the Humanization of Work?," paper delivered before the American Association for the Advancement of Science, Philadelphia, December 27, 1971.

Teague, Burton. "Can Workers Participate in Management—Successfully?," *The Conference Board Record*, July 1971.

Thompson, Donald B. "Enrichment in Action Convinces Skeptics," *Industry Week*, February 14, 1972.

Trist, E. L., Higgin, G. W., Murray, H., and Pollock, A. B. *Organizational Choice*, Tavistock Publications, London, 1963.

Vroom, V. H. *Some Personality Determinants of the Effects of Participation*, Prentice-Hall, Englewood Cliffs, New Jersey, 1960.

Walton, Richard E. "Work Place Alienation and the Need for Major Innovation," Graduate School of Business Administration, Harvard.

"Workers Learn Varied Jobs in Sweden's Auto Plants," *New York Times*, July 31, 1972.

"The Working Conditions Survey as a Source of Social Indicators," *Monthly Labor Review*, April 1971.

Chapter 5

Arensberg, C. M. and Kimball, S. T. "The Small Farm Family in Rural Ireland," in Michael Anderson, ed., *Sociology of the Family*, Penguin Books, 1971.

Bachman, Jerald G., Green, Swayzer, and Wirtanen, Ilona. *Youth in Transition (Vol. III): Dropping Out—Problem or Symptom?*, Institute for Social Research, University of Michigan, 1971.

Banta, Trudy W. and Marshall, Patricia. "Schools and Industry," *Manpower*, June 1970.

Baritz, Loren. *The Servants of Power*, Wesleyan University, Middleton, Connecticut, 1960.

Becker, Gary. *Human Capital*, University of Chicago Press, Chicago, 1964.

Belitsky, Harvey. *Private Vocational Schools and Their Students: Limited Objectives, Unlimited Opportunities*, Schenkman, Cambridge, Massachusetts, 1969.

Bendix, Reinhard and Lipset, Seymour M. *Social Mobility in Industrial Society*, University of California Press, Berkeley, 1959.

Berg, Ivar. *Education and Jobs: The Great Training Robbery*, Praeger, New York, 1972.

Blaug, Mark, ed. *Economics of Education*, Vol. 1, Penguin Books, 1968.

Block, J. H., et al. *Mastery Learning*, Holt, Rinehart and Winston, New York, 1971.

Boocook, S. and Schild, E., eds. *Simulation Games in Learning*, Sege Publications, Beverly Hills, California, 1968.

Borow, H. "Development of Occupational Motives and Roles," in L. S. Hoffman and M. C. Hoffman, eds., *Review of Child Development Research*, Russell Sage Foundation, New York, 1966.

Boschan, C. *Fluctuation in Job Vacancies—An Analysis of Available Measures*, National Bureau of Economic Research Reports, New York, 1965.

Bowlby, R. L. and Schriver, W. R. "Nonwage Benefits of Vocational Training: Employability and Mobility," *Industrial and Labor Relations Review*, July 1970.

Bronfenbrenner, Urie. *Two Worlds of Childhood*, Russell Sage Foundation, New York, 1970.

————. "The Roots of Alienation," unpublished paper, Cornell University.

Bushnell, David S. "The Value of Vocational Education," in R. A. Gordon, ed., *Toward A Manpower Policy*, New York, 1967.

————, and Yoder, D. *Training in Industry*, Stanford Research Institute, Long Range Planning Service Report No. 148, Menlo Park, California, 1962.

————, and Zagaris, Ivars. *Report from Project Focus: Strategies for Change*, American Association of Junior Colleges, Washington, D.C., 1972.

Carroll, Adger B. and Ihnen, Loren A. *Costs and Returns of Technical Education: A Pilot Study*, Department of Economics, North Carolina State University at Raleigh, July 1966.

Carter, Michael. *Into Work*, Penguin Books, Baltimore, 1966.

Cliff, Samuel H. and Hecht, Robert. "Job/Man Matching in the Seventies," *Datamation*, February 1, 1971.

"College Educated Workers, 1968–80," U.S. Department of Labor, U.S. Government Printing Office, Washington, D.C., 1970.

Corrazini, Arthur. *Vocational Education: A Study of Benefits and Costs*, Princeton University, 1966.

Cunningham, J. S., ed. *The Job Cluster and Its Curricular Implications: A Symposium*, Center for Occupational Education, Raleigh, University of North Carolina, 1969.

Davis, Louis E. "Readying the Unready: Postindustrial Jobs," *California Management Review*, Vol. XIII, No. 4, Summer 1971.

Dobell, A. R. and Ho, Y. C. "An Optimal Unemployment Rate," *Quarterly Journal of Economics*, Vol. 81, November 1967.

"Educational Attainment of Workers, March 1971," U.S. Department of Labor, U.S. Government Printing Office, Washington, D.C., 1972.

"Education of Adult Workers: Projections to 1985," U.S. Department of Labor, U.S. Government Printing Office, Washington, D.C., 1970.

Education for a Changing World of Work, report of the Panel of Consultants on Vocational Education, Washington, 1963.

Education Vouchers: A Report on Financing Elementary Education by Grants to Parents, Center for the Study of Public Policy, Harvard University, Cambridge, Massachusetts, 1970.

"Employment of High School Graduates and Dropouts, October 1970," U.S. Department of Labor, U.S. Government Printing Office, Washington, D.C., 1971.

"Employment of School Age Youth," U.S. Department of Labor, U.S. Government Printing Office, Washington, D.C., 1971.

Eninger, Max U. *The Process and Product of T&I High School Level Vocational Education in the United States: The Product,* American Institutes for Research, Pittsburgh, 1965.

————. *The Process and Product of T&I High School Level Vocational Education in the U.S.: The Process Variables,* Vol. II, Educational Systems Research Institute, Pittsburgh, 1968.

Evans, Rupert N. "School for Schooling's Sake: The Current Role of the Secondary School in Occupational Preparation," in *The Transition From School to Work,* Industrial Relations Section, Research Report Series No. 111, 1968.

————, Mangum, Garth L. and Pragan, Otto, eds. *Education for Employment: The Background and Potential of the 1968 Vocational Education Amendments,* Institute of Labor and Industrial Relations, Ann Arbor, Michigan, 1969.

Flanagan, J. C., et al. *Project Talent: Five Years After High School,* American Institute for Research and University of Pittsburgh, 1971.

Gartner, A., Kohler, M., and Riessman, F. *Children Teach Children,* Harper and Row, New York, 1971.

Ginzberg, Eli. "A Critical Look at Career Guidance," *Manpower,* February 1972.

————. "Guidance—Limited or Unlimited?," *Personnel and Guidance Journal,* Vol. 38, 1960.

————. "Vocational Education Is Not the Answer," *Phi Delta Kappa,* February 1971.

Glasser, William. *Schools Without Failure,* Harper and Row, 1969.

Godfrey, Eleanor and Holmstrom, Engin. *Study of Community Colleges and Vocational Technical Centers,* Bureau of Social Science Research, Inc., Washington, D.C., 1970.

Goodlad, J. E. and Anderson, R. H. *The Nongraded Elementary School,* Harcourt, Brace and World, New York, 1963.

Greer, Colin. *The Great School Legend: A Revisionist Interpretation of American Public Education,* Basic Books, New York, 1972.

Gregoire, Roger. *Vocational Education,* Organization for Economic Cooperation and Development, Paris, 1967.

Hall, Robert. "Prospects of Shifting Phillips Curve Through Manpower Policy," Brookings Paper on Economic Activity, III, 1971.

Hamburger, Martin and Wolfson, Harry. *1000 Employers Look at Occupational Education,* Board of Education of the City of New York, July 1969.

Hiestand, Dale. *Changing Careers After Thirty-Five,* Columbia University Press, New York, 1971.

Hillsman, Sally T. *Entry into the Labor Market: The Preparation and Job Placement of Negro and White Vocational High School Graduates*, Ph.D. dissertation, Columbia University, 1970.

Holt, C. C. and Huber, G. P. "A Computer-Aided Approach to Employment Service Placement and Counseling," *Management Science*, Vol. 15, July 1969.

———, and Smith, R. "A Job Search—Turnover Analysis of Black-White Unemployment Ratio," Proceedings of 23rd Annual Meeting of Industrial Relations Association, 1971.

———, MacRae, C. D., Schweitzer, S. O., and Smith, R. E. *The Unemployment–Inflation Dilemma: A Manpower Solution*, Urban Institute, Washington, D.C., 1971.

———. *Manpower Programs to Reduce Inflation and Unemployment: Manpower Lyrics for Macro Music*, Urban Institute, Washington, D.C., 1971.

Hoyt, Kenneth B., Evans, Rupert N., Macken, Edward F., and Mangum, Garth L. *Career Education: What It Is and How To Do It*, Olympus, Salt Lake City, 1972.

Hu, Teh-Wei, Lee, Maw Lin., Stromsdorfer, Ernest W. *A Cost Effectiveness Study of Vocational Education*, Institute for Research on Human Resources, Pennsylvania State University, 1968.

———. "Economic Returns to Vocational and Comprehensive High School Graduates," *Journal of Human Resources*, Winter 1971.

Hurbison, Frederick and Myers, Charles. *Education, Manpower and Economic Growth: Strategies of Human Resource Development*, McGraw-Hill, New York, 1964.

"Inflation, the Present Problem," Organization for Economic Cooperation and Development, Report of the Secretary-General, Paris, 1970.

Janess, R. A. "Manpower Mobility Programs," in G. G. Somers and W. D. Woods, eds., *Cost/Benefit Analysis of Manpower Policies*, Queens University, Kingston, Ontario, 1969.

"Job Opportunities at the Employment Service," U.S. Department of Labor, U.S. Government Printing Office, Washington, D.C., 1968.

Kaufman, Jacob J., et al. *The Role of the Secondary Schools in the Preparation of Youth for Employment*, Institute for Research on Human Resources, Pennsylvania State University, 1967.

———. *An Analysis of Comparative Costs and Benefits of Vocational versus Academic Education in Secondary Schools*, Institute for Research on Human Resources, Pennsylvania State University, 1967.

———, and Lewis, Morgan V. *The Potential of Vocational Education: Observations and Conclusions*, The Institute for Research on Human Resources, Pennsylvania State University, 1968.

———. *The School Environment and Programs for Dropouts*, Institute for Research on Human Resources, Pennsylvania State University, 1968.

Kohen, A. I. and Parnes, H. S. *Career Thresholds,* Center for Human Resource Research, Ohio State University, Columbus, Ohio, Vol. III, June 1971.

Kohl, Herbert R. *The Open Classroom,* Random House, New York, 1969.

Kozol, Jonathan. *Free Schools,* Houghton Mifflin, Boston, 1972.

"Less Time, More Options: Education Beyond the High School," The Carnegie Commission, January 1971.

Levitan, Sar, Mangum, Garth, and Marshall, Ray. *Human Resources and the Labor Market: Labor and Manpower in the American Economy,* Harper and Row, New York, 1972.

Little, J. Kenneth. *Review and Synthesis of Research on the Placement and Follow-Up of Vocational Education Students,* ERIC Clearinghouse on Vocational and Technical Education, Ohio State University, 1970.

MacMichael, David C. "Career Education—Prognosis for a Policy," Stanford Research Institute, Menlo Park, California, 1971.

Mangum, Garth L. "Manpower Research and Manpower Policy," *A Review of Industrial Relations Research,* Vol. II, Industrial Relations Research Association, Madison, 1971.

————. *Reorienting Vocational Education,* The Institute of Labor and Industrial Relations, University of Michigan—Wayne State University, 1968.

"Manpower Policy in the United Kingdom," Organization for Economic Cooperation and Development, Paris, 1970.

Marien, Michael. "Credentialism in Our Ignorant Society," *Notes on the Future of Education,* Vol. II, Issue 3, Summer 1971.

Myers, John and Creamer, Muriel. "Measuring Job Vacancies," National Industrial Conference Board, New York, 1967.

Newman, F., et al. *Report on Higher Education,* U.S. Department of Health, Education, and Welfare, U.S. Government Printing Office, Washington, D.C., 1971.

"Occupational Manpower and Training Needs," U.S. Department of Labor, U.S. Government Printing Office, Washington, D.C., 1971.

Okun, A. "The Gap Between Actual and Potential Output," in *1962 Proceedings of the Business and Economic Section,* American Statistical Association, Washington, D.C., 1963.

Palmer, John L. *Inflation, Unemployment and Poverty,* Ph.D., Stanford University, 1971.

Pearl, A. and Riessman, F. *New Careers for the Poor,* The Free Press, New York, 1969.

Perry, G. L. "Changing Labor Markets and Inflation," *Brookings Papers on Economic Activity,* III, 1970.

Peters, Herman J. and Hansen, James C. *Vocational Guidance and Career Development,* Macmillan, New York, 1970.

Phelps, E. S., ed. *Micro-Economic Foundations of Employment and Inflation Theory*, W. W. Norton, New York, 1970.

Piker, Jeffry. *Entry Into the Labor Force*, Institute of Labor and Industrial Relations, University of Michigan—Wayne State University, 1969.

Piore, Michael J. and Doeringer, Peter B. *Low Income Labor Markets and Urban Manpower Programs*, Cambridge, Massachusetts, 1969.

"Population Estimates and Projections," U.S. Department of Commerce, U.S. Government Printing Office, Washington, D.C., 1970.

"Procedures of the International Conference on Continuing Training and Education During Working Life," Organization for Economic Cooperation and Development, July 1970.

Pucinski, R. C. and Hirsch, S. P. *The Courage to Change: New Directions for Career Education*, Prentice-Hall, Englewood Cliffs, New Jersey, 1971.

Richardson, Elliot L. Address before the National Education Association, 1971.

Rivlin, Alice. "Critical Issues in the Development of Vocational Education," in *Unemployment in a Prosperous Economy*, Industrial Relations Section, Princeton University, Research Report No. 108, 1965.

———. *Systematic Thinking for Social Action*, The Brookings Institution, Washington, 1971.

Roomkin, Myron. *High School Dropouts and Vocational Education in Wisconsin*, Center for Studies in Vocational and Technical Education, University of Wisconsin, Madison, 1970.

"Second Careers as Way of Life: a Symposium," *The Vocational Guidance Quarterly*, Vol. 20, No. 2, December 1971.

Sharp, Laure M. and Krasnegor, Rebecca. *The Use of Follow-Up Studies in the Evaluation of Vocational Education*, Bureau of Social Science Research, Inc., Washington, 1966.

Sheets, Don R. and Dahlor, H. W. "The Cluster Concept: Kansas City Style," *American Vocational Journal*, October 1967.

Sheppard, Harold. "Mid-Career Change," unpublished paper, W. E. Upjohn Institute for Employment Research, Washington, D.C., 1972.

Smith, Harold T. and Thole, Henry C. "Secondary and Postsecondary Occupational Education in Kalamazoo County, Michigan," in Sar A. Levitan and Irving H. Siegel, eds., *Dimensions of Manpower Policy*, Baltimore, 1966.

Somers, Gerald G. *The Effectiveness of Vocational and Technical Programs*, Center for Studies in Vocational and Technical Education, University of Wisconsin, 1971.

———, and Little, J. Kenneth, eds. *Vocational Education: Today and Tomorrow*, Center for Studies in Vocational and Technical Education, University of Wisconsin, Madison, 1971.

Spitaller, Eric. "Prices and Unemployment in Selected Industrial Countries, International Monetary Fund, staff paper, 1971.

Striner, Herbert E. "Continuing Education as a National Capital Investment," W. E. Upjohn Institute for Employment Research, Washington, D.C., 1972.

Super, Donald *The Psychology of Careers,* Harper and Brothers, New York, 1957.

————, et al. *Floundering and Trial After High School,* Columbia University, New York, 1967.

Swanson, J. Chester. *Program-Cost Analyses of Vocational-Technical Education in a Junior College and in a Unified School District,* University of California at Berkeley, 1969.

Taussig, Michael K. "An Economic Analysis of Vocational Education in the New York City High Schools," *Journal of Human Resources,* Vol. III, Supplement, 1968.

Training and Jobs for the Urban Poor, Committee for Economic Development, New York, 1970.

"The U.S. Economy in 1990," The Conference Board, New York, 1970.

"The U.S. Labor Force: Projections to 1985," U.S. Department of Labor, U.S. Government Printing Office, Washington, D.C., 1970.

Venn, Grant. *Man, Education and Manpower,* American Association of School Administrators, Washington, D.C., 1970.

Vocational and Technical Education: Annual Report, Fiscal Year 1969, U.S. Department of Health, Education, and Welfare, U.S. Government Printing Office, Washington, D.C., 1971.

"Vocational Education," supplement to the *Journal of Human Resources,* Vol. III, 1968.

Vocational Education: The Bridge Between Man and His Work, U.S. Department of Health, Education, and Welfare, U.S. Government Printing Office, Washington, D.C., 1968.

Warmbrod, J. Robert. *Review and Synthesis of Research in the Economics of Vocational-Technical Education,* Center for Vocational and Technical Education, Ohio State University, Columbus, 1968.

Whitehead, Alfred North. *The Aims of Education and Other Essays,* Free Press, New York, 1929.

Wirth, Arthur G. *Education in the Technological Society: The Vocational-Liberal Status Controversy in the Early Twentieth Century.* Intext Vocational Publishers, Scranton, Pannsylvania, 1972.

Wolfbein, Seymour. *Education and Training For Full Employment,* Columbia University, New York, 1967.

"Youth Unemployment and Minimum Wages," U.S. Department of Labor, U.S. Government Printing Office, Washington, D.C., 1967.

Chapter 6

"AFDC: Selected Statistical Data in Families Aided and Program Operations," U.S. Department of Health, Education, and Welfare, U.S. Government Printing Office, Washington, D.C., 1971.

Burnside, Betty. "The Employment Potential of AFDC Mothers in Six States," *Welfare in Review,* July/August 1971.

Champagne, Joseph E. and King, Donald C. "Job Satisfaction Factors Among Underprivileged Workers," in *Guidance for Urban Disadvantaged Youth,* Vol. 45, No. 5, January 1967.

Cutright, Phillips. "Income and Family Events; Marital Stability," *Journal of Marriage and the Family,* May 1971.

————, and Scanzoni, John. "Trends in Marriage and the Family; The Effect of Past and Future Income Supplements," paper prepared for the Subcommittee on Fiscal Policy, Joint Economic Committee of the Congress, May 1972.

"Day Care Facts," U.S. Department of Labor, U.S. Government Printing Office, Washington, D.C., 1970.

Durbin, Elizabeth F. *Welfare Incomes and Employment,* Praeger Special Studies in U.S. Economic and Social Development, 1969.

Economic Report of the President: 1971, U.S. Government Printing Office, Washington, D.C.

"Findings of the 1971 AFDC Study: Parts I and II," U.S. Department of Health, Education, and Welfare, U.S. Government Printing Office, Washington, D.C., 1971.

Fine, Sidney. "Job Development for a Guaranteed Full Employment Policy," W. E. Upjohn Institute for Employment Research, Washington, D.C., 1972.

Friedlander, Stanley. *Unemployment in the Urban Core,* Praeger, New York, in press.

Fuchs, Victor. *The Service Economy,* Columbia University Press, New York, 1968.

Gans, Herbert. "Three Ways to Solve the Welfare Problem," *New York Times Magazine,* March 7, 1971.

Ginzberg, Eli. "Perspectives on a Public Employment Program," paper prepared for 33rd meeting of the National Manpower Advisory Committee, June 1972.

Goodwin, Leonard. "A Study of the Work Orientations of Welfare Recipients Participating in the Work Incentive Program," Brookings Institution, Washington, D.C., 1971.

————. "Summary of Findings and Discussion" of the Brookings Institution Conference on Manpower Services for the Welfare Poor, U.S. Department of Labor, Washington, D.C., 1971.

Gordon, R. A. *The Goal of Full Employment,* Wiley, New York, 1967.

————. *Toward A Manpower Policy,* John Wiley and Sons, New York, 1967.

Grant, D., and Grant, J. *Evaluation of New Careers Programs,* unpublished paper, Social Action Research Center, Oakland, California.

Gursslin, R. and Roach, Jack. "Some Issues in Training the Unemployed," *Social Problems,* Summer 1964.

Hannerz, Ulf. *Soulside,* Columbia University, New York, 1969.

Hapgood, David. "Beyond Welfare Reform," *Washington Monthly,* May 1970.

Herman, Melvin, Sadofsky, Stanley, and Rosenberg, Bernard, eds. *Work, Youth and Unemployment,* Thomas Y. Crowell, New York, 1968.

Kershaw, David. *The Negative Income Tax Experiment in New Jersey,* mimeograph paper, Urban Opinion Surveys, a division of Mathmatica, Inc., Princeton, New Jersey, 1971.

Komarovsky, Mirra. *The Unemployed Man and His Family,* Drydon, New York, 1940.

Koos, Earl L. *Families in Trouble,* King's Crown Press, New York, 1946.

Kreps, Juanita, ed. *Technology, Manpower, and Retirement,* World Publishing Co., Cleveland, 1966.

Lecht, Leonard. *Manpower Needs for National Goals in the 1970's,* Praeger, New York, 1969.

Levitan, Sar and Siegel, Irving, eds. *Dimensions of Manpower Policy: Programs and Research,* Johns Hopkins Press, Baltimore, 1966.

————. "Federal Manpower Policies and Programs to Combat Unemployment," W. E. Upjohn Institute for Employment Research, Washington, D.C., 1964.

————. "Reducing Work Time as a Means to Combat Unemployment," W. E. Upjohn Institute for Employment Research, Washington, D.C., 1964.

Manpower Reports of the President: 1970, 1971, 1972, U.S. Government Printing Office, Washington, D.C.

"Marital and Living Arrangements: March 1971," U.S. Department of Commerce, U.S. Government Printing Office, Washington, D.C.

Passell, Peter and Ross, Leonard. "Don't Knock the $2 Trillion Economy," *New York Times Magazine,* March 3, 1972.

Piore, Michael J. "Jobs and Training," in Samuel H. Beer and Richard E. Barringer, eds., *The State and the Poor,* Winthrop, Cambridge, Massachusetts, 1970.

The President's Commission on Income Maintenance Program, U.S. Government Printing Office, Washington, D.C., 1970.

Rainwater, Lee. "Poverty, Living Standards and Family Well-Being," paper prepared for the Subcommittee on Fiscal Policy, Joint Economic Committee of the Congress, June 1972.

————. *Behind Ghetto Walls*, Aldine, Chicago, 1970.

Schultz, David A. *Coming Up Black*, Prentice-Hall, Englewood Cliffs, New Jersey, 1969.

Sheppard, Harold L. *The Nature of the Job Problem and the Role of New Public Service Employment*, W. E. Upjohn Institute for Employment Research, Washington, D.C., 1969.

Steiner, Gilbert. *Social Insecurity: The Politics of Welfare*, Rand McNally, Chicago, 1966.

Tobin, James. "Raising the Incomes of the Poor," in Kermit Gordon, ed., *Agenda for the Nation*, Brookings Institution, Washington, D.C., 1969.

"Toward Full Employment," report of the Senate Committee on Labor and Public Welfare, Washington, D.C., 1964.

"The U.S. Economy in 1980: A Summary of B.L.S. Projections," U.S. Department of Labor, U.S. Government Printing Office, Washington, D.C., 1970.

Walther, R. H. *The Measurement of Work Relevant Attitudes*, final report, U.S. Department of Labor Contract #41-7-004-09, October 1970.

————. *Strategies for Helping Disadvantaged Groups*, paper for International Conference on Trends in Industrial and Labor Relations, Tel Aviv, Israel, January, 1972.

————, et al. *A Proposed Model for Urban Out-of-School Neighborhood Youth Corps Programs*, Manpower Research Projects, George Washington University, 1969.

"The Workfare State," *New Generation*, Winter, 1970.

"The Work Relief Employment Program: A Legislative Proposal," City of New York, Department of Social Services, March, 1972.

INDEX